Praise for *Out of the Shadows*, Volume 1

'This is intelligent writing which opens doors for imaginative preaching and roots this life giving ministry in prayer.'

The Rt Revd Alison White, Bishop of Hull

'An important, accessible and comprehensive account of the too-long silenced voices of women of the Bible. Including the women you know, the women you thought you knew and the women you hadn't heard of or had long forgotten, this book seeks them out and brings them out of the deep shadows imposed on them. This is a book for everyone seeking to challenge their own bias, conscious or unconscious, and is particularly urgent given the public conversations around violence against women and the dismantling of patriarchy. I commend it to you with urgency, it will challenge, inform and gently but surely change the way you think, speak and write about these women of faith.'

The Revd Kate Bottley, Priest and broadcaster

'I have long believed that the women in the biblical narrative have been overlooked. Sadly they are pigeon-holed to only being suitable for women's fellowship talks, a few comforting tales to entertain between the sessions on the holiday photos of the minister's tour of Greece, and the nice person from the children's charity. They are often skirted over in the lectionary without the preacher giving them the rigour of academic integration that other biblical texts in our tradition have been afforded. In the twenty plus years I have known Kate Bruce, and through Kate, Liz Shercliff I have admired her dogged determination to never let a text go, without affording it that interrogation, with her sharp mind, honest questioning heart and insightful wit, Kate's beautifully crafted use of language shines light where there once was darkness. All this is evident in abundance in *Out of the Shadows* and I wholeheartedly commend this book to all who are seeking more than a cursory glance at the women in the biblical texts. You will not be disappointed.'

The Revd Alison Wilkinson, Wesley Study Centre, Durham

'What an absolute gift Kate Bruce and Liz Shercliff have gifted the preacher. How boldly and vibrantly the women of scripture speak through their insightful telling of their stories. How dynamically they spring to life. In *Out of the Shadows*, they write of "Woman Wisdom" being an inspirational ally for the woman preacher. This book, in its entirety, is a confident, wise and powerful ally that all preachers will want to turn to, again and again. It will sit firmly on my writing desk, very close to hand.'

Jenny Cornfield, Freelance charity consultant

'This book is stuffed with scriptural sleuthery, homiletical skill, and pastoral sensitivity. Kate and Liz show preachers how honouring women's stories leads to encountering God's Wisdom.'

The Revd Matthew Allen, Diocese of Blackburn

Out of the Shadows

Out of the Shadows

Preaching the Women of the Bible

Volume 2

Kate Bruce and Liz Shercliff

scm press

Published in 2024 by SCM Press

Editorial office
3rd Floor, Invicta House,
110 Golden Lane,
London EC1Y OTG, UK
www.scmpress.co.uk

SCM Press is an imprint of Hymns Ancient & Modern Ltd (a registered charity)

Hymns Ancient & Modern® is a registered trademark of
Hymns Ancient & Modern Ltd
13A Hellesdon Park Road, Norwich,
Norfolk NR6 5DR, UK

British Library Cataloguing in Publication data

A catalogue record for this book is available
from the British Library

978-0-334-06351-3

Typeset by Regent Typesetting

Contents

Introduction   xi

1   One Who Sees and Lives: Hagar   1

2   God of the Traumatized: Lot's Wife and Daughters   9

3   God in the Muddle: Rebekah   14

4   Sisters, Wives and Servants: Rachel, Leah, Bilhah and Zilpah   24

5   A Daughter Defiled: Dinah (Genesis 34)   31

6   Sex-Trading for Justice: Tamar, Daughter-in-Law of Judah   39

7   Vilified and Vindicated: Potiphar's Wife   47

8   Acting Above Her Station: Zipporah   54

9   A Dancing 'Rebel': Miriam   60

10 Inheritance Matters: Zelophehad's Daughters   65

11 An Ambiguous Figure: Rahab   77

12 Women Warriors: Deborah and Jael   88

13 A Misunderstood Migrant: Naomi   99

14 Raped, Dismembered, Remembered: The Levite's Concubine   104

15 A Woman Who Challenges God: Hannah   111

16 A Player or a Pawn? Bathsheba   117

17 A Desolate Woman: Tamar, Sister of Amnon and Absalom   129

18 Eloquence in Word and Action: The Wise Woman of Tekoa,
    the Wise Woman of Abel-Maacah, Merab and Rizpah   134

19 A Woman of Substance: The Queen of Sheba   146

20 Wicked Women and an Unexpected Saviour: The Medium
    of Endor, Jezebel, Athaliah and Jehosheba   152

21 Nameless Presences: The Widow of a Prophet and the
   Shunammite Woman   165

22 A Slave in Syria, but a Servant of God: Naaman's Wife's Maid 174

23 Caught Up in Power Politics: The Woman of Timnah,
   Delilah, Ahinoam Daughter of Ahimaaz, Ahinoam of Jezreel,
   Michal, Abishag and Jeroboam's Wife   179

24 Prophetic Pictures: The Prophetess, the Builders, the Image
   of Exile, and the Loving Mother   193

25 Interrupting Power: Pilate's Wife   200

26 Daughters of Dysfunction: Herodias and Salome   205

27 She Answered Back: The Syrophoenician Woman   217

28 Seen by Jesus: The Widow with the Two Coins   224

29 A Faithful Prophet: Anna   233

30 Touched by Christ's Compassion: Widow of Nain   241

31 A Daughter of Abraham: Woman Bent Over for
   Eighteen Years   245

32 'Rejoice with me': The Woman with the Lost Coin   255

33 The Power of Her Testimony: The Woman at the Well   260

34 'Some Women' Encounter God: Peter's Mother-in-Law,
   Women of Jerusalem, Sapphira, Drusilla and Bernice   267

Appendix: Sermon Series Suggestions   275
Bibliography   277

List of Abbreviations

RCL	Revised Common Lectionary
CW	Common Worship Lectionary
OT	Ordinary Time (RCL)
CW, PS	*Common Worship*, Principal Service
CW, SS	*Common Worship*, Second Service

This book is dedicated to all women
who have the courage to preach;
to all women who faithfully wrestle with the Scriptures,
seeking the love of God;
to all women who refuse to settle for
easy answers and superficial platitudes
in the quest for truth, integrity and justice.

Introduction

We did not set out to write an angry book, but this *is* an angry book. Certainly, it is more angry than the first volume of *Out of the Shadows* – perhaps because we have explored the lives and stories of Bible women we avoided in Volume 1, because they are so challenging; perhaps because the previous book was largely written during the Covid pandemic, when many hoped things would not go back to the way they were; perhaps because we live in an age where 'influencers' like Andrew Tate allegedly encourage men not only to rape women but to 'enslave them',[1] and perhaps because we live in a world where some public figures, including some church leaders, collaborate to hide the misdeeds of male colleagues against women. It is an angry book, and we hope that you have already read the first book, and realize that we are not unreasonable or anti-male.

Many of our chapters address stories in which women are raped, abused and treated as objects. It could be argued that we are reading back into these stories a sense of female individualism and autonomy, alien in their original contexts. So, should we just leave it at that – these are ancient, irredeemable texts. Leave them alone. Or should we ask ourselves what a just reading of scripture looks like? How does the grace of the gospel expressed in the life and teaching of Jesus, recorded within scripture, interpret those parts of scripture that speak of cruelty and gross injustice? Right now, there is a particularly pointed questioning about the treatment of women across cultures. Reading these ancient texts in our current contexts, the cruelty, silencing and abuse of the women we uncover there finds startling similarity in the present. What *is* the correct response? Silence? Polite avoidance? Or a naming of the resonances as the horizons of text and context interact, with a consideration of what grace, love, truth and justice look like as we engage with the women of the Bible. If we opt for silence or avoidance, we send a powerful message: these issues don't matter; the church isn't interested, and God doesn't care. Be quiet? No.

It was a man, John Chalmers KHC, then Principal Clerk to the General Assembly of the Church of Scotland, who first inspired Liz to work and speak for women's rights. At an after-dinner speech in 2016, he argued that one of the most significant issues in human rights over the next decade would be women's rights. We are almost at the end of that decade. We acknowledge and honour all the men who are also angry at the way women are treated. Men too suffer at the hands of toxic masculinity and traditional patriarchy. The term 'toxic masculinity' was coined by a male psychology professor, Shepherd Bliss, in describing his own father's authoritarian behaviour and its effects. It should not be or taken as shorthand for condemning men. It is used to describe some masculine behaviour 'that diminishes women, children, other men'.[2]

Liz runs a conference about women's preaching, at which Kate often speaks too. One woman who attended said in her feedback, 'feminist "shouty-ness" puts me off'. Another said, 'If we want to win people over, we need to be gentler; if we used feminine tones, men would take more notice.' The topic that year was #MeToo! These women make shouting, being angry, the problem, not the abuse of women. The content of what is said is overlooked because the speaker seemed angry. The problem here is that determining the speaker was angry, and that anger is unacceptable, results in the speaker not being heard, and injustice not being recounted.

It's worth pausing to reflect on how anger itself is a gendered term, which may explain why we notice it in our text. Dr Pragya Agarwal comments that, 'Women are given the message that their anger is "ugly" and that no one will listen to them if they are angry. Women have to suppress their anger and are more likely to ruminate.'[3] Agarwal explores how anger is a term which in men is associated with power and strength and in women linked with lack of control.[4] We notice that the gendering of anger is further compounded by race, making the expression of anger by black and Latina women even more challenging, since they are 'frequently stereotyped with high emotionality, intense emotions, uncontrolled behaviour and a kind of exoticism that assigns them fiery traits irrespective of individual or personal characteristics'.[5] Michelle Obama was called an 'angry black woman' on the campaign trail, 'perceived to be emasculating her husband'.[6] This was an attempt to silence her.

Our anger here is an accurate emotional response to the stories we have encountered. This response has a purpose. Our anger is a catalyst to seeking change: changed perspectives, greater understanding, changed attitudes and reformed actions. Our anger is a rational response in search of justice. It is a right response in the face of silencing, misogyny and oppression. To those who would silence us we point out that rather than tell us to be quiet, attend to the reasons why we have raised our voices. Our anger is not hostile or hysterical, but an honest, measured and reasoned response to what we have encountered in these stories, themes repeated in contemporary contexts.

It is an angry book. But it is angry for good reason. The stories we present in this book too often remain untold. These women appear in the text of Christian scripture. They are our foremothers in faith. Their stories are moving and profound. God frequently honours them. Yet many are absent from our lectionaries, our sermon series, our pulpits, even our Bible reading.

The stories of these women resonate with women's lives down through the ages, as the suggested sermon on Lot's wife illustrates. Given that one in four women in the UK has been sexually assaulted, preachers must be speaking, on a weekly basis, to women who have suffered in this way. The fact that this is rarely mentioned suggests that it does not matter. The fact that it is rarely mentioned from the Bible suggests that it is not part of Christian experience. But it is. The temptation is to avoid giving sermons on difficult subjects. We need to balance the risk of triggering distressing subject matter against the risk of deafening silences. Hard subjects can be handled with good advertising and pastoral follow-up. Silence just begets more silence, and the underlying assumption that subjects like rape and abuse are not addressed because the church isn't interested. In churches where the benign presence of God in our daily lives is preached confidently, though less confidently experienced, the stories of women such as Hagar, apparently abandoned by God, could have much to say, yet remain largely ignored.

Increasingly, churches are being revealed as unjust spaces: places where marginalization is justified on grounds of theological position; places where the acceptance of women's ministry has not translated into greater numbers of women at senior levels; places where women are expected not to speak out. None of this is unique to today's church. Women have been ignored among the people of God from the beginning; they've been turned to salt or made leprous simply for questioning patriarchal decisions. Women have been taken, brought, sent, exploited and silenced.

So why this book? From the conception of the first volume, our aspiration was to equip preachers to speak holy truths from the stories of Bible women. We wanted to enable preachers who value women's lives and understandings of God to find in *Out of the Shadows* a useful and inspiring source of research, sermon ideas and collects. In short, we wanted to make it easier to acknowledge and respect women's lives. The more we read of women's lives in the Bible and in newspapers, the more we realize that they have been and are being devalued and desecrated.

Yes – there is a certain angry tone found in these pages. We won't apologize for this. Perhaps we need to reflect on the nature and purpose of our anger. Our anger is a deep rage on behalf of people pushed aside, violated and silenced. 'Anger' itself is a simple word used to map a wide territory of meaning. In the Central Australian language of Yankunytjatjara there are a number of words which denote different forms of anger: 'mipanarinyi' means anger with a sense of grievance; 'kuyaringanyi' means someone is resentful; and 'pikaringanki' means active hostility.[7] This book is written in the spirit of 'mipanarinyi', and our aim is to bring grace to the grievances in these biblical stories and in our contexts.

During his after-dinner speech in 2016, John Chalmers cited Augustine of Hippo: 'Hope has two beautiful daughters; their names are Anger and Courage. Anger at the way things are, and Courage to see that they do not remain as they are.' Anger must be accompanied by courage.

The first book in this series was dedicated to the Rt Revd Mariann Edgar Budde, Bishop of the Episcopal Diocese of Washington, who, on the night of 6 January 2021, when supporters of President Donald Trump stormed the American Capitol building with a view to staging a coup, stood in Washington National Cathedral and spoke truth to power: 'Mr President, there has been no fraudulent election ... [this violence] is not acceptable.' This book is dedicated to all those women who dare to speak out, including all those who have the courage to preach about Bible women, and address the concerns of women in the pews.

Notes

1 Multiple sources, see for example 'BBC, "The man who groomed the world"', https://www.bbc.co.uk/programmes/m001q1n6, accessed 07.10.23; or 'Andrew Tate prosecution files reveal graphic claims of coercion ahead of trial', https://www.bbc.com/news/world-europe-66581218, accessed 07.10.23.

2 Soraya Roberts, 'The classroom origins of toxic masculinity' (2019), https://longreads.com/2019/01/25/origins-of-toxic-masculinity, accessed 07.10.23; see also Shepherd Bliss, 'Revisioning masculinity: a report on the growing men's movement', *Gender* (IC#16) (Spring 1987); Context Institute, https://www.context.org/iclib/ic16/bliss/, accessed 07.10.23; and Bryant W. Sculos, 'Who's afraid of "toxic masculinity"? Class, race and corporate power', Volume 5, Issue 3, Article 6 (2017), https://digitalcommons.fiu.edu/classracecorporatepower/vol5/iss3/6/, accessed 07.10.23.

3 Pragya Agarwal, *Hyster!cal (sic): Exploding the Myth of Gendered Emotions* (Edinburgh: Canongate, 2023), Kindle edition, p. 232.

4 Agarwal (2023), Kindle edition, pp. 84–5.

5 Agarwal (2023), Kindle edition, p. 234.

6 Agarwal (2023), Kindle edition, p. 235.

7 Agarwal (2023), Kindle edition, p. 39.

One Who Sees and Lives: Hagar

LIZ SHERCLIFF

Hagar in the Revised Common Lectionary

Year A	Season after Pentecost	Proper 7 (OT 12)	Genesis 21.8–21

Hagar's Words in the Bible

'I am running away from my mistress Sarai.'
(Genesis 16.8)

'You are El-roi.'
(Genesis 16.13)

'Have I really seen God and remained alive after seeing him?'
(Genesis 16.13)

'Do not let me look on the death of the child.'
(Genesis 21.16)

Hagar's Story: Scene One

In the opening scene of Hagar's story (which is not included in the Lectionary) Hagar is her mistress's commodity, a surrogate (mother) for Abram's child. Having 'achieved' something her mistress could not by bearing Abram's child, Hagar apparently looks down on her mistress.

Sarai blames Abram, and Abram responds with the chilling permission, 'do to her as you please' (Genesis 16.6). Hagar is passed from person to person, the pawn in a domestic power game, possibly the victim of her mistress's neurosis. In a bid to take control of her own life, Hagar flees to the wilderness near her country of birth, Egypt (Genesis 16.7), where 'the angel of the LORD' finds her. God 'sees' her and calls her by name. God promises her son will be the ancestor of a great nation. Hagar becomes the first person in the Bible to be visited by a divine messenger and to receive a divine promise of descendants.[1] She is the first person in the Bible to name God. God does not, however, relieve her suffering. Rather, she is sent back to Sarai with the injunction to 'submit' (Genesis 16.9). We learn nothing of how Hagar feels about this. Her subordinate role is reinforced at the end of Genesis 16: '*Abram* named his son', despite the fact that the angel previously told Hagar she would name him (Genesis 16.11). Patriarchal power usurps even God's will for this woman.

Scene Two

In the second scene, which is included in the Lectionary, friction between Hagar and her mistress, now called Sarah, continues. Sarah notices Ishmael playing with Isaac. The incident itself is problematic. Not only are we not told what Ishmael was doing with Isaac, the Hebrew text does not include Isaac in the story at all. He appears in the Latin Vulgate. Nevertheless, Sarah demands that Abraham 'cast out this slave woman with her son' (Genesis 21.10). Sarah does not name Hagar; instead she others her by referring to her as 'this slave woman'.[2] God seems to do the same, instructing Abraham not to 'be distressed because of the boy and because of your slave woman' but to do as Sarah says. God too seems to other Hagar and Ishmael. God even attributes the promise to prosper them to Abraham – 'I will make a nation of him also, because he is your offspring' (Genesis 21.13). Some interpreters argue that Hagar was not expelled but freed, since she was not sold.[3] As a poor single mother in a foreign land, it would be fairer to assume that Hagar felt more an enforced exile than a freed woman. Abraham gives Hagar food enough to get her away from his camp so that he need not contemplate her suffering. When the bread and water are gone, Hagar hides Ishmael under a bush, and sits down some distance off. At last, the narrator allows us to hear Hagar's grief: 'Do not let me look on the death of the child,' and she lifts her voice and weeps (Genesis 21.16). Again, the narrative is problematic, for we are told not that God hears Hagar's cry but that God hears 'the voice of the boy' (Genesis 21.17). Finally, Hagar is noticed: 'What troubles you?' But again God seems only interested in the boy: 'Do not be afraid; God has heard the voice of the boy ... I will make a great nation of *him*.' Hagar's role is to look after the boy until such time as she finds him a wife, and then she disappears from the tale (Genesis 21.21). The story seems irredeemably patriarchal and oppressive for women. No wonder that when I gave Genesis 21.8–21 to a group of students as the basis for a sermon, Hagar was not in any of them. There were sermons about Abraham standing by and letting Sarah act unjustly, and even one about Ishmael not being named but being called 'the boy' even by God. But nobody mentioned Hagar.

What are we to do with this story?

Rediscovering Hagar

In contrast to my students, when I told a friend that I was writing a book about women in the Bible, she immediately jumped in with, 'You must talk about Hagar! She's my favourite.' Why such contrasting responses?

My friend is black.

There is a history, particularly in America, of black women relating to Hagar because they understand her as a victim of racism, sexism and abuse. The themes of sexual exploitation and surrogacy resonate with African-American slaves of the past and the womanist[4] movement of the present. In a womanist telling of Hagar's story there are two significant themes – surrogacy and wilderness. Hagar is a black slave whose body, and its reproductive capacity, is at the command of Sarah. Surrogacy was a common experience of black women slaves in the American South, particularly before the Civil War. They experienced coerced and voluntary surrogacy – as breeders, suffering the plight of Hagar, and as nannies or housekeepers, taking on roles usually filled by someone else.[5] Hagar goes twice into the wilderness, first to flee after enforced surrogacy and abuse by her owner, Sarah; second, as a free woman but poor, black, homeless and a single mother. What is striking about Hagar's story is that God offers no liberation from oppression; in fact, on the first occasion, God sends her back to her mistress and instructs her to submit (Genesis 16.9). On the second occasion, God meets Hagar in the wilderness, she is free. God provides for her survival and the survival of her son, but she remains in the wilderness.

In this context, womanist theologian Dolores Williams explores the doctrine of atonement. Either Jesus suffered in obedience to God, in which case he too was a victim of coerced surrogacy, or he suffered of his own accord, making him a victim of voluntary surrogacy. In both cases Jesus identifies with black women's experiences. Williams offers a third alternative: encountering suffering is always encountering sin, not holiness or God's will. Jesus' work was to place people in right relationship to each other and to God, it was not vicarious suffering. Williams argues that the oppressed community is where we are called 'to hammer out the meaning of Jesus' presence for Christian behaviour'.[6] From a womanist perspective, re-evaluating the lives of African-American women is central to this task.

Dolores Williams suggests that Hagar's wilderness experiences are 'near-destruction situation[s] in which God gives personal direction ... and helps her make a way out' where she thought there was none.[7] This is not liberation theology, however. Twice she goes into the wilderness, twice she meets God there. Neither occasion offers much hope. First, she is returned to her oppression, and is told her son will be a 'wild ass of a man' whom nobody will like (Genesis 16.12). Then it is made clear she is simply the servant of this son who will 'live at odds with all his kin' (Genesis 16.12) – presumably including her! Hagar is not offered liberation, only survival.[8] She remains alone, in the desert, without food. There is no anticipation of liberation, only perhaps the strength to continue. For African-American women Hagar has become a symbol of how to survive the injustices of slavery and exploitation, and still maintain faith in a God who works towards equality. 'By using resistance strategies to counteract prejudice, black women strive to be like Hagar and embody her qualities of nurturance, determination, endurance, and steadfastness.'[9]

Marion Taylor and Heather Weir[10] gather a collection of nineteenth-century interpretations of women in Genesis. British women understood Hagar's story from their perspectives as wealthy and privileged. Their understanding is rooted in their belief in ordered society and their experiences of having servants. One contributor approves Hagar's return to Sarah because it was wrong to 'desert one's duty', and Hagar had been 'insubordinate'.[11] Another nineteenth-century essayist writes: 'Was it wrong of her to go away like this? Yes, it was very wrong. She was Abram's wife, and she had no right to leave him; she was Sarah's servant, and her place was with her mistress.'[12] For this writer it seems that abusing a servant is acceptable, but deserting a husband or an owner is not.

Both the womanist and the nineteenth-century readings of Hagar objectify her. She has no characteristics, we know very little of her, so she becomes a kind of 'everywoman', a representative of particular oppressions. Just as the writer of Genesis eliminates her once Ishmael begins to thrive in the wilderness,[13] so many commentators and preachers eliminate her from their reflections on the Genesis passages that tell her story. Just as there is no freedom from oppression within Hagar's story, there has generally been none in the application of it subsequently.

The Preacher's Problem

The problem for me of preaching Hagar, particularly when the Lectionary only affords us the second part of her story, is that I am white and reasonably privileged. I need to be very aware of the fact that I and my congregation are probably closer, in terms of lifestyle and status, to the nineteenth-century women cited above than we are to African-American slave women. Womanist preachers like Wil Gafney preach personally and convincingly about Hagar.[14] But what can *I* do? The real hope in Hagar's story is in the first part, the part excluded from the Lectionary: 'You are El-roi'; for she said, 'Have I really seen God and remained alive after seeing him?' (Genesis 16.13). Let's start there.

Sermon Suggestion: Not Seen and Seen

I have been invisible twice in my life. I hadn't donned any kind of cloak. I wasn't even hiding. But I was invisible.

The first time, I was in a restaurant with two colleagues. Male colleagues. The waitress focused on impressing them; the wine waiter concentrated on informing them. I was invisible. One of the men was even asked what 'the lady' would like to eat!

The second time, I saw someone I recognized. I smiled. I was ignored. The situation had changed from last time I had seen them, just a day before. Then, I was on the stage, addressing a group of students from a position of authority. Now, I was serving them food, temporary staff for a friend with a catering business. First unseen because of my sex, then unseen because of my status.

I make no claim to understanding how Hagar felt in the Genesis narrative. I have an inkling, that's all. I know that to be *seen* is important. To be *seen* means someone recognizes our personhood. To be *unseen* deprives us of existence. Hagar does not exist for most of her story. She is 'my slave' to Sarai, 'your slave' to Abram, 'slave of Sarai' to the angel – though the angel does at least use her name Hagar before calling her that.

5

Later she is 'this slave woman' to Sarah, and 'your slave woman' when God speaks to Abraham. She is the surrogate, the chattel, the pawn. Even to God it seems she is there simply to nurture a son. The God of the first Patriarch, the male God – He – sends her back to oppression. Even when she is desperate and dying, the male God – He – hears the *boy's* cries.

Yet somewhere in the middle of Hagar's story, hidden away from us by the Lectionary compilers, there is hope. Hagar, the black, poor, single mother, becomes the first person in the Bible to name God. Hagar, the pawn in other people's games, names God 'the one who sees'. Hagar, who is usually known by her status instead of her name, calls God 'the one who sees'.

Hagar the invisible knows that God sees her.

As well as the oppression of being unseen, slaves also knew – know – the dangers of seeing. Slaves who see the wrongs done by their owners are harshly punished in film and in literature, and also in real life. To see means recognizing wrong, and that is fraught with the danger of wanting things to be different. Hagar was probably used to not seeing. Not seeing Abram abuse Sarai.[15] Not seeing Sarai abuse other slaves. Not seeing is a well-known means of self-protection among the oppressed. God too appears to see Hagar only as the slave of Sarai and the mother of Ishmael, yet Hagar sees God.

Hagar the unseeing sees God.

Abram too is unseeing in Hagar's story. He fails to see her abuse at the hands of his family. He fails to acknowledge her oppression in his culture. He cannot recognize her as anything other than a chattel, for the convenience of his wife and himself. When she becomes a problem, she is thrown out. Abram does not see.

I began with stories of being unseen. They are memorable because I am not used to being invisible. I end with challenges about unseeing. Come with me into the city. Let's get the bus. Just in front of us is a young woman wearing hijab. A couple of white men get on at the next stop. They sit behind her, making racist comments. Do we see her? On the way from the bus stop we see a shop doorway. In it a bedraggled-looking young man, looking up asking for money. Do we see him? What else could we see if only we would look?

God does not offer Hagar a way out of her oppression. Is that because the answer is in Sarah's hands? Or Abraham's? Or those with the power?

Hagar, the unseeing and unseen, sees God and is seen by God. What might that say to us?

Homiletic Points

1 The sermon begins on a personal note as the preacher recounts her experience of not being seen. This serves two purposes: first, the preacher draws from her own experience to create an 'inkling' of understanding of Hagar's'; and, second, it sets up the theme of seeing, around which the sermon is woven.

2 The sermon is bookended by references to our present context, implicitly conveying the view that the biblical themes are resonant and relevant now.

3 The central hope-filled image of the sermon is that the woman who has to unsee so many things, and is not seen herself, is the woman who sees and names God. She is the one with insight and awareness. The sermon, like the biblical text, inverts expectation.

Collect

God of Hagar,
who named you 'God who sees',
give us clear vision,
that we might see the overlooked
and the marginalized.
As Hagar saw you,
enable us to see you at work
in the lives of
the silenced and the oppressed,
that they might know strength and liberation.
Amen.

Notes

1 P. Trible, *Texts of Terror: Literary-feminist Readings of Biblical Narratives* (London: SCM Press, 2002).

2 Trible, *Texts of Terror*, p. 16.

3 T. Frymer-Kensky, *Reading the Women of the Bible* (New York: Schocken, 2002), p. 235.

4 'Womanist' is a term coined by Alice Walker in 1983 in her book *In Search of Our Mothers' Gardens: Womanist Prose* (re-published London and New York: Harvest Books, 2004. p. xi). 'Womanist theology' critiques feminism for being too white and reads the Bible from the perspective of the whole of black women's lives.

5 D. Williams, *Sisters in the Wilderness* (New York: Orbis Books, 2013), p. 63.

6 Williams, *Sisters*, pp. 174–5.

7 Williams, *Sisters*, p. 28.

8 E. Peecook, 'Hagar: an African American lens', *Denison Journal of Religion*, Vol. 2 (2002), p. 9.

9 Peecook, 'Hagar', p. 12.

10 M.-A. Taylor and H. E. Weir, *Let Her Speak for Herself: Nineteenth-century Women Writing on Women in Genesis* (Waco, TX: Baylor University Press, 2006).

11 Taylor and Weir, *Let Her Speak for Herself*, pp. 217–19.

12 Taylor and Weir, *Let Her Speak for Herself*, p. 226.

13 She appears in the genealogy of Genesis 25.12 but is not present at Abraham's burial in Genesis 25.9.

14 See for example https://www.wilgafney.com/2020/11/29/jesus-and-hagar-the-form-of-a-slave/, *Jesus and Hagar: The Form of a Slave*, accessed 11.05.22.

15 Genesis 12 and Genesis 20; see K. Bruce and L. Shercliff, *Out of the Shadows: Preaching the Women of the Bible* (London: SCM Press, 2021), ch. 3.

2

God of the Traumatized:
Lot's Wife and Daughters

LIZ SHERCLIFF

Lot's Wife and Daughters in the Revised Common Lectionary

Not included.

Their Words in the Bible

None.

The Story of Lot's Wife and Daughters

Those who remember anything about Lot's wife are likely to recall that she was turned into a pillar of salt because she looked back on the condemned city of Sodom. She stands for ever as both a vertical slab of salt and as a warning against disobedience. American Rabbi Sandy Sasso points out the lessons traditionally drawn from the narrative: 'Women are disobedient. They don't listen.'[1] Until recently, the story has been interpreted in almost wholly negative ways. There are richer and more nuanced ways of reading this story, however.

What would Lot's nameless wife tell us if she could speak? Some Rabbinic literature names her Idit – witness. What does she witness to, then? First, she witnesses to human-ness. In an exceptionally striking account of September 11, 2001, the fall of the Twin Towers in New York, Martin Harries recounts meeting a woman in a supermarket that same afternoon. She had been inside one of the towers, on the thirty-fourth floor. The evacuation had been orderly, she said, until people reached the lobby and saw the extent of the destruction. She was told not

9

to look back, but her first instinct was to do exactly that.² It is a normal human reaction to look back at a place where we have lived. Poet Anna Akhmatova (1889–1986) imagines this might be what happens:

> It's not too late, you can still look back
> at the red towers of your native Sodom,
> the square where once you sang, the spinning-shed,
> at the empty windows set in the tall house
> where sons and daughters blessed your marriage-bed.³

Then, Lot's wife witnesses to the pain of motherhood when families break apart. Lot must have had more than the two daughters with whom they escape – perhaps all with this woman. In Genesis 19.1–3, two angels visit Sodom. They meet Lot in the gateway. Lot invites them to stay with him, though they plan to spend the night in the square. In verses 5–8, in a story similar to Judges 19, the men of the town go to Lot's house demanding to rape the men. Lot tries to trade his virgin daughters for his guests. The angels strike the men blind, and they disperse. Later, in verse 14, Lot goes to speak to his *sons-in-law*. He therefore has two virgin daughters and at least two married daughters. When Lot escapes the city, he takes two daughters with him, and leaves two behind. Lot's wife must be distraught. For her, this is not a simple escape story; two of her daughters, because their husbands ignore Lot's warning, will be destroyed. Looking back seems natural.

Finally, Idit stands in contrast to her husband. Rabbi Sandy Sasso points out that, although the destruction is ascribed to God, Lot's wife does not see Shekhinah, the presence of God, when she turns. Rather, she sees shekhenim, her community,⁴ and is 'consumed in tears, becoming a pillar of salt'. Lot is convinced by the judgement and flees, thinking only of himself and his household. Idit shows compassion, bears witness and is paralysed. Perhaps Idit as witness has much to tell us.

A significant outcome of Idit's destruction, later in the same chapter, is the rape of Lot by his remaining daughters. Lot seeks safety in an isolated cave. His daughters realize they have no hope of a future, that is, of children, unless they have sex with their father. Theologian Miri Rozmarin argues that Lot's wife leaves her daughters a heritage of life, because her own resistance to God's destruction of the city shows them how to withstand patriarchally determined social norms, and to take things into their own hands.⁵ We may find the way they do so difficult! The relationship between father and daughters is recast, and the daughters take control.

We live in fractured times when generational relationships seem broken. Young people, concerned about climate crisis, blame those of us who have triggered it. The assumption of home ownership seems an unattainable dream to younger generations. The world is not only changing, it seems to be heading towards annihilation. Modern-day Lots assume the confidence of counterfeit Christianity, when they claim that they will be safe as the world meets catastrophe. Perhaps this is a time for modern-day Idits to witness events, give credence to the experiences of the oppressed, and challenge both the inevitability and the divine ordination of these events. Perhaps in turning, Lot's wife resists the easy assumptions of hierarchy and power to empathize with suffering.

A final understanding of the story comes from trauma theology. Considering all that Lot's wife witnesses in the space of a few days, is her becoming rigid and immobile a catatonic reaction to severe psychological trauma?[6] Was the advice not to turn back an injunction or a warning? Perhaps in Lot's wife we find a witness to extreme trauma who, like many victims, continues to be traumatized by also being blamed for their troubles. Trauma theology, and the story of Lot's wife, insist that we must rethink Christian hope. Suffering has often been presented as a positive, productive of character, resilience or greater faith, by preachers. The implication is that suffering becomes part of who we are. Trauma resists this interpretation, however. When the abused allow their suffering to become part of themselves there is no hope, they remain a victim. Trauma must be named as evil, not something from which good might come. Trauma must lead us to solidarity with survivors, and to action against abusive structures and practices.

Sermon Suggestion: Silencing Trauma

I have only once suffered trauma. I was sexually assaulted on a train in France. There was another woman in the carriage, but she decided not to intervene. I did not speak to anyone about the event for over 20 years. But I did often look back, and each time I did, I asked myself what I should have done. Had I invited the attack? Looking back was not helpful. I wasn't turned into a literal pillar of salt, but I was frozen as I relived the event and saw before me the disdainful, distanced look of the woman who failed to help.

I want to suggest that Lot's wife is a victim of trauma, rather than a disobedient woman who refused to listen to God. Consider what she has seen in the last few days. A gang of local thugs comes banging on her door wanting to rape her guests. Her husband offers the thugs their virgin daughters in place of the men. The thugs are struck blind by the guests. They are told to leave their home because the city is about to be destroyed. Her sons-in-law refuse to come with them, and so her married daughters are left to face destruction. Then, she becomes an asylum-seeker because of the wanton destruction of her home. How likely is it that she will follow the advice not to look back? I suggest it is an almost impossible instruction. It is human to look back on our traumas unless they have been dealt with.

Lot seems to find it easy to keep looking forward, abandoning family and recent home. He has no roots there; he wants to survive. He obeys the rules. He protects his tribe. I wonder how often trauma sufferers are denied help because others want to keep the rules and protect the tribe. Isn't this what has happened in the church for generations? The abuse perpetrated by leaders has been covered up to protect the tribe. Many of them, like Lot's wife, have suffered catatonic trauma, trauma that freezes them, makes them unable to act. Lot's wife, I believe, calls us to empathize with victims, to share their suffering.

In recent times significant leaders in the church, and in para-church organizations, have been either accused or found guilty of abuse. Some have been appropriately dealt with. What has been remarkable, though, has been the number of times other church leaders have asked victims to remain quiet, for the good of the church. Not to look back on what has happened but to look forward to what might be. These leaders have acted like Lot in our story. They have shown no compassion. They have been concerned only for themselves and their institution. Meanwhile, victims have suffered trauma that has turned them to pillars of salt, unable to act.

Whenever we refuse to acknowledge the horror of trauma, whenever we imagine that trauma can lead to good, we ascribe destruction and devastation to God. I suggest that God is not in the destruction, but alongside the traumatized. That is where the church should be too.

Homiletic Points

1 The opening anecdote establishes the preacher's story of trauma. This needs careful handling in a church context, as there are likely to be others with similar stories – so a sensitive content warning up front would be important.
2 The connection between the trauma response of being frozen and the pillar of salt image helped the preacher re-frame the story, bringing out the multiple traumas suffered by Lot's wife – a very different approach to that which simply condemns the woman.
3 The final move of the sermon connects her trauma to the contemporary stories of trauma within the church.

Collect

God of the traumatized,
we turn to you for mercy.
Forgive us the times we have assumed pain
always leads to good.
Give us strength to stand alongside those who suffer,
those unable to act for themselves,
in the name of Jesus,
Amen.

Notes

1 Sandy Sasso, 'Bear witness: the story of Lot's wife explored through art, poetry', News at IU (2019), https://news.iu.edu/live/news/25906-bear-witness-the-story-of-lots-wife-explored, accessed 07.10.23.

2 Martin Harries, *Forgetting Lot's Wife: On Destructive Spectatorship* (New York: Fordham University Press, 2007), pp. 103–4.

3 Anna Akhmatova, *Poems of Akhmatova*, trans. S. Kunitz and M. Hayward (Boston MA: Little, Brown and Co., 1973).

4 See http://evolve.reconstructingjudaism.org/witnessing-suffering, accessed 25.02.23.

5 Miri Rozmarin, 'Staying alive: matricide and the ethical-political aspect of mother–daughter relations', *Studies in Gender and Sexuality*, Vol. 17, No. 4 (2016), pp. 242–53.

6 Steven Luger, 'Flood, salt, and sacrifice: post-traumatic stress disorder in Genesis', *Jewish Bible Quarterly*, Vol. 38 (2010), pp. 124–6.

3

God in the Muddle: Rebekah

KATE BRUCE

Rebekah in the Revised Common Lectionary (Sundays)

Year A   Proper 9 (OT 14)   Genesis 24.34–38, 42–49, 58–67

Rebekah's Words in the Bible

'Drink, my lord.' (Genesis 24.18)

She said to him, 'I am the daughter of Bethuel son of Milcah, whom she bore to Nahor.' She added, 'We have plenty of straw and fodder and a place to spend the night.' (Genesis 24.24–25)

'Thus the man spoke to me.' (Genesis 24.30)

'I will.' (Genesis 24.58)

'Who is the man over there, walking in the field to meet us?' (Genesis 24.65)

'If it is to be this way, why do I live?' (Genesis 25.22)

'I heard your father say to your brother Esau, "Bring me game, and prepare for me savoury food to eat, that I may bless you before the LORD before I die." Now therefore, my son, obey my word as I command you. Go to the flock, and get me two choice kids, so that I may prepare from them savoury food for your father, such as he likes; and you shall take it to your father to eat, so that he may bless you before he dies.' (Genesis 27.6–10)

(His mother said to him,) 'Let your curse be on me, my son; only obey my word, and go, get them for me.' (Genesis 27.13)

'Your brother Esau is consoling himself by planning to kill you. Now therefore, my son, obey my voice; flee at once to my brother Laban in Haran, and stay with him for a while, until your brother's fury turns away – until your brother's anger against you turns away, and he forgets what you have done to him; then I will send, and bring you back from there. Why should I lose both of you in one day?' (Genesis 27.42–45)

'I am weary of my life because of the Hittite women. If Jacob marries one of the Hittite women such as these, one of the women of the land, what good will my life be to me?' (Genesis 27.46)

Betrothal

Abraham wants a wife from his family line for his son Isaac. He sends a servant to Nahor in search of a suitable spouse. The servant meets Rebekah, Abraham's great niece, and Laban's sister – certainly kindred. The servant's prayer and its immediate fulfilment (Genesis 24.12–14, 15–21) offer a sense that the meeting between Rebekah and the servant is God-ordained. Rebekah is seen by God, who is an active agent in her life.

While the betrothal scene is dominated by the servant's speeches and conversation between him and Laban, it is worth attending to the counter narrative. Rebekah is a proactive young woman, eager to assist the servant in offering him water and drawing water for all his camels. She is young, beautiful and willing to roll up her sleeves – fulfilling the prayer of the servant in her words and actions. Her decisive and energetic nature is obvious: she '*quickly* lowered her jar upon her hand and *gave* him a drink' (v. 18). 'I *will draw* for your camels also, *until they have finished* drinking.' So she *quickly* emptied her jar into the trough and *ran again* to the well to draw, and she *drew for all* his camels (v. 20). She offers hospitality to the servant without asking the head of her household (v. 25). She is bold and direct. The servant thanks God for showing 'steadfast love and faithfulness' (v. 27) towards Abraham, as though he is the central character in the story. God is no less with Rebekah than God is with Abraham. Both Rebekah's and Abraham's futures are secured by the match.

In a continued burst of energy, Rebekah '*ran*' to tell her mother's household about these things' (v. 28). This reference to her 'mother's household' is interesting. Where is her father, Bethuel? Rebekah names him to the servant (v. 24) and he is mentioned later in the text, implying he has been present, but silent, in the betrothal negotiation (v. 50) – yet the household is 'her mother's'. Although it is her brother Laban who takes the lead in the betrothal conversation with the servant, her mother is mentioned (v. 55). Laban recognizes the opportunities for wealth being offered his sister and the family – and the two men engage in what is essentially a transaction, which began at the well when the servant put a nose ring on Rebekah (v. 47) and continues as they engage in discussion about her future and the dowry. Those familiar with her story will see some irony here – Rebekah is certainly not a woman led by the nose!

Initially, no one asks Rebekah what she wants. Later her mother and brother both express a desire that she stay a further ten days before going with the servant to the future husband she has never met. Now she is offered a choice: 'Will you go with this man?' (v. 58). She affirms she will – though I wonder what would have happened had she refused. It's interesting to note that her nurse goes with her (v. 59). How old is Rebekah at this point? Is the nurse's presence the decision of a protective mother, reluctant to send her daughter out into the world alone? The departing blessing offered Rebekah by mother and brother suggests the expectation of fecundity and the hope of power (v. 60). Rebekah leaves riding a camel, with an entourage of her nurse and an unspecified number of maids (v. 61).

Meeting

Again, we see the focus on Rebekah's actions – seeing Isaac, slipping from the camel, enquiring after him, and donning a veil (24.64–65). Perhaps the most intriguing aspect of the meeting between Rebekah and Isaac is that 'Isaac brought her into his mother Sarah's tent'. This reference reminds us that Rebekah has come from a matriarchal household (see above) and marries into a household where the late Sarah has had power and influence. This points us to a small detail in Genesis 29.12 when Jacob refers to himself as 'Rebekah's son' – not as Isaac's son. The theme of female influence is clearly present in the small details of the text as well as in significant sections of the plot. It is worth reminding ourselves that alongside the patriarchs we find female power and influence expressed by the matriarchs – who are evident in the narratives.

Conception: A Struggle

Isaac was 40 years old (Genesis 25.20) when he married Rebekah who must have been much younger (Genesis 24.16). We read that 'Isaac prayed to the LORD for his wife, because she was barren' (25.21). The blessing of fecundity is not realized. We read that the Lord answered Isaac's prayer (v. 21) but it took 20 years for Rebekah to conceive. 'Isaac was sixty years old when she bore' Esau and Jacob (v. 26). This bald textual statement obscures 20 years of pain, frustration, feelings of failure, perhaps anger and resentment, and almost certainly a sense that God was not blessing the marriage, with all the inherent confusion and internal struggle that must have brought.

Pregnancy: Struggling in Utero

'The children struggled together within her; and she said, "If it is to be this way, why do I live?" So she went to inquire of the LORD' (25.22).

Put yourself in Rebekah's shoes. After 20 years, finally, she conceives twins, but all is far from blissful. What experience might lie behind 'the children struggled together within her'? Pain, discomfort, gastric problems, high blood pressure, sleeplessness, hormone fluctuations, mood swings, frequent urination. No wonder she questions her life choices. The text is demure in its phrasing, 'she went to inquire of the LORD'. Let's be honest, most women would be enquiring in strong terms, rather than in a mincing, polite little prayer. Notice too that God answers her directly: 'She is the only matriarch to receive a direct message from God (although Abraham's slave wife Hagar also receives an oracle).[1]

God's answer is far from reassuring. The conflict between these babes in the womb will continue through their adult lives and develop into a conflict between peoples. God tells her: 'one shall be stronger than the other, the elder shall serve the younger' (v. 23). Perhaps those words stick in Rebekah's mind since she is instrumental in ensuring that the younger Jacob eclipses the elder, Isaac.

Birth: More Struggle

By the time of the birth, I imagine Rebekah was more than ready to meet her turbulent twins. The Bible makes no mention of the pain of birthing two children in succession – not helped by Jacob's grasping his brother's heel. Even in birth the conflict between them is clear. His name means 'supplanter' and his relationship with Isaac bears this out. Esau's name means 'hairy' and he grows up into something of the wild man. Nothing about this pregnancy has been straightforward; nothing about the boys' relationship will be either.

Family Dynamics: Further Struggle

We don't get a sense of the relationships between the boys and their parents in childhood, but no doubt the seeds of favouritism were sown then. Esau is the outdoorsman – a hunter. His brother was a quiet man who stayed around the family home. We learn that 'Isaac loved Esau, because he was fond of game; but Rebekah loved Jacob' (25.28). The text suggests a shallowness around Isaac's love of Esau, apparently being based on his love of meat, but perhaps it is more down to his love of stereotypical masculine pursuits. Rebekah's love of Jacob is perhaps based on his more constant presence around her in the domestic sphere. She may be trying to compensate for the favouritism of the head of the household, trying to mitigate her youngest son's hurt at what might be perceived as paternal rejection.

Later, Jacob plays his naive, hungry brother into selling his birthright for a bowl of lentil stew (25.29–34). Who made it is an interesting question. Has Jacob learned more stereotypically female roles from being around the tents, spending time with his mother? Further betrayal comes later, when Jacob steals his brother's blessing, with Rebekah's hand guiding the action.

Family Friction

When Isaac settles in Gerar he passes Rebekah off as his sister. Why? She is beautiful and he fears that local men might kill him because of her attractive appearance (Genesis 26.6–7). There is no sense that he might want to protect her from the potential assaults of such men. Perhaps he has learned the trick from his father Abraham.[2] We are not told what Rebekah thinks, or if she is even aware of Isaac's self-protecting ruse.

For many years the family live a nomadic existence. Isaac is blessed by God and with increased flocks and herds he needs ready access to water – which is a source of competition with other groups (Genesis 26.1–33). Wells play a significant part in Rebekah's life from her first meeting with Abraham's servant. Rebekah is not mentioned in the account of Isaac's search for a reliable water source, yet it affected her too – she was uprooted by quarrel and division over resources.

The backdrop of conflict is never far from this family. Esau married Hittite women and they 'made life bitter for Isaac and Rebekah' (26.34). We are not told the nature of the bitterness – perhaps it revolved around religious differences, and a sense that Esau was being taken from them, or disappointment in Esau's choices, or open hostility between the in-laws. Whatever the cause, the bitterness must have been a burden and a sorrow, and perhaps a source of endless circular discussion between the parents about their awful daughters-in-law.

Notice that the bitterness exists alongside the blessing of God (Genesis 24.27, 35; 26.12, 29). The two are not mutually exclusive. Grasping that God's blessing does not erase struggle is a reminder against simplistic notions of blessing and ease.

The Theft of Esau's Blessing

How are we to read this event? Is it the nadir of this family's toxic incidents? Is it the work of a mother trying to be faithful to enacting the will of God? Undoubtedly, Rebekah drives the action. She listens in to the conversation between her husband and eldest son concerning Isaac's desire to bless Esau while he still has life in him (Genesis 27.1–4). I can't help observing that if Isaac had been less concerned with his love of savoury food (v. 4) the blessing could have been given more swiftly! That aside, the deception is entirely driven by Rebekah – she listens, acts, plans, adapts to Jacob's objections, and reassures him that any retribution for the action will come on her. So convinced is she of the rightness of her plan that she is willing for any consequential curse to fall upon her (27.13). The action pivots on the disguise and the savoury food – both of which Rebekah prepares (Genesis 26.5–16). The disguise is deliberately designed to play on her husband's sensory deprivation.

Whichever way we interpret Rebekah's behaviour, there is no escaping the fact that she causes grief to her eldest son, but he is culpable for carelessly selling his birthright, suggesting he lacks the qualities for leadership which his father's blessing would confer. Does she discern in Jacob gifts that would make a better leader than Isaac? Is she trying to enact the prophecy given before they were born?

The words Esau does receive from his father are a tad underwhelming (27.39–40). Rebekah now must manage Esau's hatred. He has decided that once his father is dead, he will murder his little brother (27.41). Once again, Rebekah acts decisively with a plan to save Jacob – sending him to her brother, Laban. There is a degree of naivety in her belief that in time Esau's anger will abate and he will forget what 'you have done to him' (27.45). Years later the brothers were reconciled (33.4), but how could Esau ever forget the deception? Rebekah's words are also questionable as she places the responsibility for the incident squarely on Jacob's shoulders. She instigated a plan he then agreed to participate in; she bears as much, if not more, responsibility.

To facilitate Jacob's flight, Rebekah raises the possibility with Isaac that Jacob might marry a Hittite woman: 'I am weary of my life because of the Hittite women. If Jacob marries one of the Hittite women such as these, one of the women of the land, what good will my life be to me?' (27.46). Consequently, Isaac sends Jacob to his uncle Laban to find a wife there. Rebekah manipulates the situation effectively to secure Jacob's safety. This is the last time we hear of her other than learning that however she died (we are not told when or how) she was buried in the cave at Machpelah (Genesis 49.31) with Abraham and Sarah, and Isaac.

Sermon Suggestion: Rebekah – a Woman Who Divides Opinion

Rebekah divides opinion. An internet search on sermons about her reveal titles such as: 'Rebekah, the mother that destroyed her family'; 'Rebekah, woman of faith'; and 'Rebekah a marvellous mate and mother'.[3] Is she a controlling and deceptive woman who destroys her family? Or is she a woman who, like Mary, has been pondering the early promises about her sons' lives, watching them grow and assessing their gifts? She is a woman who divides opinion. What do we make of her?

In the story of Jacob conning his father over his brother's blessing, Rebekah plays the archetypal role of trickster, duping her husband with a goat-hair disguise and some dirty laundry. Tricksters in folk tales use intellect, guile and resource to bring about a desired end state. From the first moment we encounter Rebekah, at the well, she shows she is decisive, active and alert. She certainly has the skill set of the trickster.

Before we get too morally tight-lipped, this story is meant to entertain. It's full of humour. Picture Jacob with goat skin covering his hands and neck, trying to pass himself off as Esau. Picture the old man puzzling over the contradiction in his sensory data – feels like Esau, smells like Esau, sounds like Jacob. There is something of the pantomime here, the viewer wanting to shout out, 'He's not Esau.' Picture Rebekah listening in to the encounter, hoping Esau doesn't return too quickly.

Isaac seems incredibly naive in not following up on the clash between the sense of touch and smell, which points to Isaac's presence, and the sound of Jacob's voice (Genesis 27.22–24, 27). Although he trembles violently (27.33) when he learns he has blessed the wrong person, Isaac seems remarkably sanguine afterwards – and we witness no harsh words between him and his wife. It is tempting to wonder if he isn't aware of the switch and colluding with the deception.

We need to ask ourselves about Rebekah's motivation in the deception. Is she really seeking to cause her eldest bitter grief? Is she trying to undermine Isaac? Is she just a nasty piece of work? Or does she have a different end point in mind – fully aware of the pain her actions will cause Esau, fully aware of the family fallout. What end point? During her pregnancy, as the turbulent twins tousled in utero, she 'inquired of the LORD', much like a prophet, what it was all about – and God came straight back to her with an oracle:

'Two nations are in your womb,
    and two peoples born of you shall be divided;
one shall be stronger than the other,
    the elder shall serve the younger.' (Genesis 25.23)

Notice how God engages with her. We are not told how the message comes or what she made of this, or what questions it provoked. But I am confident she wouldn't have forgotten it! Surely this prophecy is the motivation behind her actions. In taking control of the situation, Rebekah is fulfilling the prophecy given when her sons were born. How do we react to this?

Does God need us to bring about divine purposes? Does God work through resourceful, cunning behaviour? It's an uncomfortable question. It's messy. The Bible is full of examples of God working through flawed people and their questionable decisions – which cause pain to others. Just look at the history of the patriarchs.

Did Rebekah know that Esau foolishly sold his birthright to his brother for a pot of lentil stew? Did she ponder this? One son looking ahead, thinking strategically, one diving into the moment, unreflective. Did she see that the younger showed the talent to go on to achieve great things, and the blessing would not be lost on him? Certainly, she was determined to achieve her aim and aware of the risk. Jacob feared the trickery would bring a curse not a blessing, and Rebekah says, 'My son, let the curse fall on me.' Is this just a throwaway comment muttered by an impatient woman? I don't think so. She is prepared to risk a curse for an end purpose she perceives is in line with the will of God. This has caused some to see her as a type of Christ.[4] I did say she divides opinion! She causes great pain to her eldest son who weeps aloud when he learns of the deceit and is filled with murderous hatred, which Rebekah then must manage to keep both sons safe. It's a messy story.

What we can be sure of is that God knows and loves this woman and has walked with her throughout. God was there at the well when she was betrothed to Isaac; there in the 20 barren empty years when she couldn't conceive; there in the feelings of failure as a woman; there in the pregnancy with the turbulent twins; there in the oracle about who the boys would become; there in the years she nurtured and watched them grow, forming a particular bond with Jacob, but surely loving Esau no less; there on the day of the deception; and there in the days afterwards. God has an intimate understanding of the loves and rivalries of all the characters in this strife-ridden family.

And so what? The story reminds us that God works God's purpose amid human struggle and flawed behaviour. God is in the mess and muddle of family life – in questionable decisions and painful actions, in relationships stretched and fractured, in mistakes made. No parent survives parenthood without making a catalogue of errors. No child is perfect. Families are rarely straightforward, but God works amid mess – and Rebekah's story should give us confidence in the presence of God in difficult and painful situations.

Rebekah is a woman who divides opinion. Some laud her as a prophet, some condemn her as a monster. I think she was just trying to do her best. God works in our muddled humanity now just as he worked in the muddled humanity of the matriarchs and patriarchs. The point is God works amid it all. That gives me hope.

Homiletic Points

1 The sermon begins by making the point that Rebekah divides opinion with illustrative evidence in three online sermon titles. There is likely to be a range of opinions about her in the congregation – this is acknowledged implicitly at the outset, and the congregation are asked to consider again what to make of Rebekah

2 The visual nature of the deception scene is highlighted with the three-fold invitation to 'Picture', and the comparison with pantomime.

3 Rebekah's motivation is explored, without ducking the fact that she caused great pain to Esau. Pastorally, it matters that this is noticed given the likelihood of congregants with stories of collateral damage due to parental decisions. At the same time the point is made that all parents make mistakes and no child is perfect. Family life is complicated.

4 This acknowledgement that family life is never perfect allows the turn to application – the 'and so what' is to notice that God is actively involved in the mess of this family, working the divine purpose out – and we can be confident that God still works in the muddle of our lives. Herein lies hope.

Collect

God in the muddle and mess
of our questionable decisions and best intentions,
open our eyes to your presence;
open our hearts to those wounded in families and friendships;
open our minds to seek you and trust you,
especially when it's hard
and we are unsure where you are.
Amen.

Notes

1 Carol Meyers, 'Rebekah: Bible', in *The Shalvi/Hyman Encyclopedia of Jewish Women* (2021), https://jwa.org/encyclopedia/article/rebekah-bible#pid-13308, accessed 09.07.23.

2 See Kate Bruce and L. Shercliff, *Out of the Shadows: Preaching the Women of the Bible*, Vol. 1 (London: SCM Press, 2021), ch. 3.

3 See www.sermoncentral.com, accessed 08.07.23.

4 Oleg M. Tsymbalyuk and Valery V. Melnik, 'Rediscovering the ancient hermeneutic of Rebekah's character', *HTS Theological Studies*, Vol. 76, No. 1 (2020), pp. 1–8.

4

Sisters, Wives and Servants:
Rachel, Leah, Bilhah and Zilpah

LIZ SHERCLIFF

<table>
<tr><td colspan="3">Their Stories in the Revised Common Lectionary</td></tr>
<tr><td>Year A</td><td>Proper 12 (OT 17)</td><td>Genesis 29.15–28</td></tr>
</table>

Their Words in the Bible

Leah

'Because the LORD has looked on my affliction, surely now my husband will love me.' (Genesis 29.32)

'Because the LORD has heard that I am hated, he has given me this son also.' (Genesis 29.33)

'Now this time my husband will be joined to me, because I have borne him three sons.' (Genesis 29.34)

'This time I will praise the LORD.' (Genesis 29.35)

'Good fortune!' (Genesis 30.11)

'Happy am I! For the women will call me happy.' (Genesis 30.13)

'Is it a small matter that you have taken away my husband? Would you take away my son's mandrakes also?' (Genesis 30.15)

'You must come in to me; for I have hired you with my son's mandrakes.' (Genesis 30.16)

'God has given me my hire because I gave my maid to my husband.' (Genesis 30.18)

'God has endowed me with a good dowry; now my husband will honour me, because I have borne him six sons.' (Genesis 30.19)

Rachel

'Give me children, or I shall die!' (Genesis 30.1)

'Here is my maid Bilhah; go in to her, that she may bear upon my knees and that I too may have children through her.' (Genesis 30.3)

'God has judged me, and has also heard my voice and given me a son.' (Genesis 30.5)

'With mighty wrestlings I have wrestled with my sister, and have prevailed.' (Genesis 30.8)

'Please give me some of your son's mandrakes.' (Genesis 30.14)

'Then he may lie with you tonight for your son's mandrakes.' (Genesis 30.15)

'God has taken away my reproach.' (Genesis 30.23)

'May the LORD add to me another son!' (Genesis 30.24)

'Let not my lord be angry that I cannot rise before you, for the way of women is upon me.' (Genesis 31.35)

Rachel and Leah

'Is there any portion or inheritance left to us in our father's house? Are we not regarded by him as foreigners? For he has sold us, and he has been using up the money given for us. All the property that God has taken away from our father belongs to us and to our children; now then, do whatever God has said to you.' (Genesis 31.14b–16)

The Women's Story

The background to this story is Jacob's flight from his brother Esau to the land of his uncle, Laban. At a well he meets Rachel, who takes him to meet Laban. Jacob stays a month there, presumably impressing Laban with his work, because, after the month, Laban offers Jacob one of his daughters as wages. Note the patriarchal treatment of the women. Leah, for some reason that is not clear in the Hebrew, is not an attractive proposition – either she is short-sighted, or not stereotypically beautiful. Rachel, however, is 'graceful and beautiful' (Genesis 29.17). We are told Jacob loves her, and offers to work seven years for her. Laban perhaps realizes during these seven years that he is unlikely to marry off Leah, so he swindles Jacob and sends Leah to the marriage bed. Jacob is not best pleased. Laban gives as his reason the fact that marrying the younger daughter first 'is not done' (Genesis 29.26). Culture trumps right, apparently. Laban shows no fatherly love for either daughter: 'Complete the week of this one, and we will give you the other also' (29.27). Neither woman is treated as anything more than a commodity, subject to male transactions, although Jacob does seem to love Rachel, for he works another seven years to gain her.

As rivals for their husband's love, Leah and Rachel enter a baby competition. Leah pulls well ahead, producing not only four babies but four sons. Rachel is so distressed, she claims she will die (Genesis 30.1). He gives her maid Bilhah to Jacob, and Bilhah produces two sons. The baby competition is intense – Rachel calls it wrestling with her sister (30.8). Leah learns by example, and gives her maid Zilpah to Jacob. Zilpah likewise bears sons. So far, so competitive. The women live according to patriarchal rules that afford them significance according to looks and fertility.

The story takes a turn during the harvest when Reuben, Leah's son, finds some mandrakes. Mandrakes have millennia of mythology behind them, most interestingly that they are supposed to scream when pulled from the ground, most relevantly for our purposes that they bestow fertility on the one who eats them. Rachel asks Leah for some of the mandrakes. In doing so, she asks her rival to give her an advantage in the competition. The exchange between the sisters is short but frank. Leah tells Rachel she has taken away her husband, and now wants her

mandrakes. Rachel seems to agree, at least about the mandrakes (30.15).
The women come to an agreement – Leah can have the night with Jacob,
Rachel can have some mandrakes. It seems trivial. But in this barter-
ing, the women behave as the menfolk have done previously. Laban and
Jacob bartered for the sisters, the sisters now barter for Jacob. It seems
to be empowering. Notice Leah's proactive approach to Jacob on his
return from the field – 'You must come in to me, for I have hired you'
(30.16). Jacob too seems to be affected by these events. When Laban's
sons begin complaining about him, and it is clearly time to leave, he consults his wives. Contrast this with earlier matriarchs, who were simply
taken (Genesis 12.5; 24.50).

The response of the sisters to Jacob's dilemma is very striking. They
have been treated as foreigners by their father, they say – he 'sold' us.
Although elsewhere in the Hebrew Bible men are said to 'buy' their wives,
nowhere else do fathers sell their daughters. The implication is that Laban
treated his daughters as slaves. Together, the women name their pain.
Miri Rozmarin suggests that '[h]earing oneself attest to the injuries of
phallocentric culture is a first step in recovering a sense of meaningfulness
and authority over one's own life'.[1] The sisters gain agency in this discussion, and as a result the situation changes again. They have won over
Jacob by letting him experience something akin to their own situation.
Now they, or at least Rachel, undermines her father's patriarchal power.

When the family leave, Rachel takes with her her father's *teraphim*.
Laban chases and catches up with them (Genesis 31.30). In the act of a
fully fledged patriarch, Jacob threatens to kill whoever has taken them.
What *teraphim* actually were is unclear. They may have been household
gods, but it also seems likely they were symbols of ancestry.[2] Rachel hides
the *teraphim* in a camel saddle bag and sits on the bag. She tells her
father that she is menstruating and cannot rise. Her father is unnerved by
this, and searches no further. Leah does not intervene, though she would
have known whether Rachel was menstruating because women withdrew
from the family at that time. Laban's nervousness serves to highlight a
theological point too. Women's blood is regarded as a pollutant, where
men's is associated with atonement.[3] Women's blood makes women
dirty. Ivone Gebara writes, 'For women, evil is in their very being.'[4] In
this narrative, Rachel's blood, real or imagined, is salvific.

Sermon Suggestion: The Power of Women

Have you heard the story of the jealous woman who envied her younger sister's beauty? Or the one about the rival sisters who competed to produce sons for their husband? Or the one where a ruthless uncle tricks a beautiful and in-love couple into having an unwanted sister in their marriage?

These are all ways the story of Leah and Rachel has been told elsewhere. I want, instead, to think about the story of two women who break out of patriarchal oppression and make their own story. I want to tell the story of two sisters who are set up to be rivals but overcome that by working together. And I want to tell the story of two women, bought and sold, who win the confidence of one man and undermine the tyranny of another.

Let me introduce Leah and Rachel.

They don't have a great start to the story. Their father treats them as nothing more than goods to be sold. In fact, by a bit of trickery, he manages to get 14 years' work out of a very competent flock manager in exchange for his girls. Jacob, the purchaser of the women, also treats them as commodities. He is oblivious to their plight. Beyond his growing family, and his prestigious number of sons, he sees nothing of the women's rivalry. He has no concept of their pain.

A small, apparently insignificant incident changes all that. We just have the edited highlights, but the consequences are huge. One of Leah's sons finds some mandrakes. Mandrakes are valuable, because they were believed to increase fertility. They provide Leah with an advantage. So Rachel asks for some. 'You've already taken my husband,' says Leah. 'Now you want some mandrakes too.' Rachel admits that she does. The women come to an agreement – Leah gets a night with Jacob, Rachel gets mandrakes. Do they realize through this interaction what it must be like to be a man? Do they realize that they do have power to make decisions? Whatever happens, when Jacob gets home from work, Leah tells him she has bought him. Now *he* is the commodity.

Jacob seems to learn respect for these women after this incident, because when things come to a head with Laban and it seems time for Jacob to move on he consults them. Pause for a moment and think about that. Jacob, one of the patriarchs, a man in the line of Abraham who took Sarah to a foreign land, and Isaac who had Rebekah brought to him, consults his wives. They have made him see things differently.

The consultation leads to honesty from the sisters. Their father treated them despicably. They were nothing. But now, thanks to taking some initiative and making Jacob see, they are equals with him in this decision.

There is one more step to liberation. Throughout the story we can trace the importance of ancestry. Laban's family makes him who he is. When Jacob and his wives move away, and Laban discovers that his *teraphim* are gone, he chases after them. It is not entirely clear what *teraphim* are, but they seem to be related to either family gods or ancestors in some way. Rachel knew what she was doing when she took them. Laban searches Jacob's camp, but when he comes to Rachel she tells him it is the wrong time of the month for her to stand and greet him. He backs off. Leah says nothing. At one time, in the midst of their rivalry, she would probably have betrayed her sister, but now they work together. I suspect that some of Laban's power is undermined by this action.

So this is a story of sisters at war because of their culture, who realize their own abilities to act, and discover that together they have power to disrupt patriarchal power. What might this look like nowadays? Just as Rachel's real or imagined period deterred Laban, so women's blood has been hidden for centuries in this country. As a result, sanitary products have been expensive and there has been such a thing as period poverty, causing girls to miss school for one week a month if they cannot afford the products they need. In 2020, Scotland became the first nation to provide free period products for all. The English government followed with a limited scheme available only to girls in state-maintained schools and colleges. Women worked together to make men aware of the problem and achieved significant success.

In churches, women have been asking for years why they have been barred from ministry. Some men have behaved like Jacob, understood what women say and begun to treat them as partners. Others have behaved like Laban, been fearful and continued to treat women as inferior.

Perhaps we can pray that women will realize and release their own power, so that justice might be done.

Homiletic Points

1 Structurally the sermon runs with the text, leading up to application in the contemporary context at the end.
2 The sermon's opening move establishes how the story has been told, setting up the second move, which is the decision to offer a different take on the text, that of women cooperating to make their own story.
3 This interpretation is anchored in the incident with the mandrakes and the deception over the *teraphim*. In both cases the point is made that the women have moved from competition to cooperation.

4 The sermon then asks what such female cooperation looks like today, which sets up the move to the present moment, earthed in the examples of success in the provision of sanitary products in school, and the cooperation, at least in most cases, between men and women in church leadership.

Collect

God of Leah and Rachel,
give us courage to give up on rivalry
and seek collaboration;
give us honesty to speak our truth.
God of Jacob,
give us openness to hear the other,
and treat them with dignity.
In the name of the one who
blessed and empowered women.
Amen.

Notes

1 Miri Rozmarin, 'Living politically: an Irigarayan notion of agency as a way of life', *Hypatia*, Vol. 28, No 3 (Summer 2013), p. 472.

2 S. Nidditch, 'Genesis', in C. A. Newsom, S. H. Ringe and J. E. Lapsley (eds), *The Women's Bible Commentary* (London: SPCK, 2014), pp. 39–40.

3 Tina Beattie, *God's Mother, Eve's Advocate* (London: Continuum, 2002) p. 195.

4 Ivone Gebara, *Out of the Depths: Women's Experience of Evil and Salvation* (Minneapolis, MN: Fortress Press, 2002), p. 4.

5

A Daughter Defiled:
Dinah (Genesis 34)

KATE BRUCE

Dinah in the Revised Common Lectionary

Not included.

Dinah's Words in the Bible

None.

Summary

Dinah is the only daughter of Leah, the wife Jacob did not love (Genesis 29.31). She goes to visit the women of the region. When Shechem son of Hamor, a Hivite, saw her he raped her. He then decides he is in love with her, detains her in his house (Genesis 34.26), and gets his father to go and 'Get this girl to be my wife' (Genesis 34.4).

Meanwhile Jacob learns of his daughter's defilement but says and does nothing. In contrast, his sons are furious because of the outrage Shechem had committed, 'for such a thing ought not to be done' (34.7). There follows a scene in which Hamor outlines the benefits to Israel of marrying into the Hivites, pointing to economic prosperity (v. 10). Shechem offers a marriage present and gift 'as high as you like' (v. 12) if only he can have Dinah as his wife. She is an object to be purchased in a transaction. He seems a little obsessive.

Because of the defilement of Dinah, the sons of Jacob act deceitfully (v. 13). They lead the Hivites to believe that if the men were all circumcised there would be no impediment to widespread inter-marriage. Hamor and Shechem sell this idea to the men of their city by implying that the property of Israel will become their own (v. 23). The men all agree to circumcision. While they are still recovering, Dinah's two full brothers, Simeon and Levi, enter the city, kill all the men by the sword, and take Dinah away. The sons of Jacob then plunder the city and cart off all the women and children, as well as livestock (vv. 27–28). Jacob finally expresses some anger – but only on his own behalf – stating to Simeon and Levi, 'You have brought trouble on me ...' (v. 30). The story ends with the brothers' defence, 'Should our sister be treated like a whore?' (v. 31).

Throughout we hear nothing from Dinah, and she is only referenced once again in the Bible, as one of those who came to Egypt (Genesis 46.15). What is *her* story?

Dinah's Story

Dinah is the seventh child of Leah, her only daughter (30.21). Laban, Leah's father, tricked Jacob into taking Leah as his wife (29.23), when Jacob was in love with her younger sister, Rachel (29.18). How did this favouritism affect Dinah? The text doesn't focus on Dinah's upbringing, but what we do see is Jacob's utter indifference to his daughter's defilement. In contrast to her brothers, Jacob says and does nothing in her defence. His only concern in the matter is that the vengeance the brothers wreak on Hamor's people brings trouble on him 'by making me odious' (34.30) to the surrounding tribes. We can only speculate on what this indifference says to Dinah; it's likely it is simply an extension of the indifference she has always known as the youngest child of an ill-favoured wife.

Dinah 'went out to visit the women of the region' (34.1). Some, like John Calvin, have criticized her for leaving the private space of the family home, arguing that in going out in public she put herself in danger:

Dinah is ravished, because, having left her father's house, she wandered about more freely than was proper. She ought to have remained quietly at home, as both the Apostle teaches and nature itself dictates ... if a vain curiosity was so heavily punished in the daughter of holy Jacob, not less danger hangs over weak virgins at this day, if they go too boldly and eagerly into public assemblies, and excite the passions of youth towards themselves.[1]

Victim blaming from Calvin. Gordon Wenham says that in meeting the women of the land 'Dinah was at least sailing close to the wind.'[2] Should a woman who is confident, curious, bold and engaging really be blamed because in the course of making connections with other women she is attacked? Jessica Eaton, campaigner for victims of sexual violence, comments: 'Headphones don't rape women, nor do skirts, or dark streets, or clubs, or alcohol, or parties, or sleepovers, or school uniforms,'[3] nor, we might add, seeking connections with others. Where is the focus on the perpetrator?

A Range of Interpretations

What happened to Dinah has been interpreted in many ways. The mini-series *Red Tent* interprets it as a love story, which, although it gives Dinah a voice, is unlikely since she would not have had the freedom to pursue such a relationship, and there is no evidence for this in the text.[4] Lynn Japinga suggests that Shechem and Dinah may have known each other and Dinah is potentially a victim of 'date rape'.[5] She indicates that most commentators have 'explained the encounter as a flirtation or seduction' and Dinah at least initially 'a willing partner.'[6]

What was the nature of Dinah's defilement? Was she raped by a powerful man? Was she complicit in the relationship, and then raped? Or has she disobeyed tradition and expectation and taken a lover, as *Red Tent* suggests? Why does Shechem suddenly love her and speak tenderly to her (34.3)? Is this genuine regret or gaslighting? He wants her as his wife, what does *she* want? Does she willingly remain in Shechem's house (v. 26) or is she detained against her will? Whatever the answer, all remain possibilities for girls in today's world.[7]

Much depends on the interpretation of the three Hebrew words used to describe what Shechem did after he saw Dinah. First, *yiqah* – he 'took her'; then *yishkah* – he 'lay with her'; then *'innah* – he 'defiled' her. This latter word, *'innah*, is also used to describe Amnon's sexual attack on his sister Tamar (2 Samuel 13.14), though the word order in that text is different. In the Dinah narrative we read: 'He took her, lay with her, and *'innah*-ed her.' In the Tamar account, Amnon overpowered her, *'innah*-ed her, and lay with her. Shawna Dolansky argues that this means Dinah was not necessarily raped and we should not assume that defilement in a sexual context equates to rape.[8] She argues the defilement is about a reduction in Dinah's social status due to her no longer being a virgin and therefore no longer having the same economic and social value to her father as a potential bride, able to cement alliances. The defilement is a social defilement against her and her family.

Dolansky cautions against reading back into the text a view of female independence which did not exist within the culture in which the writing originated.

> In the case of the Dinah story, I submit that feminist literary analysis projects notions of individualism and bodily autonomy from a 21st century North American perspective back onto an ancient Israelite society that seems to have thought very differently about such things. This story is not about the rape of Dinah at all. It is about the lowering of her social and economic status as she moves from fulfilling the proper role in the proper place (virgin daughter in her father's house) to a socially ambiguous role with no proper corresponding physical place.[9]

Alert to Themes of Power

Dolansky makes a fair point about being alert to the concerns of the text. However, we also need to be alert to the concerns of the context within which that text is read. According to Rape Crisis, 1 in 4 women and 1 in 18 men have been raped or sexually assaulted, and 1 in 6 children sexually abused.[10] This text needs careful handling. If we sideline Dinah's experience, what are we saying to the people behind those statistics? We need to be prepared to highlight what is in plain sight. Dinah is powerless. She has no voice, and no rights. Other than going to visit the women of the land, she is passive. There is no textual evidence that she had a prior relationship with Shechem. He is a powerful son of a prince. He sees her and he takes her. Various Bible translations offer different words for '*innah* – 'lay with her by force' (New Revised Standard Version); 'defiled her' (Authorized Version); 'humiliated her' (English Standard Version) 'raped her' (New International Version, New Living Translation, Good News Translation, International Standard Translation). However we look at it, Shechem harms Dinah. He forces her into sexual intercourse. He brings shame upon her. He defiles her body and trashes her social status.

Following the act of violence against her we read that Shechem's 'soul was drawn to Dinah ... he loved the girl, and spoke tenderly to her' (v. 3). How utterly bewildering for Dinah! To experience violence and then tenderness in swift succession is nothing short of manipulation.

Wenham comments:

At least Shechem did not treat Dinah as Amnon did Tamar after raping her, who 'hated her with a very great hatred' and expelled her from his room (2 Samuel 13.15–17). Instead, he 'became very attached' to Dinah, lit. 'his soul stuck to Dinah,' *precisely the right bond between a married couple.*[11] (my italics)

This astonishing statement rather overlooks the fact that Dinah's feelings are never mentioned. Would she want to be married to the man who assaulted her? Wenham's reading airbrushes Dinah out of the picture. Shechem's emotional response to Dinah feels suffocating and obsessive. He is determined to have her at any cost. What she wants remains unknown. She cannot be free of him emotionally or physically. He has taken her to his house; her freedom curtailed.

Jacob does not defend his daughter; he is silent. The motivation behind her brothers' terrible, violent response is open to question. Are they bothered about her or about their social standing? They state, 'Should our sister be treated like a whore?' (v. 31). Perhaps this is a statement of concern for her but, underlying their rage, is there a sense of personal affront? Even if they are defending her honour, they don't have much care for the honour of other women. The brothers rape the women's town, penetrating skin with sword. What fate awaits those women captured in the sacking of the city (v. 29)?

Throughout the story, women are objects to be taken, used, held and captured. They are passive and voiceless. The text is not interested in them. It is therefore vital to read against the grain of the text because the very real danger is that if we allow the patriarchal assumptions to go unchallenged it is a short step to stating that God is not interested in these women, and all women are just bit parts in a male-centred drama.

Sermon Suggestion: Dinah – the Importance of Seeing and Being Seen

I once heard an incredibly powerful story from a woman in therapy. She described trying to recount her experiences of sexual abuse. In the process she turned away, facing the wall, unable to move. She described how the therapist got up, slowly moved across the room, and sat down near her. After a while the woman looked up and the two made eye contact. The woman's response is striking: 'It never occurred to me that she could move towards me. For the first time, I felt my story was seen. *I* was seen.' Being seen marked a key point in that woman's journey of integration.

35

It validated her experience and conveyed value and care. It pierced the loneliness of her situation. Seeing really matters.

Seeing really matters in our reading today. What do we see in the story and who do we miss? What does the drive of the narrative expect us to see, and should we go along with the way the story is framed? The story is often called 'The Rape of Dinah', but the focus is not on her. The focus is on the male reactions to that event: the father's indifference; Shechem's obsession to marry Dinah at any price; the greed of the men of the city for the possessions of Jacob's tribe; and the brothers' murderous fury. Dinah is an object to be taken. Shechem takes her sexually, then desires to buy her as his wife. The brothers sack an entire city in vengeance and then take her from Shechem's house. We never get any insight into Dinah as a person. Her words are not recorded. What does she want? What is her story? Do we see her?

Did we see any other women in this story? They are the ones taken as plunder, along with the children, after Simeon and Levi had murdered all the men. What future can they hope for as slaves of Jacob's tribe? Gordon Wenham, in his commentary on this text, makes no specific comment on the women and children being taken into slavery, they are just part of the 'booty'. They are overlooked. Not seen.

Why does it matter? If the women are not the focus of the text, should we simply accept that? If we take the biblical text at face value, we are assuming that the narrator's perspective is the only perspective, which means there are those on the edges whom we don't see. It is not unfaithful to Scripture to focus on the edges and the corners. How many times does Jesus see what others miss? A bent-over woman; a woman offering a tiny coin; a little child; a grieving mother. Seen.

In this story we see a woman who is powerless, whose life is damaged by the actions of the man who harms her. That harm is not a one-off, it will affect her life in ways many will not see. She bears the shame of the defilement done to her. Her reputation is damaged. She is made into an object. Many commentators have placed the blame on her for the fate of the city, arguing that if she'd not left the family home none of this would have happened. No mention of Shechem's part in it. We never hear what happens next to Dinah. Other than a brief mention as one of those who went down to Egypt, Dinah disappears. Out of sight. Out of mind. But it doesn't have to be this way. We can choose to see.

Have we lost sight of the young girls abused in Rotherham? Fourteen hundred of them according to the Jay Report. What have their lives been like? What is the legacy of their abuse? Where is the hope for them? One of them, Sammy Wood, opened a cafe as a safe space in the town, and finds that young people come and chat to her. They see her. She sees them.

What is happening to the women living restricted lives under Taliban rule, pushed into the private spheres, unable to study, forced to cover up, restricted in work, struggling for identity in an oppressive and war-torn country? Do I choose to see them?

What about those caught up in war, fleeing, travelling in unseaworthy boats, looking for a better life? Do I see them – or would I prefer them to be flown far away to another country? Out of sight. Out of mind. Seeing matters – as does being seen.

To see the other, really see, is to convey care, empathy, value and love. Another person's truth will often not be obvious – it takes imagination and the willingness to move, to shift perspective, develop curiosity and take risks. Sometimes to see we must get uncomfortable. The therapist had to move from a comfortable chair and sit in a small space on the floor to see her client. It raises a question. Are we willing to leave our comfortable chairs to really see the other? Will we shift our perspective? Seeing and being seen matter.

Homiletic Points

1 Perhaps the most obvious point with this text is to handle with care. It doesn't arise in the Lectionary, and is not a text to be used in Parish Communion, since even with advance notice of the subject matter, someone could miss that and find themselves triggered by the content. It should be used in a specific context – perhaps a healing service or retreat, with plenty of warning about the content.

2 The sermon is woven around the theme of being seen, which is established through the opening story of the woman in therapy, which bookends the whole piece. Paragraphs are topped and tailed with the repetition of the theme of seeing. This serves to pull the piece together.

3 There are four movements in the sermon: the therapist story; reference to the text with focus on the question of what we see in it; reference to examples of people we may not have in sight; ending with re-stressing the importance of seeing.

Collect

You are the God who sees.
Open our eyes to the unseen.
Make us bold in challenging dominant narratives,
unwilling to allow power to frame the story.
Draw us into discomfort, to be willing to see
and be seen.
Amen.

Notes

1 John Calvin, https://www.bibliaplus.org/en/commentaries/3/john-calvins-bible-commentary/genesis/34/1, accessed 16.07.23.

2 Gordon Wenham, *Genesis 16–50*, Word Biblical Commentary (Dallas, TX: Word Books, 1994), p. 310.

3 BBC news article, 'Victim blaming: is it a woman's responsibility to stay safe?', https://www.bbc.co.uk/news/uk-england-45809169, accessed 16.07.23.

4 Princess O'Nika Auguste, 'Rape and consent in Genesis 34 and Red Tent', https://popularcultureandtheology.com/2020/06/19/rape-and-consent-in-genesis-34-and-red-tent-part-one/, accessed 16.07.23.

5 Lynn Japinga, *Preaching the Women of the Old Testament* (Louisville, KY: Westminster John Knox Press, 2017), p. 34.

6 Japinga, *Preaching*, p. 35.

7 See for example, this article about girls in Uganda: https://www.theguardian.com/global-development/2023/sep/28/kidnapped-and-forced-to-marry-their-rapist-ending-courtship-in-uganda, accessed 30.09.23.

8 Shawna Dolansky, 'The debasement of Dinah', https://www.thetorah.com/article/the-debasement-of-dinah, accessed 14.07.23.

9 Dolansky, 'The debasement of Dinah'.

10 See https://rapecrisis.org.uk/get-informed/statistics-sexual-violence/, accessed 14.07.23.

11 Wenham, *Genesis 16–50*, p. 311.

6

Sex-Trading for Justice:
Tamar, Daughter-in-Law of Judah

LIZ SHERCLIFF

> **Tamar in the Revised Common Lectionary**
>
> Not included.

Tamar's Words in the Bible

'What will you give me, that you may come in to me?' (Genesis 38.16)

'Only if you give me a pledge, until you send it.' (Genesis 38.17)

'Your signet and your cord, and the staff that is in your hand.' (Genesis 38.18)

'It was the owner of these who made me pregnant.' (Genesis 38.25)

'Take note, please, whose these are, the signet and the cord and the staff.' (Genesis 38.25)

Tamar's Story

A careful reading of Tamar's story reveals not two key characters but three. Alongside Tamar and Judah on stage is Hirah, the Adullamite and close friend of Judah. This friendship is vital to the story. The men meet when they are young. They are powerful and influential. Their friendship is secure and mutually beneficial. As so often happens, and has happened, the powerful secure their position by judicious marriages, and so it is no surprise that it is while he is near Hirah that Judah sees and marries the daughter of Shua, whose name apparently means opulent, and who has three sons in the space of three verses. The writer dispatches two of them rapidly. Er, then (under levirate law) Onan, are married to Tamar and killed by God. Judah seems to suspect either foul play or bad luck, because he refuses to follow levirate law next time round, and withholds his third son Shelah from Tamar.

Interval

Let's pause and consider what we know about the men in the story so far. Readers of Genesis have met Judah before. He and his brothers hated Joseph of the multi-coloured coat, their younger brother, and were about to kill him when Judah asked, 'What profit is there in that? Let's sell him' (Genesis 37.26). Immediately afterwards he leaves his brothers and settles in Cana near an Adullamite called Hirah. Hirah is a Canaanite of some standing. The text emphasizes that it is when Judah is near Hirah that he sees Shua's daughter (Genesis 38.2). It seems likely that, to socially advance his friend, Hirah introduces Judah to this woman who has no name but whose father's name apparently means 'opulence'. Note how the men's friendship is sealed by controlling a woman.

The author seems keen to emphasize Judah's taking of the woman. English translations are coy. Judah marries *bat Shua* (daughter of Shua) and goes into her. The Hebrew is more direct – Judah sees *bat Shua*, 'takes her and enters her',[1] again and again. In 38.3 'She conceived and bore a son'; in verse 4 'Again she conceived and bore a son'; in verse 5, 'Yet again she bore a son.' The relationship between *bat Shua* and Judah demonstrates Judah's virility and cements his relationship with Hirah,[2] a relationship between two powerful men of the area underpinned by the transaction of a woman's body.[3] In verse 6 Judah again takes a woman, this time for his son Er. Now Tamar falls under Judah's power. Her first husband, Er, is killed by God. She is passed on to Onan, the second son, who is to produce an heir for his brother under levirate law. Onan, the second son, is a chip off the old block. Any heir produced for Er would reduce Onan's own inheritance. He practises contraception instead, and God kills him for it.

Judah's power is emphasized by his control of women, but it also seems to be aligned with God's blessing. Judah sees *bat Shua*, takes her, enters her, and she becomes pregnant – three times. Er *does* not produce children and is killed by God. Onan *will* not produce them and is killed by God.

Back to Tamar's Story

Instructing Tamar to remain a widow in her father's house binds her to Judah until he has use for her.[4] She is denied justice, either a husband or release from the levirate contract. As a result, she is also denied a future. Meantime, Judah's wife dies, and after the expected time of mourning Judah joins Hirah and the sheep-shearers for the spring festival, 'a licentious bucolic occasion',[5] where men would expect opportunities for sex. Tamar's friends are apparently alert to her plight because someone tells her what Judah is up to. She sees an opportunity, dresses as a prostitute and sits herself by the roadside. Some commentators condemn her for this. In a real sense, though, it is 'survival sex', sex traded for basic needs. Tamar may have food and shelter while her father-in-law lives, but her dependence on him makes her vulnerable. Again, Judah sees a woman and takes her. Genesis 38.16 in English Bibles reads something like, 'Let me come into you', or, 'Let me sleep with you.' The Hebrew is far more straightforward and demanding, best rendered, 'Let me f*ck you!'[6] Judah speaks from a position of power and privilege.

Tamar, however, is shrewd. She negotiates a price and a guarantee of payment. It is this guarantee that is important. The seal and staff are signs of authority and status. The seal was worn round the neck, tied by a cord. If the cord is intact, the seal has not been stolen. Notice again the friendship between Judah and Hirah. Hirah hangs around while Judah has sex with Tamar. Later, when Judah needs to recover his seal and staff, Hirah goes off with the baby goat on Judah's behalf. Judah's sex with a prostitute binds them together. Using women to promote male friendship is not unusual. It is not, I suspect, a normal part of all male relationships, but it is key to toxic masculinity. Indeed, it is not unusual for relationships among men to be mediated through sexual relations with women.[7] Hirah tries to protect Judah by asking the locals where he might find the *qedesha* (temple prostitute),[8] where the text tells us Judah thought he had been with a *zonah* (a common prostitute). When he returns empty handed, Judah says, 'Let her keep the things ... otherwise *we* will be laughed at' (Genesis 38.23, my emphasis). This casual inclusion of Hirah with himself is probably an unconscious sign of male bonding. There is another sign of unconscious male bonding in this story too – the way the story is told. There is no comment on the injustice suffered by Tamar.

Yet her husbands are killed by God for not procreating. The text is clear about Onan. Ancient Jewish exegesis claims that Er also practised contraception (Genesis Rabbah: 85:4).[9]

Three months after his encounter with the 'prostitute', Judah is told that Tamar is pregnant. In fact, he is told, 'Your daughter-in-law Tamar has prostituted herself [played the whore, NRSV]' (Genesis 38.24). In a film, the camera would pan to Judah's face, picking up perhaps a subtle blush. But Judah seems not even to hesitate. He pronounces sentence without mercy, without fear of contradiction, and without reference to the law of his own people.[10] She is to be burned. Tamar returns his goods to him with the message that she is pregnant by their owner. Judah rescinds his sentence and admits his wrongdoing in not marrying his third son to Tamar. Notice his use of a prostitute is not part of his confession. Tamar gives birth to two sons, who replace Shelah in the patriarchal lineage. Their birth is seen as a blessing from God. Tamar leaves the story.

Tamar in Context

First, we need to read Tamar's story in the overall context of Genesis. It is a book full of trickery: Abraham tricks Pharaoh and Abimelech to protect himself (Genesis 12.17); Jacob tricks Isaac (with assistance from Rebekah) to receive Esau's blessing (Genesis 27); Isaac tricks Abimelech into believing Rebekah is his sister in a reprise of Abraham's trickery (Genesis 26.7). In each case the trickery was aimed at securing the safety or profit of a man. There are two other examples of trickery: Lot's daughters and Tamar. Lot and his daughters live together in an isolated cave, because Lot is afraid for his life. His daughters realize the only way of having children is to have sex with their father, so they get him drunk and do so. Lot deprives his daughters of their rights, and they trick him into doing justice. Tamar's father-in-law deprives her of her rights, and she similarly tricks him into justice. Generally, trickery is rewarded in Genesis but on only two occasions, apparently, do women benefit from it. Where Abraham and Isaac use trickery it is to protect themselves and put women at risk. Tamar, then, stands out as an example of a woman subverting the normal hierarchy to protect herself.

Second, we need to read Tamar's story in a social context. Er and Onan seem to be killed by God for not procreating. Judah seems to be blessed by God with wealth, position and children. This theme continues to the present day, when Tamar's actions are interpreted only theologically, as a way of securing the line of Judah from which Jesus is born. But the text, especially when it hasn't been filtered through the lens of respectability, is clear. Women are pawns for men to move around. They are seen and taken; they are controlled; they disappear. Their stories are suppressed – notice that Judah confesses a sin against the law rather than against Tamar (38.26). At the end of Genesis 38, Tamar disappears. She is made invisible. Three later references to her in the Bible all make her simply the bearer of Judah's sons.[11]

Introducing Christian Aid's 2018 report *War on Women: The Global Toll of Conflict and Violence*, Elaine Storkey writes:

> If we enable women to be more economically autonomous, more educated and more aware of their rights, while also working with communities to counter patriarchal narratives that subjugate women, we will be able to take steps forward in ending all forms of violence against women.
>
> As people of faith, we must also acknowledge the painful reality that religious institutions have played a part in creating and upholding patriarchal and exclusionary structures and practices which have kept women unequal and more prone to being victims of violent acts and structural violence.
>
> We must work hard to put forward theological frameworks and understandings that highlight our belief that each and every person is made in God's image and worthy of inherent respect. Our theology must enable us to fight for the equality, dignity and justice of all, and we must reject those theological frameworks which push us towards gender stereotypes that limit women's rights, bodily integrity and agency.[12]

It seems to me that Elaine offers a challenge to preachers to tell women's stories.

Sermon Suggestion: Sex for Survival

You will have met the people in our story before, I'm sure. There's the privileged and powerful Judah. He sees and takes – he sees Shua's daughter and takes her; he sees Tamar and takes her, first for his son, then for himself. He sees Tamar's liberty as a threat and takes it from her, banishing her to her father's house while keeping her beholden to him. He sees Tamar's pregnancy as an opportunity, and proposes to take her life. He sees the risk of embarrassment and confesses a sin against the law rather than against Tamar. Judah is so confident in his position he is even willing to risk the marks of his identity and authority by leaving them with a prostitute.

Yet, in the local ale house, Judah's mate Hirah will tell everyone what a good bloke Judah is. 'You can have fun with him!' I can imagine Hirah saying. Like some defend abusers – 'It's just a laugh!' When they see the prostitute on the road, Hirah doesn't attempt to hold Judah back. They were intent on having a good time anyway, it's just come a bit early. When Judah sends him off to pay the woman for services rendered, he even tries to make Judah's action seem respectable – he asks after a temple prostitute rather than a common one.

If this lot were a gang of lads out on a Saturday night, Judah and Hirah would walk in front, filling the pavement space. Er and Onan would be behind them, basking in reflected glory of masculine virility. They give the appearance of doing the right thing, following the lead. But they don't do it, and God kills them. Funny how the deaths of the weak ones make the powerful seem right somehow, isn't it? Just as the disadvantaged in our own society are blamed for their plight, and the wealthy lauded for deserving what they have.

You may not have met Tamar. But you will have seen her. She has no background or story. She is there to serve the men, marry Judah's son when he tells her. Marry Judah's other son when he tells her. Lie with Judah when he tells her. She's an accessory, needed to enable the functioning of her society. As time goes on, Tamar realizes that she will not get justice. Judah has no intention of giving her to his third son in marriage, although he keeps her in virtual captivity, under his jurisdiction. Her food and shelter depend on her father, and on his survival. Her future is bleak. Tamar does what many women around the world, and increasingly since Covid, have been forced into – 'survival sex'.[13] Sex traded for immediate needs such as money, food, or a bed for the night. Tamar has a plan, though. She targets the source of her oppression. There is no need to entice him. She removes her mourning clothes, puts on a veil, and sits at the side of the road. How well she knows Judah!

Tamar is wise though. Although Judah addresses her without a trace of respect, she demands respect of him. To guarantee his payment she takes the signs of his status and authority. Now she can command justice. And when her pregnancy is revealed that is what she does.

Imagine the scene. Judah condemns Tamar for prostitution. 'She must die. Prepare the fire.' A show of might for the benefit of his gang. All eyes are on him. And then … Then Tamar produces the seal, and the cord, and the staff. Judah is shown to be power*less* because of Tamar's trickery. He has no choice other than to admit guilt. He doesn't admit his treatment of Tamar was wrong, of course, or his willingness to take a prostitute. What he admits to is breaking the patriarchal law – guilty of not ensuring descendants is all he will own up to. Tamar, he says, is more righteous than him because she pointed out that the patriarchal law had been broken. There is no question of Tamar deserving respect or justice.

How do we place this story in our own twenty-first-century culture? In 2020 in England and Wales, according to Rape Crisis, 85,000 women were raped. Only 20 per cent went to the police. Only 3 per cent of these cases were prosecuted, and 58 per cent of these cases were acquitted.[14] Our courts behave like Hirah. Just as he looked on as Judah abused Tamar, so they look on and allow rape to happen.

A recent Christian Aid report says this:

As people of faith ... we must work hard to put forward theological frameworks and understandings that highlight our belief that each and every person is made in God's image and worthy of inherent respect. Our theology must enable us to fight for the equality, dignity and justice of all, and we must reject those theological frameworks which push us towards gender stereotypes that limit women's rights, bodily integrity and agency.[15]

Homiletic Points

1 Notice the punchy rhetorical effect of the 'sees ... takes' riff at the start of the sermon.
2 The preacher paints an imagined picture of the biblical characters as a 'gang of lads', which earths the sermon in the everyday. Colloquial language, such as 'ale house', 'good bloke', also contributes towards this effect.
3 Notice how the sermon moves back and forth between the biblical text and the contemporary context.
4 The application is embedded within the quotation from the Christian Aid report.

Collect

God of the invisible, ignored and oppressed,
we give thanks for those who strive for justice
even at great personal cost.

Give us the courage to see those we prefer not to notice;
the determination to make their voices heard
and the faithful energy to highlight injustice.
In the name of Jesus, whose flesh too
was abused.
Amen.

Notes

1 Barbara Thiede, *Male Friendship, Homosociality, and Women in the Hebrew Bible: Malignant Fraternities* (London and New York: Routledge, 2022), p. 15.

2 A. Van Selms, 'The origin of the title "The King's Friend"', *Journal of Near Eastern Studies*, Vol. 16, No. 2 (April 1957), pp. 118–23.

3 For further reading on the ways in which male relationships depend on the use and exchange of women's bodies, see Claude Lévi-Straus' alliance theory in *Elementary Structures of Kinship* (Boston, MA: Beacon Press, 1971), or Michael Flood, 'Men, sex, and homosociality: how bonds between men shape their sexual relations with women', *Men and Masculinities*, Vol. 10, No. 3 (2008), pp. 339–59, https://doi.org/10.1177/1097184X06287761, accessed 13.11.23.

4 Tikva Frymer-Kensky, *Reading the Women of the Bible: A New Interpretation of Their Stories* (New York: Schocken Books, 2002), p. 268.

5 G. R. H. Wright, 'Dumuzi at the court of David', *Numen*, January 1981, pp. 54–63, 56.

6 Thiede *Male Friendship*, p. 24.

7 Flood, 'Men, sex, and homosociality', p. 339.

8 Robert Alter, *The Five Books of Moses: A Translation with Commentary* (New York and London: W.W. Norton and Co., 2004), p. 147.

9 He would 'plough on the roof', that is, replace procreative sex with anal sex (Genesis Rabbah: 85.4).

10 As we see in the later story of the woman caught in adultery brought before Jesus (John 8.1–11), the usual punishment for adultery or prostitution was stoning.

11 In 1 Chronicles 2.4, 'His daughter-in-law Tamar also bore him Perez and Zerah'; in Ruth 4.12 people say to Boaz, 'may your house be like the house of Perez, whom Tamar bore to Judah'; in Matthew 1.3, 'Judah the father of Perez and Zerah by Tamar'.

12 E. Storkey, 'Foreword', in C. McDonald, M. Leite, N. Saracini, K. Balfe, *War on Women: The Global Toll of Conflict and Violence* (London: Christian Aid, 2018), pp. 5–6.

13 Lauren Jacobson, Alexandra Regan, Shirin Heidari and Monica Adhiambo Onyango, 'Transactional sex in the wake of COVID-19: sexual and reproductive health and rights of the forcibly displaced', *Sexual and Reproductive Health Matters*, Vol. 28, No. 1 (2020).

14 See https://rapecrisis.org.uk, accessed 03.04.23.

15 Storkey, 'Foreword', pp. 5–6.

7

Vilified and Vindicated: Potiphar's Wife

LIZ SHERCLIFF

> **Potiphar's Wife in the Revised Common Lectionary**
>
> Not included.

The Words of Potiphar's Wife in the Bible

'Lie with me.' (Genesis 39.7)

'Lie with me!' (Genesis 39.12)

'See, my husband has brought among us a Hebrew to insult us! He came in to me to lie with me, and I cried out with a loud voice; and when he heard me raise my voice and cry out, he left his garment beside me, and fled outside.' (Genesis 39.14–15)

'The Hebrew servant, whom you have brought among us, came in to me to insult me; but as soon as I raised my voice and cried out, he left his garment beside me, and fled outside.' (Genesis 39.17–18)

What *is* the Story?

The tale of Mrs Potiphar and the/a Hebrew slave appears in the holy literature of all three monotheistic religions. Joseph arrives in the house having been bought as a slave. The Lord is with him and he prospers, as does Potiphar's house under him. Joseph is placed in charge of everything, and all Potiphar has to worry about is his food. Potiphar's wife is attracted to Joseph apparently, and pursues him. Joseph points out that she is the only thing her husband has withheld from him – note Joseph's treatment of her as a prized possession rather than a human being able to make her own choices. Joseph goes to the house when everyone else is out. Mrs Potiphar corners him, but he apparently refuses her advances.

There are several interpretations of events. In Christianity, Potiphar's wife is often interpreted as a deceitful temptress,[1] or crafty villain,[2] who wants to have sex with her husband's slave. His rejection of her renders her vengeful and scared.[3] She lies to the staff and to her husband, she resorts to racism, and she blames someone else: 'The Hebrew servant whom you have brought among us' (Genesis 39.17). Joseph's decision not to sleep with her is 'held up as a model of piety'.[4] Some Christian commentary redeems Mrs Potiphar by casting the incident as a device to bring Joseph to the Pharaoh's attention, interpreting his dreams and thus saving Israel through his subsequent management of the food crisis (Genesis 40—42).[5] Traditional Judaism is more ambivalent. The story is a *parasha* (a biblical portion) of a bigger story known as *Va-yeshev,* which is Joseph's story. The *parashot* are completed annually, and sung. The way they are set to music offers clues as to their meaning. The music to which this *parasha* is set contributes to the passage's interpretation. The cantor is instructed to sing some words three times, going up and down the scales, indicating ambivalence. The words that are ambivalent are 'he refused'.[6] James Kugel suggests that Joseph invites sexual attention, goes to Potiphar's house when everyone else is out, with the intention of having sex with Potiphar's wife, gets as far as taking his clothes off, but then flees.[7] In this case, then, some level of mutuality is implied. Rashi, a medieval Jewish rabbi and writer of comprehensive commentaries on the Hebrew Bible, excuses Mrs Potiphar on astrological grounds. She thought that she was destined to bear Joseph's children. Rashi proposes the Potiphera of Genesis 41 is the same Potiphar as in this story. Potiphera gives his daughter to Joseph in marriage; therefore Mrs Potiphar confused her own role with that of her daughter. In the Qur'an, Joseph is presented as so handsome that Mrs Potiphar can't help herself.[8]

On the day in question, Mrs Potiphar again asks Joseph for sex. What happens next, as we have seen, is unclear. Mrs Potiphar calls out to the members of the household. What she says is not 'Help!' or 'Rape!' but, 'See, my husband has brought among us a Hebrew' (Genesis 39.14). She immediately does two things – blames her husband and points out that Joseph is not one of them. When her husband returns, she doubles down on her theme, 'the Hebrew you brought among us' (39.17). In the text, there is silence from Joseph. He seems to see no need to defend himself. He is a respected man who has made his master prosper. Damon Young, writing in *The Root*, an African-American online magazine, says:

> Generally speaking, we (men) do not believe things when they're told to us by women ... other than our mothers or teachers or any other woman who happens to be an established authority. Do we think women are pathological liars? No. But, does it generally take longer for us to believe something if a woman tells it to us than it would if a man told us the exact same thing? Definitely.[9]

Perhaps Joseph took advantage of this. Whatever had happened, Potiphar is more likely to believe his slave than to believe his wife.

Focusing on Joseph and Mrs Potiphar makes the story confused and unclear. Both are oppressed in some way. Perhaps Joseph did intend to have sex with her. She was alone and a woman, her husband's possession, as Joseph makes clear. Perhaps Joseph was oppressed by the woman – she would not accept his 'no', she used his race against him. Several things have gone wrong, the greatest of them is not the sexual interaction.

'The master's tools will never dismantle the master's house'[10]

I want to suggest that Potiphar is at the centre of this story. He purchases Joseph; he benefits from Joseph's skill; with Joseph around, all he has to worry about is what he eats. The Qur'an makes it clear that an investigation into the matter was possible: 'A witness from her household suggested: "If his shirt is torn from the front: then she has told the truth, and he is the liar. But if his shirt is torn from the back: then she has lied, and he is the truthful"'.[11] This possibility is not raised in Genesis 39, where no investigation is reported. Potiphar is too comfortable to dismantle his house either to settle a dispute or to see justice done.

The narrator tells us (39.19) that Potiphar 'became enraged'. His subsequent actions do not bear an interpretation in which he is angry at either Joseph or his wife, however. The usual punishment for adultery is not invoked, neither party is executed. In Egypt at the time, adultery was considered a religious crime, and therefore partners in it were put to death to prevent the spread of immorality.[12] It was, however, only an offence if those involved chose to make it so. A husband could simply let the matter drop, as Potiphar seems to do. Neither does he seem to be enraged at Joseph. A mere foreign slave, Joseph could have been executed or put in a foreigners' jail, but instead he is placed in the king's jail, presumably still within Potiphar's jurisdiction, since he was the captain of the guard (39.1).

The master, Potiphar, does not dismantle his house because of what has happened. He seems, instead, to maintain it, as far as possible. To prosecute his wife, Potiphar would have to admit his property had been violated. To execute Joseph would mean admitting an error of judgement and losing the benefit of Joseph's wisdom, which might well still have been available in the king's prison. He is probably enraged because his comfortable house has been threatened. In order to maintain his own well-being, he denies justice to those who threaten it. In the context of Egyptian religion and law, he is guilty of a dereliction of duty for the sake of his own contentment.

Social Capital and Potiphar's House

Potiphar is an influential male in charge of his own household, part of a network of significant people, including the pharaoh, who is free to handle things as he sees fit. He has status and access to resources (even slaves) and so he has power. Having power enables him to keep his position and suppress events or people who might threaten it. In other words, privilege promotes itself – back to Audre Lorde's image: the master's tools will always maintain the master's house. I want to bring this uncomfortably close to home.

The kind of story we see enacted in Genesis 39 is also enacted in the church. Although in many denominations women can be ordained and even hold senior posts, the leadership of all churches is dominated by men.[13] Similarly, children's contributions are rarely heard, and their position is inscribed in services where they are sent out 'for their own teaching' while the adults get on with grown-up stuff. The status quo is maintained for the sake of the dominant, usually male, leaders – the Church of England's 2022 Past Cases Review serves as a chastening reminder of this. Institutions are hard to change, because the master's tools will never dismantle the master's house.

Sermon Suggestion: Keeping the Powerful Comfortable

If you watch much news, you will have heard of GDP – Gross Domestic Product. It is used to measure a country's economic health. It's applied internationally as though it is a reliable measure. It was invented in 1934 during the Great Depression by a statistician called Simon Kuznets. It became particularly important during the Second World War, because it measured a nation's potential output and what consumption would need to be sacrificed to maintain the war effort.[14] There was one major contributor to production that was not measured – unpaid domestic work. It was decided that measuring unpaid work would be too big a task, and so in official figures it was not costed, which resulted in its not being valued. The fact that work in the household was going on made the war possible, but not counting it made the leaders comfortable.

Think about that in the context of Joseph and Mrs Potiphar. Both were free household labour. Wives in Egypt at the time were often engaged in spinning and weaving domestic fabrics, and the narrator of this story tells us that Joseph ran Potiphar's house, as a slave. Both worked free of charge. Both contributed to making Potiphar's life one where he only needed to worry about his menu choices. What happens between Joseph and Potiphar's wife, then, is disruptive for Potiphar. I think that what he rages about is having his comfort disturbed. He avoids the usual punishment for adultery and neither participant in the incident is executed. And he retains the possibility of the free labour. Joseph is put in the king's jail, where Potiphar probably had jurisdiction. The outcome is that things remain largely the same for the powerful male and, whatever actually happened, there is no justice. Because justice would inconvenience the powerful.

I want to invite you to do something really difficult. How do you identify with Potiphar? How are others oppressed so that your life is more comfortable? It's easy to fall into the trap of complaining about the cost of social care, for example. To believe politicians when they tell us we can't afford to look after people properly. To turn into heroes and heroines children and young people who drop out of education to look after disabled or sick parents. When we do that, we create Josephs and Mrs Potiphars. It's easy to believe the myth of meritocracy – if you're good enough you will succeed. Joseph excelled and was a slave. It's easy to condemn those intent on getting what they want, without asking why they might want it. Perhaps Mrs Potiphar wanted to take Joseph because she had been taken. She had no control over her own life, so wanted to control someone else's.

It's easy not to ask questions, to remain comfortable. Not to ask, 'Who pays?'

Potiphar's wife has been both victimized and vindicated in the major religions. All because Potiphar wanted to stay comfortable.

Homiletic Points

1 This punchy, brief sermon is woven around the theme of comfort, with three key moves.
2 The first move explores how GDP does not measure unpaid domestic work, a major contribution to a nation's output. The argument is that this creates a sense of comfort at others' expense.
3 The second move is to the biblical text with the insight that the incident between Joseph and Mrs Potiphar has the effect of disturbing Potiphar's comfort.
4 The third move is straight to application, asking the direct and difficult question, 'Who are we oppressing for a more comfortable life?'

Collect

God who dwells among the uncomfortable and the distressed,
disturb us.
Prick our consciences so that we see the discomfort our comfortable
lives cause others.
Inspire our courage, so that we might live justly, love mercy,
walk humbly with you and with those whose lives seem not to matter.
Amen.

Notes

1 William L. Humphreys, *Joseph and His Family: A Literary Study* (Columbia, SC: University of South Carolina Press, 1988), pp. 76, 135.

2 Eric I. Lowenthal, *The Joseph Narrative in Genesis: An Introduction* (New York: Ktav Publishing House Inc., 1999), p. 39.

3 Susan T. Hollis, 'The woman in ancient examples of the Potiphar's wife motif, K2111', in Peggy L. Day (ed.), *Gender and Difference in Ancient Israel* (Minneapolis, MN: Fortress Press, 1996), p. 34.

4 Theodore Weinberger, 'And Joseph slept with Potiphar's wife', *Literature and Theology*, Vol. 11, No. 2 (1997), p. 145.

5 See, for example, https://www.gotquestions.org/Potiphars-wife.html, or, https://www.revival.com/a/6014-joseph-from-the-pit-to-the-prison-to-the-palace, accessed 13.11.23.

6 Weinberger, 'And Joseph slept with Potiphar's wife', p. 146.

7 James Kugel, *In Potiphar's House: The Interpretive Life of Bible Texts* (Cambridge, MA: Harvard University Press, 1994), pp. 76–9.

8 See, for example, A. F. L. Beeston, *Baidāwī's Commentary on Sūrah 12 of the Qur'ān* (Oxford: Clarendon Press, 1963); Al-Thalabi, *Lives of the Prophets*, trans. W. M. Brinner (Chicago, IL: Kazi Publications, 2019); and Mustansir Mir, 'The Qur'anic story of Joseph', https://www.islamic-awareness.org/quran/q_studies/mir joseph, accessed 13.11.23.

9 Damon Young, 'Men just don't trust women. And this is a problem', *The Root* (2014), https://www.theroot.com/men-just-dont-trust-women-and-this-is-a-problem-1822523100, accessed 30.09.23.

10 Audre Lorde, 'The master's tools will never dismantle the master's house', in *Sister Outsider: Essays and Speeches* (Berkeley, CA: Crossing Press, 1984), pp. 110–14.

11 Al-Qur'an: Surah Yusuf: 12.22–35, https://www.islamicstudies.info/, accessed 13.11.23.

12 https://www.worldhistory.org/Egyptian_Law/, accessed 03.01.23.

13 See, for example, Alex Fry, 'Clergy, capital, and gender inequality: an assessment of how social and spiritual capital are denied to women priests in the Church of England' (2021), https://doi.org/10.1111/gwao.12685, accessed 30.09.23.

14 Caroline Criado-Perez, *Invisible Women: Exposing Data Bias in a World Designed for Men* (London: Vintage, 2020), pp. 239–53.

8

Acting Above Her Station:
Zipporah

LIZ SHERCLIFF

Zipporah in the Revised Common Lectionary

Not included.

Zipporah's Words in the Bible

'Truly you are a bridegroom of blood to me!' (Exodus 4.25)

'A bridegroom of blood by circumcision.' (Exodus 4.26)

Zipporah's Story

No matter how often you read this story, or how many commentaries you dip into, Zipporah's story remains enigmatic. She has at least three identities within the pages of the Bible (a Midianite in Exodus 3.1; 18.1–2, 5, and Numbers 10.29; a Cushite in Numbers 12.1; and a Kenite in Judges 1.16 and 4.11). Her story seems to follow that of female predecessors. Like Rebekah (Genesis 24.15) and Rachel (Genesis 29.2), she is met at a well. Unlike them, however, she and her sisters require rescue from some bullying shepherds. Also unlike them, she is not chosen. Where Rebekah is 'very fair to look upon, a virgin whom no man had known' (Genesis 24.16) and Rachel 'was graceful and beautiful'(Genesis 29.17), Zipporah is simply one of seven sisters (Exodus 2.16). She is given to Moses by her father (Exodus 2.21). Exactly what happens on the night around which her story centres is unclear to say the least. Moses, Zipporah and their son are heading back to Egypt. 'The LORD met *him* and tried to kill *him*'

(Exodus 4.24). 'Him' could be either Moses or his son, we don't know who God tries to kill. Zipporah cuts off her son's foreskin with a flint, and touches 'his' feet – but we don't know whether it is Moses' or her son's feet she touches. 'He let *him* alone' (v. 26) is equally ambiguous. Zipporah's utterances, 'Truly you are a bridegroom of blood to me! ... a bridegroom of blood', might be spoken to Moses or to God. The closest we can get to retelling the story might be that one night as the family were travelling, God for some reason met someone and tried to kill them. Zipporah cut off her son's foreskin and touched someone's feet with it, and God backed off. The story is so strange that perhaps the question should be not what happened, but why is it told?

An Ignored Wife?

The marriage between Moses and Zipporah stands out among early biblical marriages for its apparent dissolution. Moses sends her and her two sons away (Exodus 18.2). The subsequent relationship seems to be between Moses and Jethro, his father-in-law. Various possible reasons are suggested – perhaps Moses was so busy leading the people of Israel, he thought Zipporah would be better off with her own family; perhaps the political nature of their marriage made their union too difficult – a union between Israel and Midian seems practically impossible in the Hebrew Bible; perhaps she was subservient to her father – seven times she is referred to as Moses' wife (Exodus 2.21–22; 4.25; 18.2, 5–6; Numbers 12.1), where Jethro (also known as Reuel) is referred to fifteen times (Exodus 2.18; 3.1; 4.18; 18.1–2, 5–6, 9–10, 12, 14, 17; Numbers 10.29; Judges 1.16; 4.11).

I want to focus just for a moment on the first possibility. Moses is a leader chosen by God, who does not have time for his wife. That is not an unfamiliar story. The missionary movement of the nineteenth and early twentieth centuries often required men to travel while wives stayed at home with the children. Although women are now ordained in many churches, the model of ministry promoted by churches remains a patriarchal one, in which the marriage partner, and any children, are expected to be subservient to the 'call' or 'vocation' of the minister. My recent research offers an illustration: a respondent reports her bishop claiming clergy children settle well when families move 'because of the man's obedience', forgetting that the woman would have contributed considerably to the 'settling'. Perhaps we know so little of Zipporah simply because the men in her life ignored her.

An Unacknowledged Priest?

The only part of the story made clear by the narrator is that Zipporah circumcises someone. Zipporah, a woman and a foreigner, carries out on an Israelite male the act of circumcision that sets the man apart as one of God's people. In doing so, Zipporah performs a priestly function. Susan Ackerman suggests that Zipporah takes on her father's role as circumciser and also priest (Jethro is identified as a priest in Exodus 2.16; 3.1; 18.1),[1] thus occupying an otherwise uniquely male position. Robinson suggests that Zipporah 'has taken the place of her father ... Henceforth, she is not only Moses' wife, but also his surrogate father-in-law.'[2] Ackerman suggests that Exodus 'provocatively hints at the notion of Zipporah assuming a priest-like role'.[3] In fact, if Zipporah first circumcises her son physically, and then touches Moses' 'feet' with the foreskin,[4] then Zipporah also symbolically circumcises Moses. The close association between the sacrifice of circumcision and the blood offering,[5] coupled with the fact that Zipporah saves Moses from God's anger, indicate that Zipporah performs a priestly role here. Her words then make sense as some kind of ritual/liturgical utterance following the sacrifice.

An Inter-racial Marriage

As well as stepping into a traditionally male role, Zipporah takes on a culturally Hebrew role, wife of a Hebrew leader. Whatever conclusions we draw about Zipporah, a second significant aspect of her story must be that Israel's leader from slavery, and great legislator of the Pentateuch, married a foreigner. Nowhere is he condemned for it. 'The image of Moses' mixed marriage is a standing criticism against a total seclusion over against the outside,' writes Ursula Rapp.[6] Every community that accepts these texts as scripture must also accept the peaceful egalitarian relations between Midian and Israel. Her in-laws refuse to do so, as we read later: 'Miriam and Aaron spoke against Moses because of the Cushite woman whom he had married' (Numbers 12.1). Their problem is her nationality. God is angry with Miriam and Aaron because of it, although apparently only Miriam is punished.

Why Do We Have this Story?

Zipporah's story is puzzling and unclear. Framed by events in the book of Exodus, where shed blood saves and circumcision signifies membership of God's chosen people, it surely cannot be insignificant that the leader of Israel is symbolically circumcised by a woman.

Sermon Suggestion: The First Woman Priest

'Without Zipporah, Moses would have died in book #1' might have been the message on a thirteenth-century BC t-shirt. Just as without Hermione Granger, Harry Potter would have died in book one, so Moses survived to liberate Israel from slavery in Egypt because Zipporah rescued him. The story is dramatic, dangerous – and bizarre!

For an unspecified reason, after detailed conversation and clear demonstrations of power, God sets out in the dead of night to kill Moses. We are not told why God wants to kill the planned rescuer, the leader out of slavery, the person prepared to head up the exodus experience. It isn't even really clear that it's Moses God has it in for. All we know is that the text presents us with God at the family's camp intent on murder. Seeing the danger, Zipporah grabs a sharp flint and ... she doesn't fight against God, she doesn't defend her family, she circumcises her son and touches Moses' 'feet' with the skin, symbolically circumcising him too. It is a bizarre story.

We all know that Moses was chosen by God, right? Moses led the people out of Egypt, Moses gave the law, Moses met God, Moses led the people through the wilderness. We remember the basket of bulrushes Moses' mother used to hide him. We remember his sister watching as Pharoah's daughter found him. We remember that Pharoah's daughter raised him as a prince of Egypt. But Zipporah? She's well hidden in Moses' story. Yet without her, there would be no Moses.

Zipporah is the embarrassing relative, the one you don't let on about to many people. For Moses and his family, brother Aaron and sister Miriam, Zipporah is the wrong race, wrong religion and possibly wrong family. We meet her and her sisters drawing water at a well, being bullied by some shepherds. They don't have the protection of a powerful family name. They are Midianites, people who don't get on well with the people of Israel. Zipporah's father is a priest of Midian. They are not just nominally Midianite; they are faithful Midianites. No wonder Aaron and Miriam complain to Moses about his unsuitable marriage.

But Zipporah is the daughter of a priest. She knows her religious stuff. She understands ritual and sacrament. She's used to dealing with a number of gods, and a range of sacred practices. When Moses' God shows up, she is not only undeterred, she is insightful. She knows which God this is, and what their requirements might be. She understands what Moses and their son lack. After all, she too is a descendant of Abraham.

Zipporah could have stood back – not the right gender, not the right race, not the right religion – and left Moses at God's mercy. But she didn't. She acted. She used what she knew, appeased God and saved Moses. 'Without Zipporah, Moses would have died in book #1!'

What does this strange little story have to tell us?

If Zipporah had failed to act – not the right gender, not the right race, not the right religion – nobody could have blamed her. She was bold, she took the place of a priest, she fulfilled the covenantal law, in spite of all that. And here's the thing – God accepted it. God did not switch murderous intention and kill Zipporah. God did not rebuke her for taking on the task. God accepted what she did as a sign of the covenant. She was completely the wrong person for the task, but God respected her action. And later, when Aaron and Miriam complain about Moses because of her, in Numbers 12, God takes Zipporah's side and inflicts leprosy on Miriam. Zipporah acts like a priest and is accepted as a priest by God.

Perhaps it doesn't really matter who we are willing to accept. Perhaps what's important is that God accepts them. On the other hand, perhaps too it doesn't really matter whether others accept our ministry. What really matters is that our ministries matter to God.

Homiletic Points

1 The sermon fuses the text and our context in the opening move through the parallel between Zipporah and Moses and Hermione Granger and Harry Potter.
2 The preacher twice states it is a 'bizarre story' and is unapologetic since there is much of worth in this strange account.
3 Layering up of well-known parts of Moses' story heightens the contrast with the unknown Zipporah (second paragraph). The next move explores all the things which make Zipporah strange from an Israelite perspective, and which should rule her out of effective ministry.
4 The sermon turns at this point towards application; in spite of being the 'wrong' person, Zipporah does exactly the right thing, which saves

Moses. Her priestly ministry is accepted by God – which is ultimately what matters.

Collect

God of Zipporah,
the wrong person, wrong race, wrong religion,
who saved your servant Moses, and your people who followed on:
make us willing to act,
even when we would prefer to stand back.
Make us bold to challenge,
even when it seems we might be challenging your way.
Make us confident in your love.
Amen.

Notes

1 Susan Ackerman, 'Why is Miriam among the Prophets? (And is Zipporah among the Priests?)', *Journal of Biblical Literature*, Vol. 121, No. 1 (2002), pp. 47–80.

2 B. Robinson, 'Zipporah to the rescue: a contextual study of Exodus IV 24–6', *Vetust Testamentum*, Vol. 36, No. 4 (October 1986), pp. 1–27.

3 Ackerman, 'Why is Miriam among the Prophets?', p. 75.

4 As in Ruth 3.7, 'feet' is a euphemism for male genitalia (cf Ackerman, 'Why is Miriam among the Prophets?', p. 74).

5 For example, in Exodus 12.1–28, 43–49; Joshua 5.2–12.

6 Ursula Rapp, 'The vanishing of a wife', in Irmtraud Fischer and Mercedes Navarro Puerto (eds), *Torah* (Atlanta, GA: Society of Biblical Literature, 2011), p. 327.

9

A Dancing 'Rebel': Miriam

LIZ SHERCLIFF

Miriam in the Revised Common Lectionary
Years A, B and C   Easter Vigil   Exodus 14.10–31; 15.20–21

Miriam's Words in the Bible

'Sing to the LORD, for he has triumphed gloriously;
horse and rider he has thrown into the sea.' (Exodus 15.21)

'Has the LORD spoken only through Moses? Has he not spoken through us also?' (Numbers 12.2)

Miriam's Story

Miriam is best known for engineering the survival of her younger brother Moses. The Hebrew midwives disobeyed Pharaoh and did not kill Israelite newborns. However, once babies get to a certain age, they get noisy, and keeping Moses put the family at risk. Miriam seems to be behind the plan to hide Moses in the bulrushes where the Egyptian princess bathes, so that he may be found. Miriam proposes Moses' own mother as a wet nurse for the child. She is insightful from the beginning.[1]

In the exodus from Egypt, Miriam leads the women in a joyous celebration of singing, dancing and playing tambourines. The story is unusual, for the women's celebration parallels that of Moses and the men.[2] In this liberation, women and men are equal (Exodus 15.20–21). Then, having led the women out of captivity, Miriam disappears from the story until Numbers 12, when the people are in the wilderness. Miriam speaks out against Moses, and is afflicted with a skin disease. We might ask why Miriam only is punished by God, when Aaron seems to have been complicit.[3] The context is unclear, though it relates to Moses' wife, who could be his only wife or one of several. Miriam's complaint is unclear, though her question is explicit: 'Has the LORD spoken only through Moses? Has he not spoken through us also?' (Numbers 12.2). Tamar Kamionkowski points out that the Hebrew verb is feminine singular – it is Miriam who speaks.[4] Miriam, then, questions male leadership, and asks whether God does not also speak through women. She is, after all, acknowledged as a prophet herself (Exodus 15.20–21).

For challenging male authority, Miriam is afflicted with a skin disease and banished from the community. Traditionally, Miriam's affliction is regarded as coming from God.[5] However, ancient Midrashic readings 'posit that Miriam's punishment masks a legitimate point'[6] – God does also speak through her, and has done throughout Moses' life to rescue and protect him. Phyllis Trible likewise believes that Miriam's challenge to Moses, rooted in an understanding of leadership as embracing male and female voices, is justified.[7] Justified or not, Miriam is silenced by this show of patriarchal strength, because she is not heard from again until her death (Numbers 20.1).

Miriam sets an example of strong female leadership, creating and taking opportunities to deliver her family from the threat of discovery, guarding her brother and manipulating his safety, leading women alongside men into liberation, and finally questioning exclusive male authority. As long as she is delivering others from danger, or celebrating others' victories, she is approved. Once she begins to question the status quo, she is condemned.

Miriam shows no sign of fear when she is called to enter God's presence. Perhaps her previous experiences as a co-leader mean she meets God confidently. She seems unaware of any transgression or threat. Miriam's experience here reminds me of a woman who took part in my doctoral research. She told me, 'I thought you were exaggerating [about sexism in the church] when I was an ordinand, now I'm a curate, I know how bad it is.' She entered ministry unprepared for the treatment she would receive, and was caught off guard by attempts to silence her. Miriam, I suggest, might make an excellent patron saint for women ambushed by misogyny.

Reading the story in this way leaves us with the inconvenient question of whether or not God does afflict Miriam. Here, I adopt a hermeneutic of suspicion. Taking Kamionkowski's linguistic point seriously, Miriam alone asks whether God only speaks through Moses. Aaron is not known for strength of character – he allows the manufacture of a golden calf while Moses is off communing with God (Exodus 32), although, interestingly, he is not immediately punished for this transgression, which seems more serious than Miriam's.[8] It seems likely that Aaron is not directly involved in the challenge. He and Moses, whose authority is being challenged, are the only witnesses to this event – they meet God in a cloud! Since Miriam is immediately banished outside the camp, the men's version of events spreads first. The narrative strengthens Moses' authority. This is import-ant, because earlier in the story the people had been disgruntled. Some might argue that strong, self-sufficient leadership is needed in situations of despair, and the story creates Moses as such a leader. In some ways, then, I propose Miriam as a forerunner of Vashti (Esther 1.10—2.4) a woman who challenges absolute male authority, and is silenced for it.

As if to affirm Miriam's continued leadership, the writer of Numbers tells us that once Miriam dies, the community's water supply dries up, and the people turn on Moses and Aaron (Numbers 20.1). Miriam, I sug-gest, continues to play a key part in the leadership of the nation after the dispute with Moses. Her role is as vital to its life as water, but she must submit to the patriarchal structure.

Sermon Suggestion: Leading the Women Out

'Sing to the LORD, for he has triumphed gloriously;
horse and rider he has thrown into the sea.'

These words are included in the Easter Vigil; that holy night when we liturgically 'wait' for the resurrection of Jesus, and anticipate his return to the world in glory. At that time, we focus on Jesus' glorious triumph. Now, I want to focus on the woman who led other women in singing these words and celebrating their liberation from Egypt. That woman is Miriam, Moses' sister, one of the women who ensured there *was* a Moses to lead the people out of captivity. Because of Miriam, Moses was rescued by the Pharoah's daughter and grew up a prince in Egypt. She becomes a co-leader with her brothers, and when Moses leads the men out of slavery, she leads the women, singing, dancing and playing tambourines. God works through Miriam to save not only her brother but the whole people of Israel.

So why is it that, when she asks a perfectly reasonable question, she is punished? In Hebrew, it is clear that Miriam alone challenges Moses.

'Is it just you who can lead the people?' she asks. 'Does God only speak through you?' As a result of her challenge, she is silenced.

Miriam is one of those characters who help us see that the Bible is bang up to date. Her story cannot be relegated to history. It happens regularly, millennia later – women are frequently silenced. Research at the University of Cambridge indicates that women academics are two and a half times less likely to ask questions than their male counterparts.[9] In courts of law, women witnesses are accorded less credibility than men.[10] And the Bible too silences women; it includes only 93 of them, with just 49 named. So let us not be surprised that when one of them challenges the patriarchal structure developing in her baby nation, she is silenced harshly and decisively.

What can we learn from Miriam? Women's leadership is needed – Miriam ensured Moses' survival. Women's leadership is liberating – Miriam led the women out of slavery into freedom. Women's leadership creates balance – while Miriam lived, the people had water. Let us, then, nurture women's leadership.

Women's leadership is also risky. When Miriam challenged the autocracy of Moses, she was punished. Let us defend women leaders and their right to question the status quo. Balanced, refreshed communities of faith are led by both women and men. Let us pray for more women like Miriam.

Homiletic Points

1 The sermon roots Miriam in the liturgical tradition of some churches. The words of her song are recited annually, but who is she?
2 Her silencing is linked to examples of the contemporary silencing of women.
3 The sermon concludes with comment on the importance of women's leadership as potentially liberating, creating balance, and risky for women.
4 This feeds into comment on the importance of women and men leading communities of faith.

Collect

God of the strong and the silenced,
the refreshed and the disheartened,
give us courage to challenge and change
systems that focus power instead of sharing responsibility.
Provide your church with Miriams, to lead us in joy,
refresh us in spirit, and ask good questions of others who lead.
In the name of Jesus, who himself led with gentleness and courage.
Amen.

Notes

1 See Kate Bruce and Liz Shercliff, *Out of the Shadows: Preaching the Women of the Bible* (London: SCM Press, 2021), pp. 40–1.

2 T. Kamionkowski, 'Will the real Miriam please stand up?', TheTorah.com (2015), https://www.thetorah.com/article/will-the-real-miriam-please-stand-up, accessed 30.09.23.

3 B. Schwartz, *Path of the Prophet: The Ethics-Driven Life* (Philadelphia: The Jewish Publication Society: 2018), p. 166.

4 Kamionkowski, 'Will the real Miriam please stand up?'

5 E. James, 'Miriam and her Interpreters', in C. A. Newsom, S. H. Ringe and J. E. Lapsley (eds), *The Women's Bible Commentary* (London: SPCK, 2014).

6 B. Schwartz, *Path of the Prophets: The Ethics-Driven Life* (Philadelphia, PA: The Jewish Publication Society, 2018), p. 166.

7 P. Trible, 'Miriam', *The Shalvi/Hyman Encyclopedia of Jewish Women* (1999), https://jwa.org/encyclopedia/article/miriam-bible, accessed 13.11.23.

8 He is eventually punished, by not entering the Promised Land. Perhaps this is more for not defending Moses than for criticizing him.

9 See https://www.cam.ac.uk/research/news/women-much-less-likely-to-ask-questions-in-academic-seminars-than-men, accessed 27.09.23.

10 See https://www.forbes.com/sites/patriciafersch/2023/04/05/gender-bias-in-the-courts-women-are-not-believed/, accessed 27.09.23.

10

Inheritance Matters:
Zelophehad's Daughters

KATE BRUCE

Zelophehad's Daughters in the Revised Common Lectionary (Sundays)

Mahlah, Noah, Hoglah, Milcah and Tirzah are not included.

The Words of Zelophehad's Daughters' in the Bible

'Our father died in the wilderness; he was not among the company of those who gathered themselves together against the LORD in the company of Korah, but died for his own sin; and he had no sons. Why should the name of our father be taken away from his clan because he had no son? Give to us a possession among our father's brothers.' (Numbers 27.3–4)

They came before the priest Eleazar and Joshua son of Nun and the leaders, and said, 'The LORD commanded Moses to give us an inheritance along with our male kin.' (Joshua 17.4)

Background

The story of Zelophehad's daughters comes towards the end of the book of Numbers, which follows the Israelites' wilderness wanderings. This is a journey full of complaint. Frequently, the Israelites long for the 'good old days' in Egypt (Numbers 11.1–6; 14.2, 4; 20.4–5; 21.5) – a sign of their lack of faith in God's provision and promise. Some of the men sent

65

to spy out Canaan were so sure they would not be able to overcome the people of the land that they give an 'evil report' of Canaan to the Israelites (13.32–33). This leads to further complaint and the desire for another leader to take them back to Egypt (14.4). Fundamentally, the people do not trust God or the divine promise of land (13.31—14.38). As a result, God decrees that no one over 20, except Joshua and Caleb, will enter the Promised Land (14.28–35). This does not dissuade Korah from leading a rebellion against Moses and Aaron, which infuriates Moses and incites divine wrath (16.1–35). Still the people complain, inciting more judgement, this time in the form of a plague (16.41–50). At Meribah there is more dissent, this time over lack of water. The people complain to Moses and Aaron, but the text is plain: their contention is with God (20.13). This becomes crystal clear when they yoke themselves to the Moabite gods (25.1–5). It is against this backdrop that we meet the daughters of Zelophehad.

Numbers in Numbers

The book of Numbers begins with a census in which every male over 20 is counted for the purposes of reckoning Israel's war fighting strength (1.1–4). A second census is called not only for assessing military power (26.1–2) but also in preparation for calculating land distribution when the time finally comes (26.52–56). Land is symbolic of God's covenant, a concrete sign of divine faithfulness. It is in the record of this second census that we first hear mention of the daughters of Zelophehad:

> Now Zelophehad son of Hepher had no sons, but daughters: and the names of the daughters of Zelophehad were Mahlah, Noah, Hoglah, Milcah, and Tirzah. (Numbers 26.33)

In Israel land passed from father to firstborn son (Deuteronomy 21.15–17). Zelophehad had no sons, so at his death his land would pass to other male family members, meaning his name would be lost and his daughters rendered destitute: 'The land was the critical unit of economic sufficiency.'[1]

Referring to land rights in Malawi today, Louis W. Ndekha states: 'If land is a source of livelihood and daughters and women are denied access to it, it makes them secondary citizens in the land.'[2] This is the fate these sisters will face after their father's death: 'Where property rights were concerned a woman was always a victim.'[3] However, these five women

66

choose to challenge the divinely appointed law of Sinai (Deuteronomy 21.15–17).

What's in a Name?

Each sister's name in Hebrew has connotations of moving and initiating, which is fitting given their active challenge to the inheritance law. It's also of note that the syllable 'ah', which forms the end of each name, is a contraction of the Hebrew form of Jehovah: each sister bears the name of God within her own name.[4] How appropriate given that their action reflects deep faith in God's justice and faithfulness. The daughters strain ahead in hope of the fulfilment of the divine promise of land (Deuteronomy 6.3; 8.9; 11.11–12).

> [N]ote the contrast between the men, who were afraid to enter the land and cried, 'Let us appoint a leader and return to Egypt,' and the women, who were eager to possess the land and even demanded a share in it.[5]

It is noteworthy that the sisters' names are recorded on four separate occasions (Numbers 26.33; 27.1; 36.10; Joshua 17.3). We are not meant to forget them!

Challenging the System

'The daughters of Zelophehad came forward' (Numbers 27.1). To 'come forward' to challenge an unjust system is costly. There is no guarantee they will be heard, and every possibility they will be censured. The women come before 'Moses, Eleazar the priest, the leaders, and all the congregation at the entrance of the tent of meeting' and put their case (27.2–4). Imagine the courage it took to stand before such a gathering of powerful men. They act together as a unit: female solidarity meeting male power at the tent of meeting. There is no single spokeswoman. Interesting that there are five of them and five stages in their argument – suggesting collective action, which has a number of benefits. There is no obvious ringleader to pick off. Working together in the face of what might have been a hostile response gives a sense of confidence and is a source of courage.

They begin by setting up their problem: 'Our father died in the wilderness' (27.3). They head off any objection that their father might not have been eligible for a share in the land with their second statement: 'he was not among the company of those who gathered themselves together against the LORD in the company of Korah, but died for his own sin' (27.3). This is important. Zelophehad was of the tribe of Manasseh, a member of the covenant community and he died as part of that, guilty of his own failings, but not of rebellion against God.

> If Zelophehad had not been dishonourably cut off from the covenant community, then the God of the covenant was still the God of his family. They remained heirs of the covenantal promises. Zelophehad's daughters expressed their faith in God's promise to keep his covenant, and they had every right to hold him to it. If Zelophehad's name disappeared, then God had not preserved the covenantal relationship and the daughters had no part in the covenantal community.[6]

Their third statement gets to the heart of the matter. 'He had no sons' (27.3). The law of inheritance meant that the women could not take on their father's share in the land. As unmarried women they would be left with no means of survival and others would benefit from their suffering, since the land would pass to male relatives. The fourth step in their appeal is shrewd and diplomatic: 'Why should the name of our father be taken away from his clan because he had no son?' (27.4). A sonless man stood to be erased from history, since his inheritance would pass to other male relatives and his name would be lost. Argued this way, it is in the male interest to change the law: Their argument, 'Let not our father's name be lost to his clan', was one that could find a sympathetic response in the ears of the male leaders. In using this tactic, the women displayed an understanding of the constraints of the patriarchal society in which they lived. Rather than present an unqualified demand that daughters inherit equally with sons, they limited their demand to cases in which there are no sons. Their diplomacy enabled them to get the attention of Moses, for their demand was not a threat to the patriarchal order, but rather in accordance with the male concern for continuity.[7] Their final comment is the logical extension of their argument: 'Give to us a possession among our father's brothers' (27.4). Their shrewd approach demonstrates solidarity, strength, diplomacy, wisdom and profound faith in God.

An Aside from the Talmud

The Talmud (a collection of writings by Jewish scholars) offers a fascinating midrash (a type of commentary) on this story. The wisdom of the sisters is demonstrated since they presented their case at 'an auspicious time'. Tradition teaches that Moses was teaching on levirate marriage: when a man dies and leaves a wife but no heir, her husband's brother should take her as a wife.[8] At just this moment the daughters argue that either they are legitimate progeny, in which case they should inherit, or they are not valid offspring, in which case their mother is childless and subject to levirate marriage.[9] Ingenious! No wonder Moses is stumped!

The Daughters of Zelophehad are Right!

Moses takes the case to God. God rules in favour of the women, saying:

> The daughters of Zelophehad are right in what they are saying; you shall indeed let them possess an inheritance among their father's brothers and pass the inheritance of their father on to them. (27.7)

Like Jacob, wrestling with the mysterious figure at the Ford of Jabbok, the sisters wrestle with the law of Sinai. They contend with God and prevail (Genesis 32.28). In challenging the law, they show they expect God to 'bless those who cling to God's promises'.[10]

From the specific case of Zelophehad's daughters God then gives a general statute concerning the order of inheritance, establishing a new tradition (Numbers 27.8–11). The new law still discriminates, since daughters' inheritance is an exception, but in a patriarchal context the change is significant, allowing women, who would otherwise be left with nothing, to inherit land.

In the story of Achsah we have another example of a woman being granted land and successfully demanding vital water resources (1 Chronicles 2.49; Joshua 15.16–19; Judges 1.9–15).

The Backlash Comes

Put yourself in the shoes of one of the men of Manasseh. The success of the daughters' claim means Zelophehad's close male relatives will lose out on that extra land. It's not difficult to picture them hotly discussing the case and reflecting that the land will be lost if the women marry outside the tribe.

Some of the tribal heads bring the problem to Moses. They accept the outcome that Moses 'was commanded by the LORD to give the inheritance of our brother Zelophehad to his daughters' (Numbers 36.2), before adding the issue about potential land loss. Land loss meant loss of power.

Is there also another issue of power playing out here? A desire to reassert control over these five women who have successfully challenged the established order? God upholds the tribal leaders' concern about land, saying:

'The descendants of the tribe of Joseph are right in what they are saying. This is what the LORD commands concerning the daughters of Zelophehad,
"Let them marry whom they think best; only it must be into a clan of their father's tribe that they are married."' (36.5–6)

God asserts that the men are factually correct. If the daughters marry out then the land will be lost. The daughters' choice of husbands is circumscribed and they obediently take husbands from their own tribe. At least in this are they are instructed by God to 'marry whom they think best' – which implies a large degree of agency. One solution to the problem could have been that any men from a different tribe marrying the women would be received into the tribe of Manasseh, but no one suggests this!

A Firm Reminder

The agreement to give land to the daughters of Zelophehad was made before Moses died, and before the people entered the land. Time has passed and perhaps memories are short. For example, Caleb needs to remind Joshua of Moses' particular promise to him of the land he went to explore, 45 years earlier. Caleb, now 85 years old, approaches Joshua and declares, 'Now give me this hill country of which the LORD spoke on that day' (Joshua 14.12).

In Joshua 17 we read of the land allocation for the tribe of Manasseh. Like Caleb, Mahlah, Noah, Hoglah, Milcah and Tirzah come to the leaders, including the priest Eleazar and Joshua's son of Nun, with a memory-jogging exercise: 'The LORD commanded Moses to give us an inheritance along with our male kin' (Joshua 17.4). A firm reminder ensures that their claim is not 'forgotten'.

Sermon Suggestion: 'The daughters of Zelophehad are right'

Jesus said. 'Blessed are those who have not seen and yet have come to believe' (John 20.29).

There were five women, the daughters of Zelophehad:

Five women who trusted in the gift of the Promised Land,
    long before their eyes beheld the country.
Five women who trusted in the gift of the Promised Land,
    long before their feet touched the soil.
Five women who had not yet seen but who believed.
Five faithful women.
Five blessed women.
Their names – Mahlah, Noah, Hoglah, Milcah and Tirzah –
are recorded on four separate occasions
three times in Numbers and once in Joshua.
So what's the scoop?
We meet Zelophehad's daughters in the second half of the Book of
    Numbers.
Israel was wandering around the wilderness,
frequently disgruntled, often fed-up,
complaining to Moses and in strife with God.

A census is taken, to assess Israel's fighting strength
and to reckon how the land will be divvied up once they reach it.
In this context only men over 20 were allowed to fight and able to
    inherit.
In the middle of the record of this census
we learn that Zelophehad, of the tribe of Manasseh, had no sons.
His five daughters are named: 'Mahlah, Noah, Hoglah, Milcah, and
    Tirzah' (Numbers 26.33).

Somewhere in the wilderness their father, Zelophehad, died.
    Picture the scene.

The daughters are sitting around a fire.
Listen to them.
They discuss the census and what it means for them.
Perhaps they had already tried to be included in the list
of those entitled to land inheritance and been turned away,
'Not for women!'

The sisters discuss matters.

Listen to them:

'Dad's name will be forgotten, nothing to remind people of him.'

'We'll get nothing.'

'Begging for food and somewhere to sleep.'

'Charity cases – dependent on others for a crust and a place to sleep.'

'Just because Mum and Dad didn't have a son.'

Four of the sisters look at the youngest:

'You should have been a boy!'

'Sorry to disappoint!'

'Well – what are we going to do? Who will listen to us? We have no
    say, no power, no status.'

'Look. God has promised that Israel will have land. We are part of
    that people. We belong to God. Ok, we haven't seen the land, yet.
    But let's believe that God is faithful – and act from that belief.'

'Let's act together. There's more power in five people than in one.'

'Yes, and let's hone our argument, so there's no nervous waffling.'

'Let's go together, to Moses and the rest of them and ask for our
    father's parcel of land.'

So together they work on their argument – making it clear and concise.
More of that later.

Just as an aside – remember that at the time some of the men of Israel,
full of fear, looked for another leader to take them back to Egypt, while
the daughters of Zelophehad strain ahead to land they have not seen,
trusting in a promise yet to be fulfilled.

They have not yet seen but they come to believe.

Blessed women.

Watch them:

Together they leave their tents, determined to be heard.

Together they walk through the camp, sweaty palms and pounding
    hearts.

Together they get closer and closer to the Tent of Meeting, the heart of
    power,

Together 'the daughters of Zelophehad came forward'.

Together they prepare to speak.

Perhaps people glance at them. Curious.

Perhaps they draw stares as they approach Moses.

Perhaps others are more hostile.
'What are they doing here? They have no business here.'

What courage! What faith!
Hold up your heads, daughters of Zelophehad.
Keep your nerve.

Their argument is crisp, clear and intelligent.
Hammered out on the anvil of wisdom.
They state their reality: their father's death in the wilderness.
They head off the objection: he was no rebel; he was a member of the
    community.
They state their problem: he had no sons.
They appeal to the men: why should a sonless man lose his name?
They stake their claim: give us our share of land.

Moses immediately turns to God and God responds:
'The daughters of Zelophehad are right.'

'The daughters of Zelophehad are right!'
Notice God upholds their challenge.
Notice God's reward for their trust.
Notice how when faced with a difficulty they work together.
Notice the intelligence of their argument.
Notice how, long before they have sight of it, they choose to believe
    that land will be given.
Blessed women.

But life is seldom straightforward.
Victories are often followed with lash backs.
Unsurprisingly, the daughters' brave move triggers an effect.

Picture the scene.
Their male relatives are sitting around a fire discussing recent events.
They have just lost the possibility of the extra land
that would have come their way
if Zelophehad's daughters had just toed the line.
Some might well have wanted their womenfolk pulled back into that
    line.
'Who knows where this kind of innovation in the law might lead?
Best reign them in, and stamp it out.'

However, they do have a valid point about the potential
for land to be lost to their tribe
if any of the daughters marry into other tribes.
This is the argument they present to Moses –
who declares that the word of the Lord is
they 'are right in what they are saying'.
But this does not lead to a ruling that the daughters can't inherit.
That stands.
However, they are to 'marry whom they think best;
only it must be into a clan of their father's tribe.'

The daughters of Zelophehad did as the Lord had commanded Moses.
Notice their obedience – at the close of a book
that details the disobedience of many in Israel.
The women are obedient and faithful.
They believe, though they have not yet seen.

There is no question that the daughters ever forgot
God's decree that they should inherit.
Many years later, when at last the land is being allocated, once again,
the daughters of Zelophehad came forward.
Mahlah, Noah, Hoglah, Milcah and Tirzah come to the leaders,
including the priest Eleazar and Joshua son of Nun, with a firm
    reminder:
'The LORD commanded Moses to give us an inheritance
along with our male kin' (Joshua 17.4).
Bold and blessed women.

Jesus said, 'Blessed are those who have not seen and yet have come to
    believe' (John 20.29).

The daughters of Zelophehad:
They had not seen the land, but they trusted in God.
They acted together in challenging the system.
They spoke what is right.
They waited and waited until the point came to issue a timely
    reminder.
They did this collectively, peaceably and wisely.

In challenging the divinely given law of Sinai concerning male
    inheritance

these five women challenged God.
Like Jacob in Genesis 32, they wrestled and they overcame.
Like Jacob they were blessed.

No wonder the Bible gives their names on four occasions.
Mahlah, Noah, Hoglah, Milcah and Tirzah.
They are blessed women who had not seen and yet they believed.

It raises a question in matters of faith
– are we more Thomas or more daughters of Zelophehad?

Mahlah, Noah, Hoglah, Milcah and Tirzah.
Don't forget them.
Be like them – the daughters of Zelophehad.

Homiletic Points

1 Jesus' statement 'Blessed are those who have not seen and yet have come to believe' (John 20.29) is used as a descriptor of the daughters and a way of framing the sermon.
2 The sermon retells the story of Mahlah, Noah, Hoglah, Milcah and Tirzah. It is such a little-known story that impressing the details on the hearers is important. The sermon weaves details from the biblical text in with imaginative scenes, to bring the backstory to life. The imagined scenes are not in scripture, but the inference is plausible.
3 The women's names are used frequently throughout the sermon, mirroring their repetition in the scriptures. We are meant to know these women and remember them. Notice too how patterns of five emerge in the sermon – mirroring the number of the sisters and the number of statements they make in their argument to Moses. How many patterns of five can you spot?
4 The application is largely left implicit. Attention is drawn to particular aspects of the daughters' approach – see the repetition of how they act 'together', the multiple observations of their faith, their wisdom and corporate courage.
5 The indication that they are those who 'have not seen and yet have come to believe', and are blessed in this, begs a question of the hearer which pulses underneath the surface of the sermon, before emerging explicitly at the end: 'Are we more Thomas or more daughters of Zelophehad?'

Collect

God of Promise,
thank you for Mahlah, Noah, Hoglah, Milcah and Tirzah,
these faithful daughters.
Help us like them to act together
in challenging injustice.
Give us their faith, courage, wisdom and diplomacy.
Nurture our belief in your promises,
even through the years when we cannot and do not see fulfilment.
Help us to remember and hang on to your word,
like our foremothers –
the daughters of Zelophehad.
Amen.

Notes

1 Kelly L. Schmidt, 'Strategic leadership as modelled by the daughters of Zelophehad', *Journal of Biblical Perspectives in Leadership*, Vol. 10, No. 1 (Fall 2020), pp. 102–12, https://www.researchgate.net/publication/344829038, accessed 25.06.22.

2 Louis W. Ndekha, 'The daughters of Zelophehad and African women's rights: a Malawian perspective on the book of Numbers 27:1–11', *Journal of Gender and Religion in Africa*, Vol. 19, No. 2 (November 2013), p. 46.

3 Ndekha, 'The daughters of Zelophehad', p. 40.

4 'Zelophehad's daughter's Hebrew name meanings', https://www.hebrew versity.com/zelophehads-daughters-hebrew-name-meanings/, accessed 25.06.22.

5 Mendy Kaminker, 'The daughters of Zelophehad', https://www.chabad.org/library/article_cdo/aid/2259008/jewish/The-Daughters-of-Zelophehad.htm, accessed 25.06.22.

6 Dean R. Ulrich, 'The framing function of the narratives about Zelophehad's daughters', *JETS*, Vol. 41, No. 4 (December 1998), p. 535, https://www.etsjets.org/files/JETS-PDFs/41/41-4/41-4-pp529-538-JETS.pdf, accessed 26.06.22.

7 Brenda Bacon, 'The daughters of Zelophehad and the struggle for justice for women', https://schechter.edu/the-daughters-of-zelophehad-and-the-struggle-for-justice-for-women/, accessed 25.06.22.

8 Bava Batra 119b:2 with Tosafot, https://www.sefaria.org/Bava_Batra.119b, accessed 25.06.22.

9 Abba Engelberg, 'Lessons from the Story of Zelophehad's daughters', https://blogs.timesofisrael.com/lessons-from-the-story-of-zelophehads-daughters/, accessed 25.06.22.

10 Ndekha, 'The daughters of Zelophehad', p. 40.

11

An Ambiguous Figure: Rahab

KATE BRUCE

Rahab in the Revised Common Lectionary (Sundays)

Year C	Proper 15 (OT 20)	Hebrews 11.29—12.2
	Proper 15 (CW)	Hebrews 11.29—12.2 (CW, PS)

Other readings concerning Rahab are not included in the Sunday lectionary.

Rahab's Words in the Bible

Then she said, 'True, the men came to me, but I did not know where they came from. And when it was time to close the gate at dark, the men went out. Where the men went I do not know. Pursue them quickly, for you can overtake them.' (Joshua 2.4–5)

Before they went to sleep, she came up to them on the roof and said to the men: 'I know that the LORD has given you the land, and that dread of you has fallen on us, and that all the inhabitants of the land melt in fear before you. For we have heard how the LORD dried up the water of the Red Sea before you when you came out of Egypt, and what you did to the two kings of the Amorites that were beyond the Jordan, to Sihon and Og, whom you utterly destroyed. As soon as we heard it, our hearts failed, and there was no courage left in any of us because of you. The LORD your God is indeed God in heaven above and on earth below. Now then, since I have dealt kindly with you, swear to me by the LORD that you in turn will deal kindly with my family. Give me a sign of good faith that you will spare my father and mother, my brothers and sisters, and all who belong to them, and deliver our lives from death.' (Joshua 2.8–13)

She said to them, 'Go towards the hill country, so that the pursuers may not come upon you. Hide yourselves there for three days, until the pursuers have returned; then afterwards you may go on your way.' (Joshua 2.16)

She said, 'According to your words, so be it.' (Joshua 2.21)

Rahab the Ambiguous

Whenever you think you have Rahab's story pinned down, it springs back up with an 'ah, but'. This insight hit me when we discussed Rahab at the 2022 Women's Voices Conference in Chester Diocese. I was presenting the material for this chapter and angling for an interpretation of Rahab that sees her as a faithful heroine, as I think the text pushes that view, which is endorsed by New Testament readings. But our discussion and delegates' questions reminded me to consider the untold aspects of the narrative.

In all that follows, keep in mind the 'ah, but'. Rahab is ambiguous – is she a hero or a villain? It depends on where you stand and whose eyes you look through. This is explored in the Sermon Suggestion below. If you want an easy read, look away now. Billy Kluttz argues that Rahab can helpfully be interpreted as a queer character, defining queer not as an assumption about sexual preference but as broadly representing the politicized other. Rahab is definitively 'other': triply marginalized as a woman, a sex worker and a Canaanite.[1] She stands apart from the dominant culture, an outsider in her own city. She demonstrates pro-active understanding of how to survive, an understanding schooled by her marginal position. Welcome to a story riddled with ambiguity.[2]

Rahab at the Centre of the Action

The text presents Rahab as a woman of remarkable faith. Her first words to the spies are 'I know that the LORD has given you the land' (Joshua 2.9). This knowing informs her behaviour. She is at the centre of the action – managing the hapless spies and misdirecting the suspicious king. The two spies sent by Joshua get no further than the local brothel, surely a 'nudge, nudge, wink, wink', situation is operating here. Their whereabouts are known immediately by the king. Not exactly a covert operation. It looks as though the plan of these bumbling stooges will be thwarted before it has even begun. We witness dramatic action and comedic misdirection – but there are more serious themes at work here.[3] Running with the grain of the text, Rahab demonstrates subversion and the dissenting voice – and that dissenting voice is brave and faithful. As with Mary, God looks 'with favour on the lowliness of his servant' (Luke 1.48) using 'the weak to shame the strong' (1 Corinthians 1.27). Imagine reading this as someone marginalized, subjugated and oppressed. What hope there is to be found here. Rahab and Yahweh are presented as on the same team. A straightforward reading of the narrative presents Rahab as the hero; her words support this interpretation.

Rahab's Words Examined

Her words are remarkable. In Joshua 1 God says, 'proceed to cross the Jordan, you and all this people, into the land that I am giving ... to the Israelites' (Joshua 1.2). Rahab confirms the fulfilment of the divine word, declaring to the spies, 'I know that the LORD has given you the land' (2.9). The declaration 'I know' is not mere head knowledge. It is the conviction that leads her to risk everything; a deep awareness that her people are facing the living God.

Moses declares: 'trembling seized the leaders of Moab; all the inhabitants of Canaan melted away' (Exodus 15.15). Rahab confirms the words of Israel's leader, 'dread of you has fallen on us ... all the inhabitants of the land melt in fear before you' (Joshua 2.9).

The writer of Exodus records that when the Israelites saw God's work against the Egyptians, 'the people feared the LORD' (Exodus 14.31). Like the biblical author, Rahab confirms her people's response to the divine hand, declaring to the spies that as soon as they heard about the Red Sea being dried up, and the fate of the Amorite kings Sihon and Og who were utterly destroyed (Joshua 2.10), 'our hearts failed, and there was no courage left in any of us' (2.11).

Rahab continues, 'The LORD your God is indeed God in heaven above and on earth below' (2.11b). Her words are strikingly similar to Moses' words: 'So acknowledge today and take to heart that the LORD is God in heaven above and on the earth beneath; there is no other' (Deuteronomy 4.39). Similarly, Solomon states: 'there is no God like you in heaven above or on earth beneath' (1 Kings 8.23). Rahab stands with Moses and Solomon. This is remarkable.

Intertextuality

There are similarities between Rahab hiding the spies, defying the king and playing a role in bringing about Yahweh's conquest of Jericho, and the story of the Hebrew midwives, Moses' mother, his sister and Pharoah's daughter – who all defy Pharoah, ensuring the survival of Moses (Exodus 1.15—2.10).

The picture of Rahab letting the spies out through a window recalls the scene where Michal, David's wife, saves him from a murderous Saul by letting him down through a window with a rope (1 Samuel 19.12). These stories highlight the role of female wisdom and courage in bringing about the purposes of God.

Heroine of the Faith? Rahab in the Genealogy of Jesus

In his genealogy of Jesus, Matthew names Rahab along with Tamar, Ruth, the wife of Uriah (Bathsheba, who is not explicitly named), and Mary (Matthew 1.1–16). Excluding Mary, these women were all Gentiles, outsiders named in the genealogy of the Messiah. Each woman could be seen as morally questionable, though Matthew simply includes them without any hint of disapproval. They are attributed significance by being named. Rahab stands in good company among the great-grandmothers of Jesus with brave, shrewd women.

Rahab Named in the Company of the Faithful (Hebrews 11)

The writer of Hebrews declares:

> By faith Rahab the prostitute did not perish with those who were disobedient, because she had received the spies in peace. (Hebrews 11.31)

Rahab is commended as a person of faith, along with Abel, Enoch, Noah, Abraham, Sarah, Isaac, Jacob, Joseph, Moses, the people of Israel who passed through the Red Sea, Gideon, Barak, Samson, Jephthah, David, Samuel and the prophets (Hebrews 11). Close examination of her words in Joshua 2 reveals her remarkable faith in the God of Israel, who will give Israel the land of Canaan (Joshua 2.8–10). She certainly displays 'conviction of things not seen' (Hebrews 11.1), believing that God will overthrow Canaan. She displays more faith than many in Israel (e.g., Numbers 23.31–33;14.1–4).

Rahab: Expressing Faith in Action

The writer of James uses Rahab as an example of one who expresses faith in works: 'Likewise, was not Rahab the prostitute also justified by works when she welcomed the messengers and sent them out by another road?' (James 2.25). Her knowing that God is at work directly affects what she does.

The New Testament presents a very positive assessment of Rahab as a woman of faith and action. However, there are other ways of reading Rahab.

Sermon Suggestion: Rahab – a Text for Our Times

The story of Rahab is a text for our times: either/or; in/out; good/bad; them/us – we see it all around us, binary opposition with neat and tidy categories. To one extent or another, overt or more subtle, all of us do it – we decide who is on our team and who we sideline as 'them'. A swift glance at social media threads highlights this tendency, with examples of sideswiping condemnation not hard to find. Rahab's story challenges us to beware the alluring simplicity of such thinking, and engage again with the call to deep listening to different voices. I don't find this easy. We can have such fixed ideas about whose faces fit and whose voices we are prepared to attend to. Rahab is definitely the 'other' to Israel, as well as to her own people – someone easily dismissed. Who would you push aside as definitely 'other' with nothing to say worth hearing? Rahab's story – messy and ambiguous – challenges this. It's definitely a text for our times.

Reading Rahab

How to read Rahab? Well, it all depends on where you stand – and that's so vital to remember:

- The text in Joshua 2 presents her as a heroine at the centre of the story.
- Her speech reveals her as a true Israelite in faith and action.

- But to an Israelite she is a triple outsider – a heathen, a woman and a sex-worker.
- From a Canaanite perspective she is a fifth columnist – a despised traitor.
- To her family she is their saviour.
- To her wider community, those who work with her, she may be both saviour and owner. Complex.

How do we read Rahab? Are we willing to wrestle with ambiguity and complexity and resist the dash to simple categorization?

Rahab – a Heroine at the centre of the story

Whatever else we say, it is clear that Rahab, the one banished to the edges of the city, is at the centre of this story, conducting events, while the powerful male characters are revealed as incompetent buffoons.

Rahab, the commanding strategist, hides the spies and misdirects the king, sending his men on a wild goose chase. She negotiates the rescue of herself and her family, before lowering the spies down the city wall in a basket, showing physical strength and nerves of steel. One upward glance from a passer-by and it's game over. Meanwhile the spies feel it is appropriate to attempt to negotiate further terms with Rahab while they are dangling from a basket on the city wall, in the midst of a night-time escape (Joshua 2.17–20). Not exactly a thought-through military strategy. Rahab directs them to hide from the king's men for three days and they are obedient to her command. When the hapless spies report back to Joshua they use Rahab's own words – given their reconnaissance has been a failure, they have nothing else to offer (5.24). Some spies!

Where has she learned to take such control? Her background and livelihood are significant here. She lives in the city wall – literally pushed to the edges of society. She runs a brothel. Who can guess at the story that led her into this work? There is trouble in this woman's background. She has to be on the lookout for danger – violence, opposition, the punter who won't pay. At the same time, she has to offer hospitality, welcome and warmth, or the business will fail and there will be no money for those under her care. Rahab has learned to scan a room, assess risk and react accordingly. It goes with the territory and it serves her well when trouble comes. But there is more to her than this.

Rahab as a true Israelite

In her speech to the spies, Rahab displays the faith of a true Israelite, declaring, 'The LORD your God is indeed God in heaven above and on earth below.' The only other biblical characters to use this phrase are Moses and Solomon. That's astounding! Rahab describes how her people have heard of God's deeds – drying up the Red Sea to bring the people out of Egypt, and destroying the Amorite Kings. This has caused Canaanite hearts to melt in fear. In spite of such fear Rahab acts with faith and courage, wit and wisdom, to ensure her survival and that of her family.

Ah, but ... triple outsider?

From an Israelite perspective she is an unclean, heathen woman – yet she acts with more faith than many in Israel who doubted and rebelled as they wandered through the wilderness. She is closer to Yahweh than many of Yahweh's chosen people. Just who is the true Israelite? That's a biting question.

Rahab – traitor or saviour?

From a Canaanite point of view Rahab is in league with the coming oppressor – treacherous and treasonous. The text presents her as a faithful diplomat, but read from a Canaanite perspective she is a self-serving manipulator who betrays her people to an invading, imperial power to save her skin. I wonder, if I had experienced an invasion by a foreign power and seen my community and environment wiped out, my dearest raped and murdered, would I have such a positive view of Rahab? We read in the text much of what we bring to it and we often miss themes which are out of our experience. When wrestling with this story, bear in mind the 'ah, but'. Rahab resists easy categorization – but perhaps that's the point.

Another 'ah, but'. Is it surprising she displays little loyalty to Jericho? Think about her position among those same people: she is used by men, just about tolerated by society, though pushed to the edges, living in the city wall. Perhaps being on the edges helps her to recognize the truth; she is not so embedded in the security of the status quo and has edgy insights.

She asks the spies that the kindness she has shown is reciprocated (Joshua 2.12–13). The Hebrew word for kindness is *hesed*, a word often used to describe the merciful, loving kindness of God. Rahab's actions echo this divine characteristic. She marks her family and those in her care for rescue with the symbol of the red thread hanging from her window. This is possibly the same red thread used to signify her business to passing trade, and at the same time it echoes the blood daubed on the doorposts and lintel of the houses on the night of Passover (Exodus 12.23).

We could see her as simply recognizing the power of the invader and throwing her lot in with them to save her skin. But is this too simple and too cynical? Rahab recognizes Yahweh and responds appropriately when no one else in Canaan does. She risks everything because of her faith that God is at work. Twice the text mentions 'all who belonged to her' (Joshua 6.23, 25). These are likely to be people, along with her family, whom she has rescued and taken in. These people are delivered from death. She is their saviour.

But here's an 'ah, but' again. At the Women's Voices 2022 conference, a prison chaplain asked an interesting question about this community of people Rahab had gathered around herself; people she housed and protected and who, presumably, worked for her in the sex trade. The question – 'When Rahab reached Israel, did she pimp out her entourage there?' Ouch. Do we read her as a heroine and champion of the down-trodden? Or, is she a pimp who preys on the vulnerable to build her business? Or is she both? If you want neat and tidy categories, look away now. But then, life is frequently ambiguous and messy. People are.

#Rahab-out?

Deuteronomy states quite clearly and very uncomfortably that when the Israelites take possession of the land, they must 'devour all the peoples' and 'not let anything that breathes remain alive' (Deuteronomy 7.16; 20.16). We later learn that Joshua spared 'Rahab the prostitute, with her family and all who belonged to her', and 'Her family has lived in Israel ever since' (Joshua 6.25). Rahab survives against all odds.

Even in her rescue, Rahab's ambiguous position is clear from the biblical text. What are the Israelites supposed to do with this female, Canaanite sex worker? 'She is not one of us. She is the enemy – defiled and defiling. She is "one of them".' Initially, Rahab and her family are put 'outside the camp of Israel' (6.23). However, just two verses later we read 'Her family has lived in Israel ever since' Joshua spared them (Joshua 6.25). There's a world of argument and resentment between those two verses. The tension in the text suggests that not everyone is comfortable about having Rahab the harlot in the midst of Israel. Just imagine if ancient Israel had the social media site X – #Rahab-out might well have trended.

#Rahab-in/ #All-are-welcome/ #Life-is-messy

Rahab's story hints at a new possibility, a new Israel which breaks apart the old oppositions, a new community which is changed by the inclusion of the outsider. Jesus is clear: 'Many will come from east and west and will eat with Abraham and Isaac and Jacob in the kingdom of heaven.' It's a beautiful picture of inclusion – but it's messy. Think about it ... that's a table around which oppositions are encountered and overcome. It would be easier to airbrush out the words Jesus says next, 'while the heirs of the kingdom will be thrown into the outer darkness, where there will be weeping and gnashing of teeth' (Matthew 8.11–12). The danger of insider/outside thinking is the risk of being named as the outsider, on the wrong side of the door. No one wants that for themselves; how thoughtlessly we place others there.

Rahab is like the centurion of whom Jesus said, 'in no-one in Israel have I found such faith' (Matthew 8.10). Jesus is praising one of the occupying soldiers – a representative of the dominating empire. That's uncomfortable. No one has a monopoly on faith.

In the New Testament, Rahab is held up as an example of faith and good works, but that does not mean she is an uncomplicated figure. Most, if not all, people are complicated and compromised to one degree or other. Aren't we? Thankfully, then, it's definitely a case of #Rahab-in. It's significant that this outsider becomes part of the genealogy of Jesus (Matthew 1.5), a sign of the radical inclusion that is a hallmark of Christ's community.

#All-are-welcome. Thankfully.

Rahab – and so what?

In this story, as with so many – we see how God works in and through people we might write off as beyond the pale. But people rarely, if ever, fit into neat and tidy categories. And if they do, there's a high chance some of their truth has been airbrushed out. Rahab's story strongly suggests that when we decide who are or are not God's people, God may well disagree. #All-are-welcome. Life is messy.

Wrestling with Rahab's story calls for a more thoughtful, less judgemental, more loving and inclusive stance, open to unexpected possibility. Such an approach calls for humility and mercy, and a willingness to resist neat judgements. It calls for a willingness to listen to differing points of view – to people we might instinctively want to silence. It faces all the messiness of humanity, and resists the rush to neat conclusions. This requires that we soften hardened attitudes and make space for the other, recognizing that to many we too are 'other'.

People are rarely straightforward. I'm not. Are you? God sits with us in messiness, and asks us to listen deeply and attentively. To be aware of the ambiguity and complexity of ourselves and others.

Rahab's story is a text for our times.

#All-are-welcome.

Homiletic Points

1 Rahab's story is strange, seemingly alien and irrelevant. The sermon's opening move claims up front that the ancient text speaks into the contemporary moment as a 'text for our times'. The rest of the sermon fleshes out that claim.

2 References to either/or thinking on social media seek to connect the horizons of the text and our time, as the later hashtag references seek to do.

3 The personal references in the opening and closing moves place the preacher and hearer on the same pew. The preacher is not six feet above contradiction. We wrestle with this together.

4 The subheadings could be projected, or put on a handout, as a visual map for the sermon.

Collect

God of inclusion,
forgive us when pride and fear
feed the allure of binary thinking.
Remind us that your inclusive heart embraces us –
who were once far off in a distant country.
You brought us home, into your love.
Make us like you.
Create in us open and inclusive hearts,
courageous attitudes which refuse

to close down or shut another up
because they don't fit into our neat patterns.
Re-pattern us as radically inclusive people.
Amen.

Notes

1 Billy Kluttz, 'Queers in the borderlands: Rahab, queer imagination, and survival', *The Other Journal: An Intersection of Theology and Culture* (September 2015), https://theotherjournal.com/2015/09/21/queers-in-the-borderlands-rahab-queer-imagination-and-survival, accessed 25.07.22.

2 I am indebted to delegates at the 2022 Women's Voices Conference, Chester Diocese, who encouraged, challenged and inspired me to continue to wrestle with this ambiguous story, and helped me to notice more.

3 For a fuller exploration of Rahab's story as comedy, see Melissa A. Jackson, 'Rahab, Comedy, and Feminist Interpretation', Oxford Biblical Studies Online, https://global.oup.com/obso/focus/focus_on_rahab/, accessed 08.08.22.

12

Women Warriors:
Deborah and Jael

KATE BRUCE

Deborah and Jael in the Revised Common Lectionary (Sundays)

Year A   Proper 28 (OT 33)   Judges 4.1–7

Note the Church of England for the second Sunday before Advent (equivalent Sunday) does not offer this reading.

Their Words in the Bible

Deborah

'The LORD, the God of Israel, commands you, "Go, take position at Mount Tabor, bringing ten thousand from the tribe of Naphtali and the tribe of Zebulun. I will draw out Sisera, the general of Jabin's army, to meet you by the Wadi Kishon with his chariots and his troops; and I will give him into your hand."' (Judges 4.6–7)

'I will surely go with you; nevertheless, the road on which you are going will not lead to your glory, for the LORD will sell Sisera into the hand of a woman.' (Judges 4.9)

'Up! For this is the day on which the LORD has given Sisera into your hand. The LORD is indeed going out before you.' (Judges 4.14)

The Song of Deborah. (Judges 5)

Jael

'Turn aside, my lord, turn aside to me; have no fear.' (Judges 4.18)

'Come, and I will show you the man whom you are seeking.' (Judges 4.22)

Troubling Characters in a Troubling Book

The story of Deborah and Jael sits within the uncomfortable narrative of the Israelite possession of the Promised Land, involving war and the enslavement of the resident population in God's name. Perhaps we should draw a veil over this difficult part of the scriptural landscape? The Revised Common Lectionary certainly takes this approach, including only Judges 4.1–7 of the entire book. Yet, the themes of Judges are strikingly contemporary: struggles over land, rival groups, war, violence against women, child abuse, the rejection of God in the search for other objects of worship, and the consequent descent into moral chaos. This is exactly why we need to delve into this book: it's 'an invitation to think also about ourselves and our world in *theological* terms'.[1] It is not a book to be taken simply at face value; we must wrestle with many questions, not least that the God of Genesis 1 and 2, the ultimate sovereign Creator over all, is presented here as particularistic, favouring Israel over the indigenous peoples of Canaan. Too easily this has been taken as 'God is for us and against them' and used to justify wiping out 'the other' in the name of 'our God'. All this before we even get to considering Deborah and Jael. Are they characters to be praised and celebrated – strong women, acting decisively – or are their actions morally questionable, or both? The watchwords for this exploration are 'wrestle' and 'question'.

A Canonical and Symbolic Approach

A helpful approach to this difficult book with its ambiguous characters is to read it both canonically and symbolically. Read canonically we interpret Judges against the backdrop of Genesis, which presents God as the Creator of all life. Later texts which stress the particularity of Israel, chosen to act as witness to all nations, need to be held in tension with Genesis. Judges explores the issue of Israel's faithfulness to God. The pattern throughout is a downward spiral into disobedience and failure.

If we understand that the whole of scripture interprets the parts then Judges cannot be used to pit the 'chosen' against whoever is deemed as a 'Canaanite'. This approach denies the

> Bible's witness to a God who claims all humanity as God's own, who wills justice, righteousness, and peace among all nations, and who, when designating any people as 'chosen', wills them to be agents of a world-encompassing reign of justice, righteousness, and peace.[2]

Reading Judges symbolically, the Canaanites, rather like Pharoah and the Egyptians in Genesis, represent 'ways of organizing social life that perpetuate injustice and ultimately produce oppressive inequalities that threaten human life'.[3] Rather than adopting an easy identification with the 'chosen', we can usefully ask to what extent does my society and my part in it contribute to symbolic Canaanism? Symbolically, Canaan represents forces in opposition to God, rather than acting as a sign of God's hatred of particular peoples. Such an interpretation is inconsistent with the God who creates and 'it was good' (Genesis 1.4, 12, 18, 21, 25, 31), the One who desires the entire cosmos (John 3.16).

A Text of Warning and Hope

The cycle in Judges is repeated many times. Israel turns aside from God to worship the Baals. Provoked to anger, God punishes them. The people cry out for mercy and God raises up a judge to deliver them. When the particular judge dies, the people return to their apostasy. As the book unfolds, the moral chaos deepens. The final verse reads, 'all the people did what was right in their own eyes' (Judges 21.25). Judges holds together the themes of judgement and grace. Failing to live lives centred on God has consequences, and at the same time we see how God keeps on reaching out in grace to restore the people. The twin bells of warning and hope toll out across the landscape of this text, as relevant now as in the period of its formation. Generally thought to be set in 1200–1020 BC, it is likely the material was reworked over centuries following this before arriving at its final form.[4]

Deborah – A Woman of Fire

Deborah is the fourth and only female judge. Her story, like that of Jael, is told in a prose form (Judges 4) and in poetic form in the Song of Deborah (Judges 5). While many think the poetic form is the older version,[5] we will look at the two accounts in the order they come in the text.

Deborah is the 'wife of Lappidoth' (Judges 4.4). 'Lappidoth' is a feminine plural, which is odd if it signifies a man's name. Elsewhere the word *lap·pî·ḏō·wṯ* is associated with light and fire. If she is married, her husband is never mentioned again. However, there is plenty of evidence that she is a woman of fire and light: she is a prophet, a judge and a commanding military leader. Barak's name means 'flash of lightning', which connects with Deborah as a woman of fire.

Deborah's story begins with the Israelites in yet another cycle of disobedience: they 'did what was evil in the sight of the LORD' (4.1). As punishment they are cruelly oppressed for 20 years by King Jabin of Canaan whose commander was Sisera (4.2). Enter Deborah.

She is described as a prophetess who sits 'under the palm of Deborah' (4.5) where the 'Israelites came up to her for judgement' (v. 5). In this she is like Moses who also sits and judges (Exodus 18.3). 'This palm tree was the ancient equivalent of a judge's courthouse, a place where people went when they needed a dispute settled.'[6] Deborah's role shows her as a trusted leader.

She summons Barak, a military commander, using the authoritative prophetic voice, 'The LORD, the God of Israel, commands you ...' (Judges 4.6). She instructs him to raise tribesmen to come and face Sisera. Barak is able to raise 10,000 men as instructed (4.10), suggesting their trust in him and in Deborah. This rabble of volunteer fighters will face a technologically advanced force with 900 chariots of iron (4.13). The divine plan Deborah outlines is to 'draw out Sisera, the general of Jabin's army', to meet them by the Wadi Kishon 'with his chariots and his troops' (v. 7). Barak is informed that if he follows the instructions given, the Lord will give Sisera 'into your hand' (vv. 6–7). However, he refuses to go on this offensive unless Deborah goes with him (v. 8). Perhaps he sees her as a sign of God's presence with them or possibly he thinks the idea is strategically flawed and he wants to put her off. Deborah is positive about accompanying the army into battle (v. 9), prophesying confidently that 'the LORD will sell Sisera into the hand of a woman' (v. 9). She is a powerful prophetic, legal and military leader.

Sisera's army is routed and he flees the battle on foot (v. 17). The only conceivable reason for leaving an iron chariot is that the chariot won't move. It's likely the chariots were bogged down in the mud of the Wadi Kishon, trapping Sisera's force and exposing them to attack by the tribesmen. Sisera heads to the camp of an ally. His encounter with Jael is explored below, but first some analysis of Deborah.

Deborah – Should We Celebrate or Condemn Her?

That Deborah, a woman, is there at all is striking. She is presented as a more fully rounded leader than the earlier judges since she combines spiritual and legal wisdom with military prowess. Julia Esquivel, a Guatemalan, sees her as a woman of decisive action who 'breaks the tradition of submission'. For Esquivel, Deborah's story 'breaks through the false understanding of pacifism that masks the face of God, reducing God to ineffectual neutrality in the face of injustice and oppression'.[7] You can hear the pain and frustration in Esquivel's assessment. Are the oppressed expected to stay oppressed in order not to transgress the bounds of moral nicety? King Jabin had his boot on the Israelite neck for 20 years! For Esquivel, Deborah enacts justice. Jabin's entire army was wiped out (4.16). Do we read this and see justice done, or do we recoil from the violence? The questions are disconcerting. Is Deborah a female warrior to be admired or a woman engaged in brutal, retributive violence? Again, we must wrestle with the text. Uncritically celebrating her as a strong role model blinds us to her lack of compassion; if an entire army is decimated, what of their women and children? Are they now Israel's chattels? However, squeamish condemnation of her actions suggests an inability or unwillingness to see through the eyes of the oppressed. Certainly, Deborah shows courage, decisive leadership, and trust in God (4.6–10). That much is certainly to be celebrated.

Jael – Israel's Ally

Jael is married to Heber the Kenite. Heber had separated himself from the descendants of Moses' father-in-law (Judges 4.11) and made peace with the Canaanite King Jabin (4.17). When Sisera fled the battle after his troops had been routed, he could reasonably assume that Heber's camp would offer safe refuge. However, Jael's name suggests 'Yahweh is God' (yā·'êl) and her behaviour is unquestionably pro-Israelite.

Jael's actions are similar to Judith in the Apocrypha. Both women are perceived as safe by the men they murder. Both women act independently of male support, with breathtaking violence. Jael hammers her tent peg into Sisera's head while Judith beheads Holofernes (Judith 13.4–10; Judges 4.21–22). Both women are celebrated for their powerful actions which benefit Israel (Judith 13.17–20; Judges 5.24–27).

> Both of these women are unequivocally celebrated and raised high, regardless of their ability to fit nicely in any preconceived notions of womanhood. They are sung about because of their strength not their weakness, their boundary-breaking abilities and nation-saving status, rather than their passivity.[8]

Jael demonstrates a calm cunning, inviting 'my Lord' to 'turn aside and have no fear' (Judges 4.18). She appears to have her own tent, or has at least ensured access to a tent where she would be undisturbed. Her behaviour is open to interpretation. Is this an apparent invitation to a sexual encounter? Sisera enters and she covers him with a 'rug'. There is ambiguity here; the words could refer to an animal skin or have inferences of human skin, supporting a euphemistic allusion to sexual intercourse. However, when Sisera asks for a drink of water, Jael gives him milk and tucks him in like an infant. He asks her to stand guard at the entrance of the tent. He wants her as his protector; she appears to take a maternal role (vv. 19–20). Whichever way we understand her cover story, femme fatale or maternal protector, the result is the same – Sisera is murdered in cold blood.

According to stereotypical gender roles, Jael should be the weaker party. However, she behaves with power and conviction, hammering the tent peg into Sisera's head as he slept. And for this, in the poetic form of the story, she is described as 'most blessed' (5.24). Analysis of Jael is offered in the Sermon Suggestion below.

The Song of Deborah and Barak

This is a song of celebration and praise following the victory over Jabin. Because the people have offered themselves willingly to God, liberty has come (Judges 5.2). The victory is framed as God's victory (5.4–5). The change in fortune of Israel is described as due to Deborah who 'arose as a mother in Israel' (v. 7). Here the word 'mother' has connotations of leadership, protection and aggression. The song describes the willing response of the tribes who gathered for war and a criticism of those who stayed away. The war itself is framed in cosmic terms – the stars fighting from heaven (v. 20). This is not a mere tribal spat; the very existence of Israel is in question. The imagery demonstrates the heightened stakes.

In contrast to the inhabitants of Meroz who did not come 'to the help of the LORD against the Mighty' (v. 23), Jael did act. For this she is celebrated as 'of tent-dwelling women most blessed' (v. 24). The theological implication of the reference to her as 'most blessed of women' is startling. Tracing this thread will open up a theological gateway into assessing her actions. Her actions are described in a matter-of-fact tone; with a tent peg and a workmen's mallet 'she struck Sisera a blow, she crushed his head ...' (v. 26). The symbolism of crushing Sisera's head also bears theological consideration. (See Sermon Suggestion below.)

Sermon Suggestion: Jael – Twisted Sister or Most Blessed of Women?

Woman offers safe refuge to military leader. Promises to stand guard while he rests. Hammers a tent peg into his skull as he sleeps. What do you make of that?

Confession time. In my last sermon on this passage, I condemned Jael out of hand as one twisted sister. Looking at the passage again I think I could have been less keen to rush to judgement, more questioning, more willing to wrestle with scripture. What's Jael's agenda? Is it possible that God is with Jael? She is, after all, described as 'most blessed of women'. That phrase alone should provoke some theological sleuthery. I'm going to stick my neck out: while I'm not advocating hammering tent pegs into people's heads, I don't think we can just write Jael off as a 'twisted sister'.

But first, let's think ourselves into Jael's shoes. War is afoot and in war women have always been at risk of gender-based violence, sexual abuse, forced marriage and displacement. In 2020, the UNHCR reported that in Afghanistan 87 per cent of women had experienced some form of gender-based violence, and 62 per cent had experienced psychological, physical and sexual abuse.[9] There are countless other examples over the millennia. Towards the end of the Song of Deborah and Barak is a little detail which tells us that the plight of women in the war between Israel and King Jabin of Canaan is no different. Sisera's mother is pictured gazing out, wondering why her son has been delayed in returning from the battle. Her 'wisest ladies' give the answer: '"Are they not finding and dividing the spoil? A girl or two for every man ...?"' (5.28–30). There might be peace between Jael's husband and King Jabin, but that does not mean Jael is safe when Sisera flees the war seeking refuge. Heber, Jael's husband, is not mentioned – it appears Jael is alone.

What should she do? Even if Sisera means her no harm, and there is no guarantee of this, the Israelites, in hot pursuit of the general, are hardly going to be warm towards anyone harbouring their enemy. Jael is in a perilous position. It's easy to condemn Jael's violence as an armchair commentator. Try to read the story from her point of view. She is surrounded by danger. What would you have done?

Her response is far from passive – she is incredibly quick thinking. She hatches a plan and enacts it swiftly. Jael 'came out to meet Sisera'. She is deceptive, cunning, courageous and violent. She reverses expectation in her seduction of Sisera; she literally penetrates him with the tent peg. The potential victim becomes the aggressor. She stands as a woman at risk, among women at risk. She is a hero for the marginalized, immortalized in song. The text interprets Jael's actions as part of the divine plan: 'on that day God subdued King Jabin of Canaan' (4.23). Jael is seen as acting with and for God. What do we make of this? Are we perhaps squeamish over Jael's behaviour, but pass over the general violence of battle with less difficulty? Do we condemn her harshly because she is a woman behaving assertively and aggressively, because she bucks expected gender stereotypes?

The biblical text has no such difficulty with Jael. In the Song of Deborah and Barak we read:

Most blessed of women be Jael,
    the wife of Heber the Kenite,
    of tent-dwelling women most blessed.
He asked water and she gave him milk,
    she brought him curds in a lordly bowl.
She put her hand to the tent-peg
    and her right hand to the workmen's mallet;
she struck Sisera a blow,
    she crushed his head,
    she shattered and pierced his temple.
He sank, he fell,
    he lay still at her feet;
at her feet he sank, he fell;
    where he sank, there he fell dead. (Judges 5.24–27)

We need to be alert to the theological reverberations set up by the double reference to Jael being 'most blessed of women'. Where else have we heard that phrase? In Luke, Elizabeth greets Mary, saying, 'Blessed are you among women' (Luke 1.42). Jael and Mary ... both 'blessed women'. This should give us pause.

What about this language of 'crushing heads'? This takes us back to Genesis 3, after the Fall, when God says to the serpent:

> I will put enmity between you and the woman,
>   and between your offspring and hers;
> he will strike your head,
>   and you will strike his heel. (Genesis 3.15)

Sisera can be read as a symbol of the serpent – the enemy of God, the bringer of death. Jael crushes Sisera's head, symbolically foreshadowing the work of Mary's son, the Christ who ultimately crushes the serpent's head. Suddenly, my squeamish condemnation of Jael as a twisted sister is starting to look a tad theologically anaemic. Faced with the forces of death symbolized by Sisera, agent of oppression on an industrial scale, Jael summons the agency she has to fight this.

The text challenges us. Jael marshalled the resources she had in opposition to the serpent's agency. How do we use our resources and power against the serpent – the power that opposes goodness, love, hope, life and justice? Rest assured, I am not suggesting actually hammering tent pegs through heads, but where do we crush the serpent's head? Are we challenging dominion and oppression through truth-telling; raising up the voices of the poor and vulnerable? Do we champion the weak, embracing our own weakness in the face of the Goliaths, and yet trusting God? Where do we name corruption – in our world and in our hearts? How are we acting as agents of disruption, offering love and hope where the serpent desires only despair, dismay and destruction?

Jael is not an easy character to interpret, but it is only as an armchair commentator that we can tritely write her off as one twisted sister. In opposing the serpent, she stands, like Mary, as 'most blessed of women'.

Homiletic Points

1 No preacher stands six foot above contradiction – no matter the height of the pulpit. Beginning by challenging a previous interpretation, the preacher models the reality that scripture 'works on us', and won't let us rest easy in comfortable armchair conclusions.

2 The horizons of text and context are fused with reference to the plight of women in war in the passage (Judges 5.29–30) and a reference to UNHCR statistics relating to women in Afghanistan.
3 The sermon picks up on the theological inferences of Jael as 'most blessed of women' and one who crushes the enemy's head – linking this to Mary's as 'blessed among women' (Luke 1.42) whose son will crush the serpent's head. Scripture is allowed to interpret scripture.
4 This allows the interpretation to move from the literal crushing of Sisera's head to a symbolic reading of Sisera as representative of the serpent – all that opposes God.
5 The application then lands in the question of how we use our resources to call out such powers of oppression.

Collect

God of the oppressed and violated,
thank you for the courage of Jael,
who alone and unsupported opposed the serpent.
We pray for all who are abused, displaced, unheard:
women and men, in war and in peace.
Provoke us to respond in attitude, word and action,
offering our power and resource
in identifying, unmasking and undoing
the serpent agenda,
for the sake of the fruit of Mary's womb,
our Saviour, Jesus Christ.
Amen.

Notes

1 Clinton McCann, *Judges*, Interpretation Series (Louisville, KY: Westminster John Knox Press, 2002), p. 2.
2 McCann, *Judges*, p. 18.
3 McCann, *Judges*, p. 19.
4 McCann, *Judges*, p. 6.
5 McCann, *Judges*, p. 48.
6 Elizabeth Fletcher, 'Who was Deborah in the Bible' (2006), https://womenin thebible.net/women-bible-old-new-testaments/deborah-and-jael/, accessed 29.11.22.
7 Julia Esquivel, 'Liberation, theology, and women', in John S. Pobee and Bärbel von Wartenburg-Potter (eds), *New Eyes for Reading: Biblical and Theological*

Reflections by Women from the Third World (Oak Park, IL: Meyer-Stone Books, 1987), p. 99.

8 Allison J. van Tilborgh, 'Deborah, Jael, and gender reversal: God favors the troublemakers', https://medium.com/interfaith-now/deborah-jael-and-gender-reversal-dc144e2ac908, accessed 07.05.23.

9 Khanyi Mlaba, 'How do women and girls experience the worst of war?', https://www.globalcitizen.org/en/content/women-and-girls-impacts-war-conflict/, accessed 07.05.23.

13

A Misunderstood Migrant: Naomi

LIZ SHERCLIFF

Naomi in the Revised Common Lectionary (Sundays)		
Year B	Proper 26 (OT 31)	Ruth 1.1–18
Year B	Proper 27 (OT 32)	Ruth 3.1–5; 4.13–17

Naomi's Words in the Bible

'Go back each of you to your mother's house. May the LORD deal kindly with you, as you have dealt with the dead and with me. The LORD grant that you may find security, each of you in the house of your husband.' (Ruth 1.8–9)

'Turn back, my daughters, why will you go with me? Do I still have sons in my womb that they may become your husbands? Turn back, my daughters, go your way, for I am too old to have a husband. Even if I thought there was hope for me, even if I should have a husband tonight and bear sons, would you then wait until they were grown? Would you then refrain from marrying? No, my daughters, it has been far more bitter for me than for you, because the hand of the LORD has turned against me.' (Ruth 1.11–13)

'See, your sister-in-law has gone back to her people and to her gods; return after your sister-in-law.' (Ruth 1.15)

'My daughter, I need to seek some security for you, so that it may be well with you. Now here is our kinsman Boaz, with whose young women you have been working. See, he is winnowing barley tonight at the threshing-floor. Now wash and anoint yourself, and put on your best clothes and go down to the threshing-floor; but do not make yourself known to the man until he has finished eating and drinking. When he lies down, observe the place where he lies; then, go and uncover his feet and lie down; and he will tell you what to do.' (Ruth 3.1–4)

Naomi's Story

In many ways, Naomi dominates the book of Ruth. Naturally, at the start of the book she is subordinate to a man, she and her children are 'his' (Ruth 1.1–2). On his death, however, the roles are reversed – he was *her* husband and she is left with *her* sons. Naomi loses everything in Moab, husband and sons. When she hears that the famine in Judah is over, Naomi decides to go home. She asks her God to be faithful to her daughters-in-law (Ruth 1.8–9). Unusually, Naomi invokes God's blessing, *hesed*, on the younger women because of the kindness they have shown not only to the dead men but also to her (Ruth 1.8), though she expects this blessing to take the form of a husband (Ruth 1.9). Naomi thus articulates a paradoxical theology in which she both subverts and preserves the patriarchy. Although she tells the villagers to call her Mara, when she returns home, because God has dealt bitterly with her (Ruth 1.20–21), there is clearly something beguiling about Naomi's personality, for Ruth refuses to leave her (Ruth 1.14, 16–18).

As the story continues, so does Naomi's prominence. The next part of the story begins with her, and establishes a link with the wealthy, prominent man Boaz. When she discovers what a good day Ruth has had, Naomi first blesses the man who has dealt fairly with her, then blesses God when she discovers the man's identity (1.19–20). Naomi may praise God but, based on her past experience, she does not trust her future to God. Knowing the weaknesses of men replete with food and drink, she hatches a plot to ensnare Boaz, one that depends on him being honourable. The plan succeeds, and Naomi is not heard from again.

Naomi is a divisive figure, Phyllis Trible points out.[1] She is variously understood as: promoting patriarchal values; being an independent character; behaving overbearingly; showing care for her daughters-in-law; rivalling Ruth for prestige; using Ruth for her own ends; an embittered woman; and a woman of faith. Given so many diverse views, debating the merits of each seems a time-consuming task of limited value. Let's turn to an intriguing alternative.

Naomi as an Image of Mother God

In Ruth 1.20–21, Naomi uses the word *Shaddai* for God. It means literally, 'God with breasts'.[2] She says, then, 'The God with breasts has dealt bitterly with me ... the God with breasts has brought calamity upon me.' Virginia Ramey Mollenkott regards this as an indication that, for Ruth, Naomi is the image of Mother God.[3] 'God-in-Naomi' arises from the circumstances of the story, there is no one-to-one equivalence as in a metaphor.[4] God as female emerges from the story, and some of Naomi's characteristics as experienced by Ruth are attributable to this God. She is a nurturer, saviour, leader, provider and problem-solver. She blesses Ruth and accepts her devotion – her people will be Ruth's people and her God Ruth's God from now on. One of Mollenkott's arguments is that Ruth commits herself to a God she has only known through Naomi.[5]

Sermon Suggestion: Empathizing with Naomi

I didn't used to be keen on Naomi. She seemed like an embittered older woman stealing the limelight from the beautiful heroine Ruth. I was younger then! I used to look down on her lack of faith when things went wrong, and wonder why she couldn't have been more faithful to God. I was younger then, too! I used to suspect her motives in sending Ruth out to a drunken man with the aim of getting him to marry her. I was younger then, too.

Now I am a mother-in-law, doing my best to walk the tricky line between supporting and interfering. I have children who have their own lives. I can look back and confess that I have been bitter about some things. I have blamed God for some things. Sometimes I would rather hatch a plan than leave things in God's hands, too. Now, I can empathize with Naomi.

I understand her struggles a bit, too. She knows that Ruth will have to make her way in a patriarchal society if she doesn't find a husband. That's not going to go well. So she bows to social pressures and makes sure that Ruth uses what she has to get herself a wealthy man.

At the same time, she also seems to know, or at least suspect, that women are as important to God as men, and that she can commend her daughters-in-law for their kindness to *her* as well as for their kindness to the menfolk. She is entitled to bless them.

I like Naomi now, because she seems real. She alternates between blaming God and praising God. She doesn't pretend to praise God when she's fed up; she doesn't proclaim faithfully that God will be with her, when apparently that hasn't been the case recently. There is wisdom in such honesty. It's also an expression of trust in God that she speaks her truth.

When Ruth decides to remain with Naomi, Naomi doesn't teach her some kind of catechism or some systematic theology. She allows her to accompany her. Naomi's faith is real and lived, gentle and reassuring. God doesn't charge through the book of Ruth, or through Naomi's life, offering slam-dunk demonstrations of power and authority. She, the God who has breasts, as Naomi calls her, is simply there. Naomi's God weaves through life's ups and downs, gentle, faithful, ever present.

When I read about Naomi, I want to reject the sentimental interpretations of her as an embittered woman who comes to her senses and praises God again. I want to say that she is honest and strong and courageous. She sets out on her first adventure as her husband's companion, but she makes the bold decision to return. She knows the risks – she explains them to Ruth and to Orpah. She has no great expectations, for she feels abandoned by God. She decides nevertheless.

So what might we learn from Naomi? I suggest it's this: sometimes we might be confident and strong, sometimes we might be full of doubt; sometimes we might feel alone, sometimes we might be in companionship. Whatever, whoever we are, God is there alongside, weaving through our lives. Sometimes seen, often not. I wonder whether Naomi's faith was like that of R. S. Thomas, which he describes in his poem 'Folk Tale'. 'Prayers', he says, are 'like gravel flung at the sky's window', hoping to attract attention. He would have given up long since, except for the fact that once, 'through locked fingers I thought I detected the movement of a curtain'.[6] For me, Thomas's line is reassuring. When I was a child, I remember feeling quite grown up when my sister and I were allowed out to play. But my mother knew we were safe, because neighbours were always looking out for us, the movement of their curtains sometimes giving them away. I may not see God, but God sees me and God's presence is woven through my life, even when I don't notice it.

Homiletic Points

1 Notice how often the first person is used. The preacher does not airbrush themselves out of the sermon. The sermon arises from the preacher's lived experience, showing how perspective and interpretation changes with experience.

2 The image of God as mother, based on Naomi's naming of God, is also woven into the sermon, along with analysis of how this God is present in Naomi's life.

3 The application comes in the final move, which is comforting in its realistic assessment of the ups and downs of the journey of faith.

4 The memorable image of prayer like gravel 'flung at the sky's window', from the R. S. Thomas piece, is connected to the preacher's childhood experience, offering a reassuring picture of the presence of God.

Collect

God, who always hears us,
even in those times when we seem to be throwing gravel
at a heavenly window;
grant us faith to know that you know our pains and our joys,
and confidence to admit our doubts.
In the name of your Son
who himself doubted.
Amen.

Notes

1 See https://jwa.org/encyclopedia/article/naomi-Bible#:~:text=Naomi%20is%20featured%20prominently%20in,that%20God%20has%20forsaken%20her, accessed 01.04.23.

2 David Biale, 'The God with breasts: El Shaddai in the Bible', *History of Religions*, Vol. 21, No. 3 (February 1982), pp. 240–56.

3 Virginia Ramey Mollenkott, *The Divine Feminine: The Biblical Imagery of God as Female* (Eugene, OR: Wipf and Stock, 2014), pp. 54–9.

4 Mollenkott, *The Divine Feminine*, p. 54.

5 Mollenkott, *The Divine Feminine*, p. 55.

6 R. S. Thomas, in *R. S. Thomas Selected Poems* (London: Penguin, 2003).

14

Raped, Dismembered, Remembered: The Levite's Concubine

LIZ SHERCLIFF

The Levite's Concubine in the Revised Common Lectionary

Not included.

Her Words in the Bible

None.

Weapons of Domination

As I began the research for this chapter, news came out of Ukraine that women and girls were being raped by Russian soldiers. 'Rape is an under-reported crime and stigmatized issue even in peaceful times. I am worried that what we learn about is just going to be the tip of the iceberg,' said Kateryna Cherepakha, President of La Strada Ukraine, a charity that sup-ports victims of trafficking, domestic violence and sexual assault.[1] We should not be surprised, then, to find rape in the Bible. What is surprising is that when these chapters of Judges are discussed, which isn't often, the abused concubine alone is the focus, as though the mass rapes at the end of the story didn't happen.

The incident begins with 'the most horrible story of the Hebrew Bible'.[2] An unnamed woman, a *pilegesh* (concubine or secondary wife) gets angry with her Levite husband and returns to her father's house. About four months later, the man follows her in an attempt to win her back. It seems that the company of her father is more alluring than returning home, however, for the Levite remains several days eating and drinking. On the fifth day, the man again chooses to feast with his father-in-law rather than set out on the journey home. Later that same day, against advice, the Levite sets off, with his concubine and his servant. Near Jebus (Jerusalem), his servant urges him to seek lodging in the city, but he refuses and they continue to Gibeah. A man on his way home from work warns them not to spend the night in the city square and offers lodging for the night.

As the men eat and drink together, a male mob pounds on the door wanting to rape the Levite. The men refuse to go out, but offer the concubine and the daughter of the house. The mob insist on having the Levite, until he pushes his concubine outside. She is raped and abused all night. In the morning the Levite finds her on the doorstep, puts her on his donkey and returns home where he chops her into 12 pieces and sends her throughout Israel.

The tribes of Israel meet together at Mizpah. The Levite recounts his version of the story: the 'lords' of Gibeah rose against *him* and wanted to kill *him*; they raped his concubine until she died (Judges 20.5). Notice how he avoids the idea that he might have been raped – we will return to this point later. The account leads to war being declared on the tribe of Benjamin. The war is not straightforward and many die. The other tribes swore not to marry their daughters to Benjaminites, and so the tribe seems likely to be cut off from Israel (Judges 21.6). The problem is presented in acutely phallocentric terms:

'What shall we do for wives for those who are left, since there are no women left in Benjamin?' And they said, 'There must be heirs for the survivors of Benjamin, in order that a tribe may not be blotted out from Israel. Yet we cannot give any of our daughters to them as wives.' (21.16–18)

The solution is to invite the Benjaminites to abduct young women and claim them for themselves (21.8–23).

Re-membering the Story

The patriarchal nature of Israelite society at the time can hardly be missed in this story. The concubine never speaks, she has no voice. Her return to her father is her only independent action. We are not told why she returns, just that she became angry with her husband. Some feminist scholars assume that she was abused, so left.[3] It is significant that she returned to her father for protection and found none. The father is referred to six times in the first pericope (19.3–9), yet even if she left her husband because of abuse, her father shows no concern. He fails to offer the protection for which his daughter hoped, preferring instead to eat and drink with his son-in-law. She is alone.

The story seems to briefly acknowledge other forms of oppression when the Levite refuses to listen to his servant and instead presses on to the next town. Here we face another interpretive problem. Why is the host happy to send the women out to be raped, but not his male guest? Michael Carden suggests that here lies a lesson in compulsory hetero-sexuality. Men affirm their maleness through penetration. A woman's status is low anyway, and penetration will not reduce it. For a man to be penetrated reduces him to the status of a woman.[4] Shockingly, when the Levite finds his concubine on the doorstep in the morning, he first gives her a command: 'Get up, we are going' (Judges 19.28). He shows no understanding of the situation or compassion for the woman he had set out 'to speak tenderly to' (Judges 19.3). When she cannot reply, he puts her on his donkey, returns home and chops her in pieces. He kills her, because she is no longer of any value to him – whether this is as a result of being gang raped or because she cannot recover from her injuries is unclear.

Even this is not the end of the story. The phallocentric nation of Israel realizes that it has lost a tribe. More women are sacrificed to bolster the nation and maintain the patriarchy. Misogyny, rape and war are presented as interrelated weapons of oppression. Women are there to be used and abused in the pursuit of male dominance, apparently sanctioned by a patriarchal god. The victimization of the concubine is followed by genocide and mass rape – no wonder this story is regarded as a 'text of terror'.[5]

Many commentators and preachers whose work is readily available interpret these chapters in the light of the final verse of Judges: 'In those days there was no king in Israel; all the people did what was right in their own eyes' (21.25). This seems to be a way simply of saying that in order to control abusive male power what is needed is a dominant male power. The problem becomes the solution simply by becoming more forceful. Is there another way of preaching this passage, then?

Sermon Suggestion: Being Powerless

How on earth did this story make it into the Bible? *It's appalling!*

This is what it's like to be powerless. The one independent action of this woman is to leave her husband and return to her father. But when her husband came calling, she likely had no choice about returning – her father could simply have pushed her out of the door. She leaves when she is told to, after her husband and father have spent enough time carousing together. She stays where she is told to on the way home. She is offered no protection by their host in Gibeah. She's at best an afterthought. When a gang wants to rape her husband, it's called a 'vile act' by their host, but when she is sent out the man simply tells the gang to do what is 'good in their eyes'.[6] In the morning, having struggled to the door of the house, the woman is simply told to get up and get moving. She is powerless.

Even in the story-telling this woman is powerless. The writer makes no comment on the behaviour of anyone involved. Contrast these events with those in Genesis. When Abraham takes a knife to kill his son Isaac, God intervenes.[7] When the Levite takes a knife to kill his concubine, God is silent. Nobody defends her. Nobody speaks for her. In the face of such awful suffering, God and the narrator are silent.

How do such things happen?

A few years ago, I went to a seminar run by Christian Aid at a well-known Christian conference. The presenter spoke movingly of the fate of women around the world, and the use of rape as a means of oppression. At the end I waited by the door for a time. I noticed a very profound thing. Many left the room promising never to forget what they had heard; many left feeling emotional. But some, a vociferous minority, left saying things like, 'You don't know how reliable the statistics are', or, 'I think that was a bit over the top.' In other words, some people were looking for reasons to be silent. The Levite's concubine suffered, because nobody spoke in her defence. It's how similar stories still come about.

Let's look at some statistics. In September 2021 the highest ever number of rapes was recorded by police in England and Wales – 63,136 women. Five in six women who are raped don't report it to the police. If those 63,136 women represent just one in six rapes in one month, then over 300,000 rapes might have taken place. And the church spends more time talking about who should have sex with whom than it does talking about the abuse of women.

Let's be clear: this story in the Bible is horrendous – but it happens.

Perhaps the really big question is this: why did God, why does God, not speak?

I wonder whether it has something to do with the fact that God works through human beings. And we are selective about what we will do, just as the old man in the story would not send out the Levite to be abused, but was prepared to send out the woman. Churches too can be selective: perhaps we support work among abused women overseas, but don't ask our councillors and MPs for abuse figures in our own area. Perhaps we can admit that women in other cultures are abused, but are reluctant to concede there is a problem in our parish, and even in our congregation, as in every congregation that meets together up and down our land. We have a God who, through Amos called for justice to roll on like a river, and through Micah told the people that what God requires is justice, mercy and humble walking with God, and through Isaiah told us to learn to do good and seek justice.[8]

Back to our story of the Levite and the concubine. Society allows this abuse to happen: the men of Gibeah are invited to do what is right in their own eyes with the women; the men are defended. The Levite is so affronted that his concubine has been abused he chops her up and sends her bits to the tribes of Israel. War and more death ensue. To avert the risk of the tribe of Benjamin dying out, more women are abused, and rape is again condoned. How does it happen? Nobody stands up for justice. Even God is silent.

Why do we have this story?

It's a challenge to us.

Robert F. Kennedy said this in 1966:

It is from numberless diverse acts of courage and belief that human history is shaped. Each time someone stands up for an ideal, or acts to improve the lot of others, or strikes out against injustice, he sends forth a tiny ripple of hope, and crossing each other from a million different centres of energy and daring those ripples build a current which can sweep down the mightiest walls of oppression and resistance.[9]

It's the little things. Imagine if the Levite had simply gone to woo his concubine, and then gone home; or if he had listened to his servant instead of his prejudice and spent the night in Jerusalem; or if the old man had simply barred the door until the men of Gibeah had sobered up. Little things make a big difference. It doesn't take much to raise our eyes above our home groups, our parishes, our Bible study and to look for opportunities to fight for justice – use online petitions from Tearfund or Christian Aid; write to our MPs; ask questions about justice.

Don't ignore the issues. When we ignore them people die.

Homiletic Points

1 The awful nature of the story is named at the outset.
2 Many examples are given to establish a clear sense of the woman's powerlessness – from the events in the text and the narrative silences.
3 The anecdote from the seminar bridges the theme of silence then to silence now.
4 Statistics are explored to give a sense of the scale of the contemporary problem of violence against women.
5 The Robert Kennedy quote bridges into the application, stressing the value of small actions.
6 The last line is punchy and emphasizes the critical importance of attending to these issues.

Collect

Ever loving God,
who created each member of the human race in your image:
give us the courage to speak on behalf of the oppressed and abused;
to look honestly at the state of our world, and point to what is wrong.
May our voices be your voice
so that justice might flow like a river through
our community, our country and our world;
through Jesus Christ our Lord.
Amen.

Notes

1 Reported in *The Guardian*, 4 April 2022.
2 A. Brenner, *A Feminist Companion to Judges* (Sheffield: Sheffield Academic Press, 1993), p. 209.
3 P. T. Reis, 'The Levite's concubine: new light on a dark story', *Scandinavian Journal of the Old Testament*, Vol. 20, No. 1 (2006), pp. 125–46.
4 M. Carden, 'Homophobia and rape in Sodom and Gibeah: a response to Ken Stone', *Journal for the Study of the Old Testament*, Vol. 82 (1999), pp. 83–96.
5 Phyllis Trible coined the phrase in 1984. The fortieth anniversary edition was published in 2022: P. Trible, *Texts of Terror (40th Anniversary Edition): Literary-Feminist Readings of Biblical Narratives* (Minneapolis, MN: Fortress Press, 2022).
6 Judges 19.24.
7 Genesis 22.1–19.
8 Amos 5.24.; Micah 6.8; Isaiah 1.17.

9 Day of Affirmation Address, 6 June 1966, in John F. Kennedy Presidential Library and Museum, https://www.jfklibrary.org/learn/about-jfk/the-kennedy-family/robert-f-kennedy/robert-f-kennedy-speeches/day-of-affirmation-address-university-of-capetown-capetown-south-africa-june-6-1966, accessed 26.07.23.

15

A Woman Who Challenges God: Hannah

LIZ SHERCLIFF

<table>
<tr><td colspan="3">Hannah in the Revised Common Lectionary (Sundays)</td></tr>
<tr><td>Year B</td><td>Proper 28 (OT 33)</td><td>1 Samuel 1.4–20
1 Samuel 2.1–10</td></tr>
<tr><td>Year C</td><td>First Sunday after Christmas Day</td><td>1 Samuel 2.18–20, 26</td></tr>
</table>

Hannah's Words in the Bible

'O LORD of hosts, if only you will look on the misery of your servant, and remember me, and not forget your servant, but will give to your servant a male child, then I will set him before you as a nazirite until the day of his death. He shall drink neither wine nor intoxicants, and no razor shall touch his head.' (1 Samuel 1.11)

'No, my lord, I am a woman deeply troubled; I have drunk neither wine nor strong drink, but I have been pouring out my soul before the LORD. Do not regard your servant as a worthless woman, for I have been speaking out of my great anxiety and vexation all this time.' (1 Samuel 1.15)

'Let your servant find favour in your sight.' (1 Samuel 1.18)

'I have asked him of the LORD.' (1 Samuel 1.20)

'As soon as the child is weaned, I will bring him, that he may appear in the presence of the LORD and remain there for ever; I will offer him as a nazirite for all time.' (1 Samuel 1.22)

'Oh, my lord! As you live, my lord, I am the woman who was standing here in your presence praying to the LORD. For this child I prayed; and the LORD has granted me the petition that I made to him. Therefore I have lent him to the LORD; as long as he lives, he is given to the LORD.' (1 Samuel 1.26–28)

'My heart exults in the LORD;
   my strength is exalted in my God.
My mouth derides my enemies,
   because I rejoice in my victory.[1]
There is no Holy One like the LORD,
   no one besides you;
   there is no Rock like our God.
Talk no more so very proudly;
   let not arrogance come from your mouth,
for the LORD is a God of knowledge,
   and by him actions are weighed.
The bows of the mighty are broken,
   but the feeble gird on strength.
Those who were full have hired themselves out for bread,
   but those who were hungry are fat with spoil.
The barren has borne seven,
   but she who has many children is forlorn.
The LORD kills and brings to life;
   he brings down to Sheol and raises up.
The LORD makes poor and makes rich;
   he brings low, he also exalts.
He raises up the poor from the dust;
   he lifts the needy from the ash heap,
to make them sit with princes
   and inherit a seat of honour.
For the pillars of the earth are the LORD's,
   and on them he has set the world.
He will guard the feet of his faithful ones,
   but the wicked will perish in darkness;
   for not by might does one prevail.
The LORD! His adversaries will be shattered;
   the Most High will thunder in heaven.
The Lord will judge the ends of the earth;
he will give strength to his king,
   and exalt the power of his anointed.' (1 Samuel 2.1–10)

Hannah's Story

The scene for this story is set clearly at the beginning. Elkanah is introduced by male lineage and geographical location: 'a certain man of Ramathaim, a Zuphite from the hill country of Ephraim ... son of Jeroham son of Elihu son of Tohu son of Zuph, an Ephraimite' (1 Samuel 1.1). Men occupy history and land. Contrast the introduction to his two wives: 'the name of one was Hannah, and the name of the other Peninnah. Peninnah had children, but Hannah had no children' (1 Samuel 1.2). Women have children – or not. The Hebrew word for co-wife means adversary (1 Samuel 1.6). Accordingly, Peninnah provokes Hannah, apparently on an annual basis when they go on pilgrimage to the Temple. Peninnah may have provoked Hannah on two counts: she has no children and so does not fulfil her role as a woman, and she has no future, for when Elkanah dies, she has no son to take her in. At the feast, Peninnah and her children get what is due to them from Elkanah. Hannah, however, is treated lavishly, because Elkanah loves her (1 Samuel 1.4–5).

Whether Hannah's desire for a male child is simply to ensure she has a future, or whether it is to validate her as a woman, or whether she simply wants to give her husband what all husbands at the time wanted – a 'truth universally acknowledged', as Jane Austen might say[2] – is unclear. It is perhaps telling that her prayer focuses on herself: 'look on the misery of your servant (my misery) ... remember me' (1 Samuel 1.11).

Elkanah seems to have no empathy with his wife. Basically, he says, 'Aren't I enough for you?' So full is he of his own importance that he asks, 'Am I not more to you than ten sons?' (1 Samuel 1.8), the assumption of a privileged man, who believes he alone is enough to give any woman purpose. Hannah decides to seek God. It is symbolic that the male priest, Eli, is at the doorway to the Temple. Men have long acted as gatekeepers to women. When he sees Hannah praying, her lips moving, he assumes that she is drunk and tells her to behave. Eli is not pastorally gifted! Hannah brokers a deal with God – 'Give me a boy and I will loan him back to you.' She will thereby gain the status of mothering a boy, God will gain a nazirite. There is no consideration that a child of any gender would be a blessing. Once the deal is done, Hannah has a son, worships God, and disappears from the story.

As Karen O'Donnell points out, 'Hannah has been wielded like a weapon to the distress and misery of many people who struggle to conceive.'[3] She is presented in the text as the 'virtuous infertile woman' whom God blesses. Alexandra Kimball argues that Hannah's response to her situation is 'almost a parody of appropriate feminine submission'.[4] Her submission includes denying herself food and drink, submitting 'immediately to the orders of the male priest ... it's as if she is trying to redeem her deviance, her failure as a woman, by doubling down on femininity'.[5]

Redeeming Hannah

I want to suggest an alternative reading of Hannah. This woman, who could have been ground down by the provocations of her co-wife and her husband's lack of understanding, does not creep submissively into the Temple. She bypasses the man at the entrance and 'presented herself before the LORD' (1 Samuel 1.9). She is a woman on a mission. Her prayer is assertive, she offers God a deal. She will not *give* her child to God, she loans him. She will ensure he is marked out as a man of God by his diet (he will not drink alcohol) and by his appearance (he will not cut his hair). Hannah is clear later too that Samuel is only on loan to God (1 Samuel 1.28).

Hannah's boldness before God seems to empower her speech to others. She firmly corrects Eli's wrong assumptions, although she has apparently not responded either to Peninnah's taunts nor Elkanah's self-indulgence. Notice, too, that although for years Hannah tags along with her husband's household on their annual pilgrimage, Hannah now goes along on her own terms – when she has weaned her child (1 Samuel 1.22). Hannah has become more than a two-dimensional pastiche of a compliant wife.

Hannah's prayer when she takes Samuel to the Temple is not about barrenness or motherhood, but about all oppressions, in some way a precursor of the Magnificat. That is problematic, for the specific anguish of the barren woman is eclipsed by generalities that inevitably transition to male normativity – there are bows and girded loins before there are children (1 Samuel 2.4–5). The prayer brings together the oppressed and finds victory and protection in God, and I am tempted to ask whether solidarity is enough. In general terms I can often say with Hannah, 'My heart exults in the LORD', or see where God raises up the lowly. But I am left with the question, 'What happens when God doesn't?' In some ways, the story of Hannah is too neat – there is a problem, there is a prayer, there is a solution.

I have not, then, redeemed Hannah entirely. I have argued that she becomes a full person in her own right by saying what she wants and acting on her own terms. The story remains, however, that she is an inadequate woman rescued by a male God, a male priest, a husband and a son. Hannah's story remains a man's story.

Sermon Suggestion: Challenging the 'Father'

I was asked, during my ordination selection process, to name a hero. I gave the name of a woman I much admired. 'I knew you would name a woman,' said the selector. 'Do you have any men heroes?' For the selector in question, women clearly were not heroes.

I suspect that the story of Hannah is read through similar lenses. She is a woman without a baby, so she is upset. Once she has a baby, everything is fine. I wonder if there is more to Hannah than that, though. She is also a woman constantly provoked by her co-wife, with a husband who assumes he is enough to fulfil her every need. Nobody empathizes with her, no one is on her side.

Eventually, she has had enough. She decides to take her complaint to the top – the very top. She goes to the Temple, where she finds the priest at the door. How often have women found men at the door, withholding women's rights, blocking women's ordination, deciding women's roles for them? Apparently, Hannah ignores the priest and presents herself to God. She tells God exactly what she wants.

In fact, she offers God a deal.

Which God accepts.

The successful negotiation gives Hannah courage. Next time her husband tells her it's time to go on the annual pilgrimage, she refuses. She will go on her own terms, later, when she, and her son, are ready. Of course, once Hannah has met her side of the bargain, she disappears from the story and it turns out to be all about her son.

For some time, Hannah puts up with the provocation of her co-wife and the self-absorption of her husband. She suppresses her emotions, she avoids reacting. Then, something makes her act – it seems to be her husband's complacency. He rates himself as better than ten sons! She doesn't argue back, she doesn't complain. She goes to God. And just for a short time in this story we have a woman who negotiates with God, and who is heard.

The incident leaves her less compliant than usual. Next time Elkanah says it's time for the annual pilgrimage, Hannah refuses to go. She will go later, on her own terms. She has become a strong woman.

Of course, in the end, once Hannah has handed her son over to the patriarchal institutions of religion and government, she disappears from the story.

But we are left with Hannah, a woman who challenges God.

Homiletic Points

1 The sermon is concise and explores one overriding theme, which challenges how Hannah has been interpreted. The sermon focuses on Hannah as a strong woman who takes matters into her own hands and challenges God.
2 The opening move takes the form of a personal anecdote, taking us into the theme of how Hannah has been interpreted.
3 Her isolation is detailed with multiple examples.
4 The use of two short sentences concerning the deal with God and its acceptance communicate a matter-of-fact tone.
5 This feeds into a statement about how her confidence gives her agency and choice.
6 The final moves of the sermon are a summary of her story, re-emphasizing the point that Hannah is a strong woman who deals directly with God.

Collect

God of our mothers
Who heard Hannah's challenge,
Give us courage to speak clearly
To resist openly
And to be the people you intend us to be.
Amen.

Notes

1 Some versions say 'your victory'.

2 Opening sentence, *Pride and Prejudice* (London: Penguin Classics, rev. edn, 2003).

3 Karen O'Donnell, *The Dark Womb: Reconceiving Theology through Reproductive Loss* (London: SCM Press, 2002), p. 138.

4 Alexandra Kimball, *The Seed: Infertility is a Feminist Issue* (Ontario: Coach House Books, 2019), p. 28.

5 Kimball, *The Seed*, p. 28.

16

A Player or a Pawn?
Bathsheba

KATE BRUCE

Bathsheba in the Revised Common Lectionary (Sundays)

Year A	Second Sunday before Advent	Second Service 1 Kings 1.15–40 (*or* 1–40) (CW, SS)
Year B	Proper 12 (CW)	2 Samuel 11.1–15 (CW, PS)
Year C	Proper 6 (CW)	2 Samuel 11.26—12.10, 13–15 (CW, PS)

Bathsheba's Words in the Bible

'I am pregnant.' (2 Samuel 11.5)

'My lord, you swore to your servant by the LORD your God, saying: Your son Solomon shall succeed me as king, and he shall sit on my throne. But now suddenly Adonijah has become king, though you, my lord the king, do not know it. He has sacrificed oxen, fatted cattle, and sheep in abundance, and has invited all the children of the king, the priest Abiathar, and Joab the commander of the army; but your servant Solomon he has not invited. But you, my lord the king – the eyes of all Israel are on you to tell them who shall sit on the throne of my lord the king after him. Otherwise it will come to pass, when my lord the king sleeps with his ancestors, that my son Solomon and I will be counted offenders.' (1 Kings 1.17–21)

'May my lord King David live for ever!' (1 Kings 1.31)

'Do you come peaceably?' (1 Kings 2.13)

'Go on.' (1 Kings 2.14)

'Go on.' (1 Kings 2.16)

'Very well; I will speak to the king on your behalf.' (1 Kings 2.18)

'I have one small request to make of you [Solomon]; do not refuse me.' (1 Kings 2.20)

'Let Abishag the Shunammite be given to your brother Adonijah as his wife.' (1 Kings 2.21)

Bathsheba and the Blame Game

Mention Bathsheba and it won't be long before someone blames her for taking a bath where she could be overlooked, making her responsible for all that follows. The Crown Prosecution Service offers a comprehensive list of 'assumptions which prosecutors may need to challenge', 'rape myths', such as: 'The victim provoked rape and automatically implied consent by their dress/flirtatious behaviour.'[1] Keep these in mind as we read some assessments of Bathsheba.

Josephus admits David's 'very grievous sin', but states David 'fell' into it, 'overcome by that woman's beauty'. Unable to 'restrain his desires', he 'sent for her, and lay with her'.[2] The *Ancrene Wisse*[3] says: 'Bathsheba, by uncovering herself in David's sight, caused him to sin with her.'[4] Hertzberg accuses Bathsheba of entrapment through her 'feminine flirtation'.[5] Bailey regards Bathsheba as 'a willing and equal partner to the events that transpire'.[6] All assume she is aware of her visibility, that she has agency in unfolding events.

Close examination of the text clarifies that Bathsheba is not a seductive player but a pawn in David's game. At the outset she is an innocent victim. Over time she grows in power and influence.

Letting the Text Speak

The story begins ominously. In the season when kings go out to battle, David remains at home. This is when '*it* happened' (2 Samuel 11.1–2). '*It*' happens at the juncture between David's rise and David's fall; from public triumph into moral chaos and personal pathos (2 Samuel 12—20).[7]

What is the '*it*'? A picture of indolence: David rises late, walks aimlessly on the roof and sees a beautiful woman bathing. He looks 'down' (*yarad*) on Bathsheba's house (11.8–10, 13). From the palace roof, David had a view down over all the local houses. There is no need to assume Bathsheba was engaging in exhibitionism. The text makes no comment about why she is in David's eyeline. There is no sense that she has any awareness that she can be seen, and no suggestion anywhere in the story that she has done anything amiss. How different the story would have been if David had simply looked away.

> It is not unreasonable to assume that the generally accepted code of decency in David's day included the understanding that it was inappropriate to look out from one's rooftop or upper-story down into the courtyard of a neighbor's property at this time of day, out of respect for privacy, since this was the normal time for baths to be taken.[8]

Bathsheba is close enough that David can see her beauty, but not close enough that he can recognize she is Uriah's wife. He sends a messenger to inquire who she is. Without regard for her vulnerability, he invites another to look on her. Bathsheba is well connected, 'daughter of Eliam, the wife of Uriah the Hittite"' (2 Samuel 11.3), two of David's top warriors (2 Samuel 23.34, 39). Ahithophel, Bathsheba's grandfather, was at one stage a trusted counsellor (2 Samuel 15.12; 1 Chronicles 27.33). These were loyal and trusted men who deserved better from their leader. These details signal David's skewed judgement. Bathsheba is named only through her relationships with them, signalling her lack of agency.

It's All in the Verbs

The text itself is clinically brief. David sees, sends and seizes (2 Samuel 11.2, 3, 4a).

> There is nothing but action. There is no conversation. There is no hint of caring, of affection, of love – only lust. David does not call her by

name, does not even speak to her. At the end of the encounter, she is only 'the woman' (v. 5).[9]

She comes to him because he is the king and he holds all the power.[10] The verb translated 'fetch' (NRSV) is better rendered as 'take' (*laqach*). This 'implies coercion'.[11] Who is going to step in to help her should she resist? David has her simply because he can. Bathsheba cannot dissent, therefore she cannot consent. While there is no sense of physical violence here, unlike the rape of Dinah (Genesis 34.2) and of Tamar (2 Samuel 13.14), Bathsheba is a woman abused.

> Given the context of (at least psychological) coercion in this passage, the best modern expression to describe David's action is 'power rape,' in which a person in a position of authority abuses that 'power' to victimize a subservient and vulnerable person sexually, whether or not the victim appears to give consent.[12]

When David is done with her, 'she returned to her house' (2 Samuel 11.4b), to her place as the wife of Uriah the Hittite. When she becomes aware of the conception, she '*sent* and told David, "I am pregnant"' (v. 5). Her act of sending echoes David's. In this she effectively says, 'This is what you have done to me.' Her fear must be of the penalty for adultery – death (Leviticus 20.10).

David continues to control events, no longer driven by lust but by a desperate scramble to manage the story. He sends for Uriah (2 Samuel 11.6–7) and Uriah, like Bathsheba, complies. David arranges for Uriah's murder: 'David's power rape of Bathsheba is paired with his "power murder" of Uriah.'[13]

A Ritual Bath? Taking Issue with Translations

Many connect 11.5 back to verse 2, interpreting Bathsheba's bathing as a ritual washing following menstruation. This establishes David's paternity beyond question. It is a fair interpretation. However, the child cannot have been Uriah's anyway. He is away at war and when he does return he will not seek pleasure while the ark, Israel and Judah are in the field (11.11). Palace messengers would have been aware of events between David and Bathsheba; this open secret must have implicated David as the father.

There is another way of reading the text which aligns us more closely with Bathsheba's suffering. The key words in 11.2 and 11.5 are *rōḥeṣet* (bathing/washing), *mitqaddeṣet* (purifying), and *miṭṭum'āṭāh* (rendered here as 'period').

Forms of the verb *rḥṣ* (*rōḥeṣet*), 'to wash', are found in various conjugations 77 times in the Hebrew Bible and are never associated with washing following a period.[14] Furthermore, according to Leviticus (15.19) a woman is unclean from the start of her period for seven days. Purification is a matter of time and the only washing required is of a man who touches her bed, who must wash his clothes and bathe in water (Leviticus 15.20–21). 'Menstrual impurity is regular and time-linked, and time itself, rather than water, brings an end to it.'[15] Given this, perhaps Bathsheba is simply having a bath at the start of the story and this is unrelated to the purification of the later verse.

The NRSV translates *miṭṭum'āṭāh* as 'period' (v. 5). However, *miṭṭum'āṭāh* has 'a wide semantic range, mostly unrelated to menstruation ... it can refer to uncleanliness related to 'men, Gentiles, food and objects'.[16] In the Masoretic text and the Septuagint the word is simply rendered as 'uncleanness' without further definition.[17]

If Bathsheba is simply taking a bath in verse 2, what uncleanliness is she later purifying herself from (v. 5)? The last action running up to this in the text is David's 'power-rape'. Her worth is utterly subjugated to the fulfilment of David's desire; her body a means to his end. No wonder she is seeking to purify herself, to distance herself, from the effect of his abuse. This reminds us of the deep and ongoing trauma of sexual violation. As Frymer-Kensky puts it, 'She can purify herself from the ordinary pollution of sexual intercourse, but the defilement of illicit sexuality is not so easily washed off.'[18]

This interpretation makes Bathsheba's purification attempt more than a narrative device establishing David's paternity (which is obvious anyway). It brings into focus the profound suffering of all who are raped and abused, highlighting a longing to undo the defilement.

Contrasting Attitudes to Uriah's Death

Bathsheba laments the death of her husband acutely. The verb *wat·tis·pōd* (11.26) used in the text, signifies intense grief – beating the breast, wailing and making lament. Bathsheba's anguish is raw. She is treated as a pawn, raped, wronged and grievously widowed. The narrator refers to her as 'the wife of Uriah' (v. 26), signalling that she is faithful to her husband to the end. Whether she ever learns the truth about the murder, we do not know, though surely she must have some suspicion? Contrast her grief with David's response to his murder of Uriah: 'Do not let this matter trouble you, for the sword devours now one and now another' (v. 25). He has become the king Samuel warned against – the despotic taker (1 Samuel 8.10–22). After the mourning period, he '*sent* and *brought* Bathsheba to his house, and she became his wife, and bore him a son' (2 Samuel 11.26). This is not a woman engaged in a dalliance, playing for power, as Randall Bailey argues.[19] Rather, Bathsheba is gathered in, harvested by her rapist.[20]

The Effect of David's Behaviour

God condemns the rape of Bathsheba and the murder of Uriah through Nathan's parable and twice in his oracle (12.9–10). The punishment relates directly to the taking of Bathsheba (v. 10) but is visited on women and the expected child:

'Thus says the LORD: ... I will take your wives ... and give them to your neighbour, and he shall lie with your wives in the sight of this very sun. For you did it secretly; but I will do this thing before all Israel, and before the sun.' (12.11–12)[21]

'Nevertheless, because by this deed you have utterly scorned the LORD, the child that is born to you shall die.' (12.14)

Bathsheba must bear the child conceived in rape, and then deal with his illness, and death. The narrator is concerned only with David's grief (12.15–23). All we learn of Bathsheba's suffering is that 'David consoled his wife' in such a way that she conceives another child (12.24), as though one might simply replace the other. Bathsheba's grief is passed over. I wonder how consoled she felt. The text is silent.

Ultimately, Bathsheba

will receive her identity, her significance, her status, not from any husband – not from the first one – who loved her; not from the second, who raped her – but from her son. It will prove to be nearly the most any woman in the court of Jerusalem could hope for.[22]

From a Pawn to a Player

When we next meet Bathsheba, David is in decline: old, bedridden and cold. A virgin is brought to warm him up. Note again the use of women in David's service. The text is candid: 'the king did not know her sexually' (1 Kings 1.1–4). He is impotent. Bathsheba is in the ascendancy. Cue a power struggle.

Adonijah tries to stage a coup. Nathan the prophet advises Bathsheba how to save herself and her son (1 Kings 1.13–14). She, however, is no ventriloquist's dummy. She has become independent, shrewd and persuasive. Rather than ask, as advised, she boldly states, 'you swore to your servant by the LORD your God'. Nathan had not mentioned God. Bathsheba stresses Adonijah's betrayal and David's ignorance: 'you, my Lord the king, do not know it'. Adonijah has enacted a coronation; Joab, who collaborated in Uriah's murder, is with him. David is betrayed. Bathsheba's knowledge is greater than Nathan's at this point. She is no longer a pawn; now she is a player – a woman who has found her voice.

Cleverly, Bathsheba refers to David as 'my lord' and 'my lord the king' (1 Kings 1.17–18, 20–21), reminding him of his position and pandering to his ego. She exonerates Solomon of rebellion. She reminds David that 'all Israel' is waiting for him to appoint his successor (v. 20). David is failing while all Israel watches. Finally, Bathsheba warns that she and Solomon will be at risk after David's death if this challenge to the throne is left unchecked (1 Kings 1.17–21). Where once David harmed Bathsheba, now, at the end of his life, he can help her, and she has found the power to speak.

Nathan reports to David that people are saying, 'Long live King Adonijah', confirming the extent of the betrayal (v. 25). Bathsheba is summoned again. 'She came into the king's presence, and stood before [him]' (v. 28). The first time Bathsheba was summoned by David she was fetched and raped (2 Samuel 11.4). The second time she was 'gathered' to his house and taken as his wife (11.27). This time there is no mention of obeisance as she comes before him. She stands and receives what she wants – her 'son Solomon' (v. 30) on the throne. David honours Bathsheba and secures her future as queen mother by decreeing that Solomon shall accede (v. 30). Now, perhaps, as she bows her face to the ground, with the words 'May my lord King David live for ever!' (v. 31), there is genuine gratitude.

Bathsheba's Final Scenes: Adonijah's Request
(1 Kings 2.13–18)

Bathsheba is queen mother. Adonijah comes to her: 'May I have a word with you?' (2.14). He desires Abishag as his wife, the woman chosen to 'warm up' the dying king David. He complains that 'the kingdom was mine, and ... all Israel expected me to reign', before conceding that the Lord gave the throne to his brother (v. 15). The text gives no hint of Bathsheba's thoughts on the matter. She simply agrees to speak to the king on Adonijah's behalf (v. 18).

Presenting the Request to Solomon
(1 Kings 2.19–24)

Bathsheba makes no obeisance to this king. Solomon bows before her, and has a throne brought and placed in the position of honour at his right hand. She does not instruct her son; she draws Adonijah's request to his attention and lets him do the maths. Solomon perceives the request as a challenge for the kingdom and remembers that Joab and Abiathar also need dealing with (2.22). Bathsheba's 'small request' is a catalyst for Solomon to establish his position.

Bathsheba, initially a pawn in David's game, becomes a player, a woman of influence who subtly helps to secure her son's throne and her own position as queen mother.

Sermon Suggestion: Bathsheba in Her Own Words

Bathsheba in her own words
Springtime. The men are off to war. I've just waved off Uriah. When will he be back? They said I shouldn't marry a Hittite. But what do they know? He is a good man.

Time passes
A messenger came, early evening, summoning me to the palace. I went, of course. I thought Uriah was dead.
But there was no news.
The king wanted me. Had me fetched. Lay with me. No one could stop it. No one.

I'm numb. No amount of washing ...
No amount ...
He saw me bathing, he said. I caught his eye – so he sent the messengers.
They saw me; know me, where I live, who my husband is. I can never go
out again. What if Uriah finds out?
Is it my fault?
It must be.
Now what? Pretend, carry on as if nothing happened.
God, where are you? Do you even care?

Sometime later
God. God. God.
I'm pregnant. The penalty is death. Could anyone really believe I'd choose
this?
I'll send that king a message.
God help me.

Later
Uriah has been at the palace. Seen with the king. He didn't come home,
he slept at the gate. Got really drunk one night, apparently. I don't know
what happened.
He's gone back to the front line now. When will I see Uriah again? Does
he blame me?

Time passes
Uriah is dead.
Gone.
The heaviness in my soul echoes the heaviness in my womb.
I am nothing.
My name is Grief.

Days of weeping bleed into each other
Again, I am sent for. Fetched. Put in his hareem. Owned.
Nights of pain are broken by the dawn of my son's first cry.
The light soon fades.
He is ill.
David fasts and prays for days – 'Let the child to live'. He dies anyway.
I am in a wilderness, yet his consolation is to lie with me again.
As though another child will take away my grief, or heal my wracked
body.

Nine months later
Another child. A son. Solomon.
I watch my back, now. I listen and observe. I know who is where, and where danger might lie. I am learning how to operate here. I need to – for my baby's sake.
I do have a friend: Nathan. He understands more than he says. He raged at David – incandescent fury – before the first child died. Others blame me – 'seductress, adulteress, whore'. But not Nathan. He's kind – respectful. I think he knows the truth.

Years later
The king is old and cold. Even a young woman, another young woman brought to him, fails to warm him.
Rumours fly around the court. Who will replace the dying king? Haggith and her son lust after power. The harem call her 'Queen mother in waiting'. Nathan tells me to save myself and Solomon. He gives me a steer.
I'll appeal to David. Remind him he promised God Solomon would be king. I'll make him realize Adonijah is planning a coup – enacting his own coronation. Making a fool of his old father. I'll remind him he's still king – he should make the succession clear. He needs to know Solomon and I are at risk. Who knows, perhaps he will act?
He has named his successor: Solomon. My son. Haggith is not best pleased.

A little later
David is dead.
An odd encounter today. Adonijah came to me – 'in peace'. He wants me to ask Solomon if he can take Abishag, David's waiting girl, as his wife. He must think I'm a fool. The king's woman and then the throne. I wonder if Haggith is behind it. We're still not safe. I said I'd ask..
I played it down. A small request. Predictably, Solomon erupted at the threat; 'I'm the king', he stormed. He is clear; the opposition will be dealt with – all of them.

I have known injustice, abuse, grief and sorrow. I have been shamed and humiliated, broken on the wheel of a powerful man's desire. These are my truths and I will not deny them.
First, I was summoned, ordered, used – a powerless pawn in one king's game. Now I am the queen mother, welcomed in the presence of the king, my son, and graced with my own throne. This does not magic away the losses. The grief still stabs. But these are not the final truths.

In the end there is hope, even in the mess and struggle.
Hope, sometimes elusive, other times easier to grasp.
Hope from ashes.
A new season birthed from anguish, full of new possibility.
Hold on to that.

Homiletic Points

1 The monologue form allows an insight into Bathsheba's perspective. It makes educated inferences, building on careful reading of the text. The points of application are implicit.
2 All preaching is performative. Performance is not a dirty word, but a means to the expression of deeper truth. The monologue form relies particularly on effective delivery, and works best when delivered without reliance on a text. Tone, body language, movement and gesture will all add to the overall effect.
3 The piece requires a health warning. People should know the subject matter beforehand to give the potential for them to opt out. Since it deals with painful subject matter – sexual assault and the loss of a child – pastoral sensitivity is needed, with the possibility of support in place afterwards for any who wish to reach out. The fact that the subject matter is sensitive is not a reason to avoid it, but a powerful reason to deal with it well.
4 People may want to study the biblical text closely in forming their own response to the piece, so take-away materials could usefully be made available.

Collect

God who rages against injustice,
we rage for all who have known Bathsheba's plight,
taken and misused for the entertainment of powerful players.
We give you thanks for enlightened witnesses,
who like Nathan speak truth to power.
Give us such courage and insight,
to speak boldly, challenge clearly and offer ongoing support.
With them we cry out to you – for vindication and hope.
Amen.

Notes

1 See https://www.cps.gov.uk/legal-guidance/rape-and-sexual-offences-annex-tackling-rape-myths-and-stereotypes, accessed 01.08.22.

2 Josephus, *Antiquities of the Jews*, VII, 7, https://www.gutenberg.org/files/2848/2848-h/2848-h.htm#link72HCH0007, accessed 08.10.22.

3 *Ancrene Wisse* is a thirteenth-century manual for anchorites.

4 Anne Savage and Nicholas Watson (trans.), *Anchorite Spirituality: Ancrene Wisse and Associated Works* (New York: Paulist Press, 1991), p. 68.

5 H. W. Hertzberg, *I and II Samuel: A Commentary*, Old Testament Library (London: SCM Press, 1964), p. 309.

6 Randall C. Bailey, *David in Love and War: The Pursuit of Power in 2 Samuel 10–12* (Sheffield: JSOT, 1990), p. 86.

7 Walter Brueggemann, *First and Second Samuel*, Interpretation Series (Louisville, KY: Westminster John Knox Press, 1990), pp. 271–2; Richard M. Davidson, 'Did King David rape Bathsheba? A case study in narrative theology', *Journal of the Adventist Theological Society*, Vol. 17, No. 2 (Autumn 2006), p. 82.

8 Davidson, 'Did King David rape Bathsheba?', p. 85.

9 Brueggemann, *First and Second Samuel*, p. 273.

10 Katharine Doob Sakenfeld, *Just Wives? Stories of Power & Survival in the Old Testament & Today* (Louisville, KY: Westminster John Knox Press, 2003), p. 73.

11 Garsiel, Moshe, 'The story of David and Bathsheba: A different approach', *The Catholic Biblical Quarterly*, Vol. 55, No. 2 (April 1993), p. 256, https://www.jstor.org/stable/43721228#metadata_info_tab_contents, accessed 25.09.2022.

12 Davidson, 'Did King David rape Bathsheba?', p. 89.

13 Davidson, 'Did King David rape Bathsheba?', p. 90.

14 J. D'Ror Chankin-Gould, Derek Hutchinson, David Hilton Jackson, Tyler D. Mayfield, Leah Rediger Schulte, Tammi J. Schneider and E. Winkelman, 'The sanctified "adulteress" and her circumstantial clause: Bathsheba's bath and self-consecration in 2 Samuel 11', *Journal for the Study of the Old Testament*, Vol 32, No. 3 (2008), pp. 339–52, http://jot.sagepub.com, p. 342, accessed 09.10.22.

15 Tikva Frymer-Kensky, *Reading the Women of the Bible: A New Interpretation of Their Stories* (New York: Schocken Books, 2002), p. 147.

16 Chankin-Gould et al., 'The sanctified "adulteress"', p. 348.

17 See http://qbible.com/hebrew-old-testament/2-samuel/11.html#4; https://biblehub.com/sep/2_samuel/11.htm, accessed 09.10.22.

18 Frymer-Kensky, *Reading the Women of the Bible*, p. 147.

19 Bailey, *David in Love and War*, pp. 84–90.

20 Trevor Dennis, *Sarah Laughed: Women's Voices in the Old Testament*, 3rd edn (London: SPCK, 2010), p. 151.

21 Later, when David flees the palace, running from Absalom, he leaves ten concubines to 'look after the house' (2 Samuel 15.16), abandoning them to his enemy, his over-indulged son Absalom. Predictably, on the same roof from which David spied Bathsheba, Absalom 'proves' his virility by raping his father's concubines (16.22). On David's return he imprisons them for the rest of their lives (20.3). David's ego and his son's 'prowess' condemn these women to a life sentence.

22 Dennis, *Sarah Laughed*, p. 158.

17

A Desolate Woman:
Tamar, Sister of Amnon and Absalom

LIZ SHERCLIFF

Tamar in the Revised Common Lectionary

Not included.

Tamar's Words in the Bible

'No, my brother, do not force me, for such a thing is not done in Israel; do not do anything so vile! As for me, where could I carry my shame? And as for you, you would be as one of the scoundrels in Israel. Now therefore, I beg you, speak to the king; for he will not withhold me from you.' (2 Samuel 13.12–13)

'No, my brother, for this wrong in sending me away is greater than the other that you did to me.' (2 Samuel 13.16)

Tamar's Story

Tamar was the daughter of one of David's most high-ranking wives, Maacah, daughter of King Talmai of Geshur, a neighbouring kingdom. Maacah had two reputedly good-looking children, Absalom and Tamar (2 Samuel 13.1; 14.25). As a princess and a virgin, Tamar was closely watched by the harem eunuchs. She was a valuable political asset, probably with a marriage arranged for her once she hit puberty. Amnon, her half-brother, became so obsessed with her that his apparent illness was noticed. As David's eldest son, his health concerned the whole court, but it is to his friend Jonadab that Amnon confesses the truth. Together the men hatch a plan to get Tamar in a room alone with Amnon so that he can possess her (2 Samuel 13.2–5).

Amnon asks David to send Tamar to him, and David does so. Since he is king, Tamar has no choice but to obey. She prepares food and takes it to Amnon, who feigns a fit of petulance and dismisses the servants. As next in line to the throne, he too must be obeyed, and the servants go. He goes into the sleeping area of his apartment and calls Tamar to him (2 Samuel 13.5–10).

Tamar has no chance of fending him off, but resists as best she can. She makes it clear that what he is doing is wrong. She offers to marry him. She pleads for her life – if she is no longer a virgin, she has no marriage prospects even if she is the king's daughter. Amon is too powerful for her, and rapes her (2 Samuel 13.12–14). Once he has done so, he is filled with self-loathing and orders 'this *thing* [to be taken] out from me'.[1] Being discarded in this manner, 'Tamar is then the victim of shame'[2] and her actions demonstrate its power. 'It shifts blame onto the wrong person, onto the powerless one – the victim.'[3] Abusers depend on the power of victims' shame to make them keep quiet. Shame is the way power works in patriarchal societies; accountability and justice are side issues at best, irrelevant at worst. Challengingly, Judith Plaskow and Carol Christ assert that 'the Christian scriptures are inextricably interwoven with this history of belief systems that support the view of women as scapegoats'.[4]

Casting Tamar out, then, continues the abuse; she is unwanted, cast out and shamed by the man who has possessed her. Tamar falls to the floor, covers her hair with ashes from the fire and tears her robe. She returns through the palace to the harem, her hand on her head – the sign of a bereaved woman. The women of the harem realize what has happened (2 Samuel 13.19). Presumably the harem is thrown into disorder because Tamar, her mother Maacah and Amnon's mother Ahinoam live together there. Perhaps other women considered how to take advantage of the demise of David's beautiful daughter.

Tamar's brother Absalom finds out what has happened and takes Tamar into his house. He visits David, demanding that Amnon marry his sister, but Amnon refuses. David typically refuses to chastise his son or get him to do the 'right' thing, protecting the abuser rather than the victim.

Although David is content for Tamar to drop out of the story, Absalom is not. He waits for two years, then has Amnon killed, Mafia style, at a party. He then escapes to Geshur, his grandfather's kingdom. The murder, of course, does not help Tamar. Absalom assumes the crown, and, in a show of power, publicly rapes ten of David's wives (2 Samuel 13.20–38; 16.21–22).

Sermon Suggestion: No Means ...

'No.'
Tamar speaks twice. Both her speeches begin, 'No'.
'No, do not force me ...'
'No, this is wrong ...'

Yet she is forced, and wrong is done to her. Wrong is done to her from among God's people – David, God's chosen king, and his family. So, as we contemplate this story, I do not want to point a finger at the world beyond the church, as though these things happen only outside our walls. I want, as sensitively as I possibly can, to speak about Tamar's story in full knowledge that there are women and men here who have been through similar trauma. Perhaps, as you heard the story read, you felt yourself draw into your protective shell, hoping not to recall what happened to you. Perhaps you empathize with Tamar as she flees, rubs ashes in her hair, tears her robe and sobs for her lost future. Perhaps you feel her shame.

If so, please be confident that I am not going to offer any easy answers. I am not going to try to cheer you up by telling you God knows all about it. I am not going tell you that what happened does not matter, because I know that just as surely as what happened to Tamar became part of her identity, what happened to you has become part of yours too.

One of the things I want to say is that shame is a mechanism that silences us. Shame makes us feel unworthy, and so we deprive ourselves of a voice. We can feel as though shame permeates our being, taints everything that we are. I remember feeling as though even strangers in the street knew I was shamed. I think it helps to name things. To describe how we feel as shame, and then to call it what it is – sin. Not my sin, someone else's, perhaps one person, or a group, or society, or the church. Gradually, we might come to a place where we know that how we feel about ourselves is not the truth about us, but something pushed on us from somewhere else.

When I was 11 years old, my history teacher said that I would never 'make anything' because I was too quiet. My wise mother encouraged me to say to myself, whenever I felt the shame caused by this verbal abuse, 'I am a child of God.' We don't know what happened to Tamar, the Bible goes quiet on her. But I wonder whether at some stage she came to a point where she could say, 'I am a child of God.' I hope so.

Then, I want to say that you should not be expected to 'get over it'. Trauma is not a sign of weakness, it is a sign of damage, done by others to you. In her book about reproductive trauma, Karen O'Donnell says that we do not recover or get healed from trauma, we re-make ourselves. And that takes time.

What might Tamar's story tell those of us who have not suffered trauma or shame? Amnon gets rid of her; Absalom hides her in his house and gets dreadful revenge. Tamar goes through the palace, probably back to the harem and the other women. She makes her pain visible. What is she hoping for? One of the most important things we can do for someone who has suffered trauma is to witness with them that it is wrong. To hear their pain, to trust what they say, and to assure them that it was evil. There are no easy answers, but sweeping things under the carpet, trying to ignore them, re-victimizes survivors.

Tamar's story hangs on dysfunction. Power is used to impose first David's will, then Absalom's will on Tamar. David refuses to use his power either to punish Absalom or care for Tamar; he makes Tamar a victim again by his injustice. Absalom objects to his sister's abuse, but uses it as an excuse to kill Amnon, usurp his father's throne and rape ten more women.

Dysfunction can only be dealt with by being brought out into the open.

We live in a dysfunctional world, and a dysfunctional church, but we do have a choice. Shall we silence the already abused in an effort to save the reputation of the church, or shall we call dysfunction out into the open, where it can be dealt with?

Homiletic Points

1 The subject matter of text and sermon is hard hitting and requires careful advertising and handling. However, as with other sermons that deal with tough subject matter, this is not a reason to avoid the material. Truth needs naming.
2 The opening word 'No' clearly establishes Tamar's lack of consent.
3 The piece openly addresses the failure of the church in the area of safeguarding, and calls for an honest calling out of dysfunction.
4 The preacher acknowledges survivors in the congregation, exploring their possible reactions to the story and aligns herself with them.

5 Tamar's story is explored, with commentary on shame, trauma and dysfunction, and the importance of acknowledgement.
6 The sermon is an honest appraisal of the story, framed in pastorally sensitive language and comment, and earthed in a plea for honesty and openness.

Collect

God of the oppressed, abused and abandoned,
forgive us when our own dysfunction causes others to suffer;
forgive us when our desire to make things seem good
means we hide evil deeds.
Give us courage to seek truth,
to hear the disempowered,
and to do what is right.
Pour into us a spirit of humility
so that we are ready to admit our fault.
In the name of the one who is truth,
Jesus Christ your Son.
Amen.

Notes

1 J. Kirsch, *The Harlot by the Side of the Road: Forbidden Tales of the Bible* (London: Rider Books, 1997), p. 278.
2 P. Tribble, *Texts of Terror: Literary-feminist Readings of Biblical Narrative* (Philadelphia, PA: Fortress Press, 1984), p. 49.
3 K. L. Casey, 'Surviving Abuse: Shame, Anger, Forgiveness', *Pastoral Psychology*, Vol. 46 (1998), p. 225.
4 S. Brooks Thistlethwaite, 'Every two minutes', in J. Plaskow and C. P. Christ (eds), *Weaving the Visions: New Patterns in Feminist Spirituality* (New York: HarperCollins, 1989), p. 302.

18

Eloquence in Word and Action: The Wise Woman of Tekoa, the Wise Woman of Abel-Maacah, Merab and Rizpah

KATE BRUCE

Their Stories in the Revised Common Lectionary (Sundays)

None of these women are included in the lectionary.

Their Words in the Bible

The Wise Woman of Tekoa

'Help, O king!' (2 Samuel 14.4)

'Alas, I am a widow; my husband is dead. Your servant had two sons, and they fought with one another in the field; there was no one to part them, and one struck the other and killed him. Now the whole family has risen against your servant. They say, "Give up the man who struck his brother, so that we may kill him for the life of his brother whom he murdered, even if we destroy the heir as well." Thus they would quench my one remaining ember, and leave to my husband neither name nor remnant on the face of the earth.' (2 Samuel 14.5–7)

'On me be the guilt, my lord the king, and on my father's house; let the king and his throne be guiltless.' (2 Samuel 14.9)

'Please, may the king keep the LORD your God in mind, so that the avenger of blood may kill no more, and my son not be destroyed.' (2 Samuel 14.11)

'Please let your servant speak a word to my lord the king.' (2 Samuel 14.12)

'Why then have you planned such a thing against the people of God? For in giving this decision the king convicts himself, inasmuch as the king does not bring his banished one home again. We must all die; we are like water spilled on the ground, which cannot be gathered up. But God will not take away a life; he will devise plans so as not to keep an outcast banished for ever from his presence. Now I have come to say this to my lord the king because the people have made me afraid; your servant thought, "I will speak to the king; it may be that the king will perform the request of his servant. For the king will hear, and deliver his servant from the hand of the man who would cut both me and my son off from the heritage of God." Your servant thought, "The word of my lord the king will set me at rest"; for my lord the king is like the angel of God, discerning good and evil. The LORD your God be with you!' (2 Samuel 14.13–17)

'Let my lord the king speak.' (2 Samuel 14.18)

'As surely as you live, my lord the king, one cannot turn right or left from anything that my lord the king has said. For it was your servant Joab who commanded me; it was he who put all these words into the mouth of your servant. In order to change the course of affairs your servant Joab did this. But my lord has wisdom like the wisdom of the angel of God to know all things that are on the earth.' (2 Samuel 14.19–20)

The Wise Woman of Abel-Maacah

'Listen! Listen! Tell Joab, "Come here, I want to speak to you."' (2 Samuel 20.16)

'Are you Joab?' ... 'Listen to the words of your servant.' (2 Samuel 20.17)

'They used to say in the old days, "Let them inquire at Abel"; and so they would settle a matter. I am one of those who are peaceable and faithful in Israel; you seek to destroy a city that is a mother in Israel; why will you swallow up the heritage of the LORD?' (2 Samuel 20.18–19)

'His head shall be thrown over the wall to you.' (2 Samuel 20.21)

Merab and Rizpah

None.

The Wise Woman of Tekoa

Background

Absalom's sister Tamar is raped by her half-brother Amnon in a plan hatched by his 'crafty' friend Jonadab (2 Samuel 13.4). Absalom waits two years before enacting vengeance (13.23). He has Amnon murdered and then flees, remaining in exile for three years (13.38). Joab, a ruthless military leader in David's entourage, perceives that David is yearning for Absalom, so he enlists the wise woman of Tekoa to enact his plan to make the king relent and allow Absalom to return. The wise woman acts as a counterbalance to the crafty Jonadab whose plan instigated the whole episode.

We are not given any background about her, and no explanation about how Joab knew of her. Why doesn't Joab approach the king directly regarding the matter? Perhaps he knows that a direct approach could bring trouble on his head – send in the woman instead! She is not just any woman; she is an example of 'a woman exercising public power in a village setting',[1] who, based on reputation, is called to address the king. Like Nathan the prophet, she broaches the king's situation through analogy (2 Samuel 12.1–7). We never learn whether she thinks the plan for Absalom's return is a wise one; with hindsight it might have been better to keep Absalom away, given the ensuing power struggle (2 Samuel 14.28—19.4). However, she addresses the king on this sensitive issue with diplomacy and rhetorical skill.

A *dangerous encounter*

Summoned by the powerful Joab, it is unlikely the wise woman could have refused. Initially the language suggests she is a pawn in Joab's plan. He 'sent' and 'brought' her, directed her appearance and 'put the words into her mouth' (2 Samuel 14.2–3). However, her conversation with the king is complex, Joab cannot have given her much more than an outline of the plan. She demonstrates the ability to think on her feet and adapt, guiding the conversation with intelligence and intuition. She is no pawn!

It is likely that Joab is present, or at least nearby, since the king addresses Joab directly (14.21), implying he has been there throughout. The woman is in a very difficult position: coerced by one powerful man to address a sensitive issue with another very powerful man. Like Nathan, the wise woman takes considerable risk in speaking to the king on a personal matter; Joab mitigates the risk to himself by using her.

Eloquence in action

The wise woman of Tekoa enacts Joab's fabrication in which she is a widow with two sons. One son has killed the other and the family demand this brother's life, leaving no heir. In taking the role of a widow seeking the king's mercy, she adopts the position of the powerless petitioner. The irony is this wise woman has more power than the king imagines. She is an accomplished wordsmith and actor. Throughout the encounter, she addresses David as 'the king' and 'my lord the king' and herself as 'his servant'. Twice she compares the king to 'the angel of God', able to discern good and evil and 'know all things' (14.17, 20). Her weapons are words – deferential and flattering, deployed within a skilfully layered argument. She adopts strong imagery in referring to her fictitious family's demand to destroy her son: 'Thus they would quench my one remaining ember, and leave to my husband neither name nor remnant on the face of the earth' (14.7). She paints a picture of a bleak, cold and dark life, adding that her husband's memory will be obliterated. The powerful king cannot resist the 'helpless' widow: 'Go to your house, and I will give orders concerning you' (v. 8).

If the king intervenes the blood guilt will not be avenged. She reels the king in further, 'On me be the guilt, my lord the king, and on my father's house; let the king and his throne be guiltless' (v. 9). The woman offers the image of a mother willing to take her child's guilt upon herself – in a move which, read from a New Testament perspective, foreshadows the work of Christ. Read within the narrative context, the wise woman is trying to draw the king in to see that, if she can make this sacrifice for the sake of her son, surely a great king can do likewise with his son. 'When the "killer" is acknowledged to be a beloved son, vengeance can be overcome.'[2]

Again, the king asserts his power: 'If anyone says anything to you, bring him to me, and he shall never touch you again' (v. 10). He aligns himself fully with her cause. The threat of harm is clear. Now the wise woman asks the king to keep the 'LORD your God in mind, so that the avenger of blood may kill no more, and my son not be destroyed' (v. 11). She enlists God's support, implying a theological justification against taking the life of the guilty son. She is ratcheting the pressure up so that when the penny finally drops the king will allow Absalom's return. With the king's response, 'As the LORD lives, not one hair of your son shall fall to the ground' (v. 11), the wise woman nearly has him in her verbal snare. She ups the pressure by stating that the king convicts himself, since he 'does not bring his banished one home again' (v. 13). This has implications 'against the people of God' (v. 13). She doesn't elaborate, but the sense is that the actions of a king affect his people. Failing to pardon his own son sets a tone of bitter unforgiveness in his rule, damaging all. She continues to build up the pressure with her argument. Everyone is destined to die 'like water spilled on the ground, which cannot be gathered up' (v. 14). The underlying point is that Amnon is dead and cannot be brought back, but Absalom lives. 'God will not take away a life; he will devise plans so as not to keep an outcast banished for ever from his presence' (v. 14). Her argument is clear: if this is how God is, what about you?

For the king this is a jaw-dropping moment. He sees what the conversation has really been about. How will he respond? I imagine the woman's speech becoming more rapid as she gets her defence in, eliding her own situation with that of the fictitious widow:

'Now I have come to say this to my lord the king, because *the people* have made me afraid. Your servant thought, "I will speak to the king; it may be that the king will perform the request of his servant. For the king will hear, and deliver his servant from the hand of *the man* who would cut both me and my son off from the heritage of God." Your servant thought, "The word of my lord the king will set me at rest"; for my lord the king is like the angel of God, discerning good and evil. The LORD your God is with you!' (14.15–17)

Surely Joab lies behind the reference to 'the people' who have frightened her. When she speaks as if she is the widow and refers to 'the man' who would cut her off, she is indirectly referring to Joab. She cannot name him directly until the king does. Finally, he sees it clearly: 'Is the hand of Joab with you in all of this?' Her speech is full of flattery as she praises the wisdom of 'my lord the King' and ensures that Joab is firmly in the frame (14.18–20). Her petition is successful, and Absalom is summoned back. She has convinced the king, at least for now, with her 'extravagant speech' that 'true wisdom consists in moving beyond vengeance to forgiveness'.[3] She is a mediator and reconciler, eloquent in action. We never hear any more of her.

The Wise Woman of Abel-Maacah

After the failed rebellion of Absalom, the northern kingdom of Israel and the southern kingdom of Judah are still at odds. A separatist movement springs up in the north, led by Sheba, a Benjaminite. Pushed back by an army led by Joab, Sheba flees to the city of Abel-Maacah. Joab lays siege to the city, and the stage is set for the destruction of many innocents. Enter another wise woman.

The siege ramp is thrown up against the city wall, which is being battered by Joab's forces, and a wise woman calls down, 'Listen! Listen! Tell Joab, "Come here, I want to speak to you"' (2 Samuel 20.16). Take that in for a moment. During battle a woman demands an audience with the commanding officer, and he obeys; he recognizes her authority. She further endorses her position as one who is 'peaceable and faithful in Israel', implying that she is one with a history of reconciling skill (vv. 18–19). She is eloquent and uses language strategically, portraying the city as 'a mother in Israel'. The image is freighted with ideas of nurture, protection and significance. She increases the rhetorical pressure, 'why will you swallow up the heritage of the LORD?' (v. 19). The city is valued by God, to be handed down – and she accuses Joab as being a devourer. Joab vehemently disavows this (v. 20) and explains his hunt for Sheba son of Bichri. The wise woman negotiates with Joab and with her people, both recognize her authority in matters of politics. The head of Sheba is the brutal price for the freedom of the city; the siege is averted by the courage and eloquence of a wise woman.

Rizpah and Merab (2 Samuel 3.7; 21.8–14)

We first hear mention of Rizpah, one of Saul's concubines, when Saul's son, Ishbosheth, now king, accuses his general, Abner, of having sex with her (2 Samuel 3.7). The drive of the accusation is the fear that Abner is seeking Saul's position. There is no sense in the text of Rizpah's vulnerability as a marginalized slave to an overthrown king.

Rizpah next emerges in a horrifying account which underlines her courage and contrasts with the brutality of David's actions. There has been a famine for three years and David asks God the reason. The text tells us that the Lord told David that there is blood-guilt on the house of Saul for trying to wipe out the Gibeonites (2 Samuel 21.1). God advocates for the marginalized Gibeonites but does not tell David what to do to put this right.[4] David asks the Gibeonites how expiation might be made and they demand seven of Saul's sons to be impaled before the Lord at Gibeon. Notice they claim a religious framework for their vengeance – it is not one God demands. David hands over the two sons of Rizpah and the five sons of Saul's daughter Merab (2 Samuel 21.1–9), thus perpetuating the cycle of aggression: 'Their violent acts to restore themselves left new victims and new traumas.'[5] David doesn't question this 'solution', which conveniently weakens the house of Saul.

Rizpah has no say in the matter, although her subsequent actions are profoundly eloquent. Merab is mentioned and then fades from the story, but it doesn't require much imagination to feel her turmoil and grief. Five sons, probably young, are taken from her and brutally killed, their bodies left to rot. She is left devastated by trauma and economically vulnerable:

> Merab is like so many victims of too many wars and acts of violence. The news and history narratives rush on to the next momentous events, but the victims who survive are silent ... What is hidden in the silence?[6]

Rizpah's eloquent action

What happens next is staggering. Strange that Walter Brueggemann, who analyses David's motives in detail, says nothing about Rizpah. Odd too that *The Women's Bible Commentary* makes no mention of her remarkable actions, she is simply alluded to as 'one of Saul's secondary wives', no name given, no comment on her actions.[7] The sons are put to death at the beginning of the barley harvest. Rizpah takes sackcloth, a symbol of mourning, spreads it on a rock by the impaled bodies and stays by them until the rain comes. Wil Gafney estimates this time as six months.[8] Rizpah expresses her grief publicly, drawing attention to the atrocity. She drives the birds away by day and the wild animals at night (2 Samuel 21.10), preventing the desecration of the bodies as the Gibeonites wanted. This is an act of civil disobedience.[9] People are aware of her presence, but there is no mention of any support for her.

Just pause and stay with Rizpah in your mind's eye. Her ordeal is grotesque. In unimaginable grief she bears witness to the stages of decay of those she loves. They have no burial, yet she honours their bodies, week after week, in an expression of love, grief, rage and horror. Her eloquence is silent but speaks powerfully. Attention must be paid! The stench of their bodies is at least natural, unlike the stench of their murders. Notice that God does not respond to supplication to heal the land when the men are impaled. God neither applauds nor rewards this wanton act. It is only when the bodies are buried that we learn that God intervenes for the land (21.14). It is only because of Rizpah's vigil that the remains are, eventually, treated with respect. She shames David into action, which enables him to complete a stage of his own grief process in retrieving the bones of Jonathan and Saul. We learn that '*they* gathered the bones of those who had been impaled. *They* buried the bones of Saul and his son Jonathan' (21.14). Who are 'they'? David must have encountered Rizpah, directly or by reputation, at the site of the sons' death. Having been there for months it's hard to imagine Rizpah would sit passively as David, or his servants, collected the bones; they do it together. Finally, David does the right thing. Finally, God intervenes for the land, because of Rizpah's effect on David.

Hers is a courageous act of resistance, which changes the heart of the king. Though her sons are gone, and her trauma will be a lifelong struggle, her actions speak eloquently and effect change, but the cost is immense. No neat and tidy ending here. The Rizpahs of the world need to be enabled to give voice to their trauma in the patient, ongoing pastoral and political work of bearing witness.

Sermon Suggestion: Hope in the Heart of Darkness

Often sermons begin in the Bible and work out, seeking connections with the contemporary world. Today we begin with two stories and work back to the Bible. Our quest? Hope in the darkest of places. In this reflection God will be unnamed, but if you look and listen carefully you will see the God of the traumatized at work, the advocate for the stamped-on is present for those with eyes to see and ears to hear. The author of compassion and justice is shaping these stories. But it's not comfortable. It's not easy. It's raw.

Mamie Till-Mobley – ever heard of her? She is the late mother of Emmet Till. In August 1955, in the town of Money, Mississippi, 14-year-old Emmet was accused of disrespecting a white woman. Four days later he was kidnapped, beaten, shot in the head, lynched and thrown into the Tallahatchie River. His mother Mamie insisted that her son's body be placed in an open casket for the funeral so the full horror of what had been done to him could be seen. Thousands upon thousands attended the funeral. It's estimated 1 in 5 had to be assisted from the building after seeing the body.[10] Amid terrible grief, Mamie was not willing to allow the atrocity perpetrated against her son to be neatly boxed away. Her actions were an eloquent protest, an act of courageous resistance, which became a catalyst for the civil rights movement. In July 2023, Joe Biden established a national monument honouring Emmet and his mother, Mamie Till-Mobley. She was an agent of change.

Mamie Till-Mobley. Remember her name

Ever heard of Hatidža Mehmedović? (*Pronounced as hah-tih-jah mehmeh-tow-ich*). She was a Bosnian Muslim. Her husband and two sons were among the 8,000 men murdered in Srebrenica by Bosnian Serb troops and paramilitaries under the command of General Ratko Mladić. She founded the Mothers of Srebrenica in 2002, an activist group, advocating for justice, seeking to identify and bury bodies, and raising money for the survivors. In 2003, due to the work of the Mothers of Srebrenica, a memorial and cemetery was opened. Seven years after that she was able to bury her husband and sons – what was left of them. Traumatized and vulnerable, Hatidža Mehmedović spoke truth to power. Not long before her death in 2018, she witnessed General Mladić sentenced to life for war crimes and crimes against humanity.

Reflecting on events she said:

I am a woman that once had a husband. I am a mother that gave birth to two sons. But I have no one anymore. I go to bed alone and I wake up alone. I gave birth to children who played, went to school, who laughed, yet all I had to bury were just two bones.[11]

Hatidža Mehmedović was an agent of justice.

Hatidža Mehmedović. Remember her name.

Mamie Till-Mobly and Hatidža Mehmedović stand in a long line of women who have spoken truth to power by their eloquence in action, choosing non-violent resistance and a refusal to allow hideous atrocities to be designated as 'unspeakable' and hidden away. There are many others we could name, if space allowed.

Buried in 2 Samuel is the story of Rizpah – arguably the mother in spirit of the women we have mentioned, and many more besides. We need to exhume her story. Like Mamie, Rizpah refused to allow what David and the Gibeonites had done to her sons and those of other women to go unmarked. Seven young men were impaled and left to rot, handed over by David as reparation for Saul's genocidal treatment of the Gibeonites. Rizpah held vigil for months by their corpses, living on sackcloth, spread upon a rock, preventing the birds and wild animals from homing in on them. Where do we imagine God to be? Applauding the atrocities, or sitting with these brave and traumatized mothers, Mamie and Rizpah?

Like Mamie, Rizpah said in her actions, 'Look and see what has been done by powerful men to my children. Notice this atrocity.'

Like Mamie, she brought about change, shaming David into action. Finally, he did the right thing by the house of Saul – burying the bodies of David and Jonathan and the murdered sons.

Like Mamie, Rizpah's actions initiated political change, bringing the house of Saul and David closer together, as Mamie's action was a catalyst for the civil rights movement.

Like Hatidža, Rizpah cared for the dead – acting from the place of trauma and apparent hopelessness.

Like Hatidža, Rizpah had little left to bury – just bones.

Like Hatidža, Rizpah ensured the memorialization of the murdered. They were not forgotten.

Rizpah, Mamie, Hatidža – seemingly powerless and voiceless women acting with eloquent courage, advocating for justice. Where do we imagine God? With the agents of violence and vengeance, hatred and fear, or with these brave and wounded women?

Rizpah, Mamie, Hatidža – a trinity of trauma and a trinity of hope. Here in the heart of their darkness we see them break out of the cycles of violence, with determined insistence that the truth be known. Each woman unveiled abusive power, named truth, and cried for justice. Here is hope. Genuine hope can never paper over the truth. It must face it down. These are women of hope, truth-tellers.

What do these three women say to us? Rizpah and all her spiritual children down the ages call us to notice, to see, to listen, to act, to empathize, to hear the trauma – to join our voices to theirs. In such unity, even from the heart of darkness, there is hope. Where there is hope, there is God.

Rizpah, Mamie, Hatidža – remember them.

Homiletic Points

1 The sermon begins in recent stories and links them back into Scripture – closing the gap between the horizon of now and then.

2 The sermon focuses on the women but identifies God at work implicitly. So often it is hard to discern God, and yet the women reveal goodness, love and hope – pointing us back to the God who advocates for the traumatized and violated. The phrase 'Trinity of trauma, trinity of hope' implies the connection between the work of the women and the work of God.

3 The pain and suffering are not muted but acknowledged. There are no easy answers that would not further abuse these women.

4 The image of Rizpah buried and needing to be exhumed is an acknowledgement that this outstanding woman has been lost, and resonates with the burial imagery weaving through the sermon.

5 The repetition of the 'like Mamie/like Hatidža, Ritpah' trope seeks to collapse the time between these women, seeing the connections between their actions.

6 The sermon lands in a final 'and so what' move which is a call to pastoral and political action for all, regardless of whether we have experienced the horror or not – we must respond.

Collect

God, Eternal Word,
thank you for the women
who use their voices and actions
to speak truth to power:
wise women who use words deftly,
brave women who act with eloquence,
even from the place of trauma,
seeking justice, showing compassion.
Exhume us from the sleep of apathy,
to join with them,
to join with you,
insistent, determined, advocates.
Amen.

Notes

1 Carol A. Newsom, Sharon H. Ringe and Jacqueline E. Lapsley, *The Women's Bible Commentary* (Louisville, KY: Westminster John Knox Press, 1992), p. 161.

2 Walter Brueggemann, *First and Second Samuel*, Interpretation Series (Louisville, KY: Westminster John Knox Press, 1990), p. 293.

3 Brueggemann, *First and Second Samuel*, p. 294.

4 Sharon A. Buttry and Daniel L. Buttry, *Daughters of Rizpah: Nonviolence and the Transformation of Trauma* (Eugene, OR: Cascade Books, 2020) Kindle edn, loc. 566.

5 Buttry and Buttry, *Daughters of Rizpah*, loc. 363.

6 Buttry and Buttry, *Daughters of Rizpah*, loc. 229.

7 Brueggemann, *First and Second Samuel*, pp. 336–8; Newsom, Ringe and Lapsley, *The Women's Bible Commentary*, p. 158.

8 Wil Gafney, *Womanist Midrash: A Reintroduction to the Women of the Torah and the Throne* (Louisville, KY: Westminster John Knox Press, 2017), pp. 200–1.

9 Buttry and Buttry, *Daughters of Rizpah*, loc. 537.

10 See https://www.pbslearningmedia.org/resource/arct.socst.ush.tillfuneral/emmett-tills-funeral, accessed 02.07.23.

11 Buttry and Buttry, *Daughters of Rizpah*, loc. 1757.

19

A Woman of Substance:
The Queen of Sheba

LIZ SHERCLIFF

The Queen of Sheba in the Revised Common Lectionary (Sundays)
Not included.

The Queen of Sheba's Words in the Bible

'The report was true that I heard in my own land of your accomplishments and of your wisdom, but I did not believe the reports until I came and my own eyes saw it. Not even half had been told me; your wisdom and prosperity far surpass the report that I had heard. Happy are your wives! Happy are these your servants who continually attend you and hear your wisdom! Blessed be the LORD your God, who has delighted in you and set you on the throne of Israel! Because the LORD loved Israel for ever, he has made you king to execute justice and righteousness.' (1 Kings 10.6–9)

'The report was true that I heard in my own land of your accomplishments and of your wisdom, but I did not believe the reports until I came and my own eyes saw it. Not even half of the greatness of your wisdom had been told to me; you far surpass the report that I had heard. Happy are your people! Happy are these your servants who continually attend you and hear your wisdom! Blessed be the LORD your God, who has delighted in you and set you on his throne as king for the LORD your God. Because your God loved Israel and wished to establish them for ever, he has made you king over them, so that you may execute justice and righteousness.' (2 Chronicles 9.5–8)

The Queen of Sheba's Story

As far as the Bible is concerned, the Queen of Sheba is a powerful ruler who visits Solomon, gives him gifts, questions him to prove his wisdom, and declares that God has blessed his nation through him. She has also been identified with the black beauty in Song of Songs 1.5.[1] For a woman given so little biblical attention, the Queen of Sheba has shown remarkable longevity and her story has undergone extensive revision at the hands of narrators from cultures as diverse as fourteenth-century Ethiopia and twenty-first-century America. In Ethiopian folklore Menelik I, the first Emperor of Ethiopia, is the child of Solomon and the Queen of Sheba.[2] The Talmud holds that Sheba was not a woman, but a kingdom that visited Solomon.[3] The Qur'an interprets the story as the conversion of the queen from polytheism to monotheism. More recently the story has been used to explore philosophies of knowledge[4] and attitudes to race in the Hebrew Bible.[5]

The story of the Queen of Sheba functions in a number of ways. It offers an alluring woman, 'beckoning and voluptuous', encompassing 'outlandish exoticism, sensuality, wonder and luxuries.[6] It highlights the extent of Solomon's influence in international trade.[7] It illustrates Solomon's largesse and wisdom.[8] In these interpretations, the Queen of Sheba becomes merely a device to spotlight the male hero, Solomon. How else might we read this intriguing woman?

An Alternative Reading

The first book of Kings includes two significant female stereotypes. First, we have the image of the virtuous mother. In 1 Kings 3.16–28 two women come to the king claiming that a baby is theirs. The king solves the problem by suggesting the division of the child into two parts. The real mother is discerned by her reaction: 'do not kill him. She is the mother.' Thus, a mother's love is seen as redemptive. Mothers are assumed to hold their children's lives in highest value.[9] The story works by making assumptions about the nature of women. Second, the mothers are also prostitutes (1 Kings 3.16). They are therefore assumed to be liars and worse.[10] Solomon, in his wisdom, plays off one characteristic against the other. Neither the reign of Solomon nor the account of it seem fertile ground for thinking women. Chronicles seems even more barren. Roland Boer calls it 'one of the first men-only utopias ... this male-only world relies on the silencing of women'.[11]

The Queen we meet in 1 Kings and 2 Chronicles is eloquent and highly intelligent. She understands Solomon's God better than the religious leaders later admonished by Jesus,[12] and formulates astute theological judgements.[13] She offers a rare example of female rulership, adventurousness, understanding and political skill. Whatever it was that inspired her journey across the desert to see Solomon, her story is so compelling that the three monotheistic religions celebrate her legacy, and she has become an icon of feminism. The Queen of Sheba knew what she wanted and how to achieve it, her personal agency seems complete. Perhaps she threatens patriarchal order, for traditional extra-biblical tellings of her story have Solomon admonish her for behaving like a man and appropriating a man's prerogative to rule.[14] A further compelling characteristic of the Queen of Sheba is her acuity. Miriam Ma'at-Ka-Re Monges argues that the Queen's desire for knowledge from Solomon and his reciprocal desire for knowledge from her generate new understandings of God.[15] In the context of a reign where women are silenced or used, the Queen's acknowledgement of a God who puts kings in place to execute justice is significant.

A composite Queen of Sheba might be a powerful black woman who carved out for herself a high-ranking and respected position in a world dominated by non-black men. Her quizzing of Solomon shows acuity and boldness. She demonstrates wisdom and statecraft. She truly is a woman of substance.

Sermon Suggestion: A Woman of Substance and Wisdom

The image of the Queen of Sheba standing before the powerful and wise King Solomon is sometimes read simplistically as two heads of state engaging, two religions entering into conversation, and two world-views appreciating each other. The story of this Queen can be found in all three monotheistic religions, in countries around the world, from the ancient kingdom of Israel to modern Mexico and the United States. It ignites imagination and inspires courage.

We are not certain where Sheba was. Commentators have it in places as diverse as Ethiopia and Yemen. Let's just take it that wherever it was, it wasn't round here. And not being from round here means we expect a certain amount of respect from this woman. We expect her to respect our status, our customs, our understanding. A hymn written in the 1700s[16] portrays an awestruck queen overcome by the glory of Solomon and his court. But I find no fainting violet here. The Queen, it seems to me, is not overcome by the impression Solomon makes; rather she sums it up accurately.

The Queen of Sheba offers an antidote to the kinds of Christian women we see portrayed in stained glass, with averted eyes and shy smiles. She visits Solomon on equal terms – the questions she asks are penetrating and challenging, we're told that she quizzes him, or tests him. She discusses with him what is on her mind – possibly a trade deal, given that Solomon's kingdom was on a route she needed. She is assertive on behalf of her people, taking with her the best that they have to offer. And she names what God has done and is doing through Solomon, clarifying the challenge set before him, to reign with justice and righteousness. She is a woman to reckon with, the kind of woman the church needs.

How can I say all this based on such a brief narrative repeated in 1 Kings and 2 Chronicles? Because her story itself is so enduring. Because it has inspired oppressed women from around the world to believe in themselves. Because the criticism of her that is commonly repeated is that she behaves like a man.

So what can we learn from the Queen of Sheba, this woman of substance, in encouraging and equipping women of God?

The relationship we see between the Queen of Sheba and King Solomon discloses some key characteristics of trusting, respectful, safe relationships. There is empathy. The Queen understands Solomon's role as king and shows herself his equal. She has heard of his wisdom and shares what is on her mind too. She is not fearful of his power, but shows she understands it. She brings appropriate gifts, things that he cannot provide for himself, wood and spices that his land does not grow.

The Queen is concerned for truth. She comes to find out for herself, rather than believe the rumours. She does not protect her own reputation by avoiding Solomon's court; she visits to find out how great it is. Probably she talks to him about her need of a trade route through his land, being open about what she needs.

Finally, when she has talked and questioned, examined and understood the blessings of the King, she points out to him what God requires. 'God has delighted in you and set you on the throne of Israel! He's done it because this is what he expects: that you execute justice and righteousness.' 'Your riches are great, your understanding is profound, but you have it for the sake of justice and righteousness.'

This strong, powerful, foreign woman understands what God has done and what God wants to see done. She models the kind of woman God wants us to be, faithful women, seeking truth and speaking justice. She models the kind of relationship that is safe for women and for men, empathetic, truthful and just. She welcomes questions and inquiry, confident in her own authority. Imagine someone asking her who she thinks she is. I'm sure she would simply say, 'I'm the Queen of Sheba'.

For all of us who are asked, or ask ourselves, 'Who do you think you are?' perhaps we should shout 'The Queen of Sheba'. The wise, strong, empathetic woman who calls the powerful to righteousness and justice.

Homiletic Points

1 The opening image of the Queen of Sheba and King Solomon facing each other gives a sense of their equality. This theme is picked up later as the respectful, mutual nature of their relationship is developed further in conversation with details in the text.
2 The second move establishes the Queen's power and independent thought.
3 The third move develops this, celebrating her assertive nature.
4 Then there are comments on how the church needs this kind of woman, an inspirational figure for the oppressed.
5 The exploration of her theological insight offers us more to celebrate about her.
6 The final lines celebrate the attributes gathered under her name, 'The Queen of Sheba' – a worthy role model.

Collect

God of truth-seeking queens like Sheba,
and wise kings like Solomon,
we pray for all those in power, that they might seek to live
righteously and administer justice;
we pray for those they govern or employ
or have power over,
that they might stand for truth and mutual respect.
Give your church the determination
to seek respectful, wise and safe relationships,
in the name of the one who is truth and wisdom.
Amen.

Notes

1 John McClintock and James Strong (eds), 'Canticles', *Cyclopaedia of Biblical, Theological and Ecclesiastical Literature*, Vol. 2 (New York: Harper & Brothers, 1891), pp. 92–8.

2 See http://www.blackhistoryheroes.com/2010/05/queen-of-sheba.html.

3 Bava Batra 15b (this is the third of the three Talmudic tractates and speaks of individual responsibilities).

4 Miriam Ma'at-Ka-Re Monges, 'The Queen of Sheba and Solomon: exploring the Shebanization of knowledge', *Journal of Black Studies*, Vol. 33, No. 2 (2002), pp. 235–46.

5 Jillian Stinchcomb 'Race, racism, and the Hebrew Bible: the case of the Queen of Sheba', *Religions*, Vol. 12, No. 10 (2021), p. 795.

6 Marina Warner, *From the Beast to the Blonde: On Fairy Tales and their Tellers* (London: Vintage, 1995), p. 106.

7 Marvin Sweeney, *I and II Kings: A Commentary* (Louisville, KY: Westminster John Knox Press, 2007), p. 141.

8 Daniel Durken, *New Collegeville Bible Commentary* (Collegeville, MN: Liturgical Press, 2015), p. 618.

9 Cameron Howard, '1 and 2 Kings', in Carol Newsom, Sharon Ringe, Jacqueline Lapsley, *The Women's Bible Commentary* (Louisville, KY: Westminster John Knox Press, 2014), p. 168.

10 A later story, the death of Ahab, reinforces the Israelite attitude to prostitutes. They wash themselves in the dead king's spilled blood (1 Kings 22.38).

11 Roland Boer, '1 and 2 Chronicles', in Deryn Guest, Robert Goss, Mona West and Thomas Bohache (eds), *The Queer Bible Commentary* (London: SCM Press, 2006), p. 251.

12 Luke 11.31

13 Greg Forbes and Scott Harrower, *Raised from Obscurity: A Narratival and Theological Study of the Characterization of Women in Luke–Acts* (Eugene, OR: Wipf and Stock, 2015), pp. 121, 205.

14 Jacob Lassner, *Demonizing the Queen of Sheba: Boundaries of Gender and Culture in Postbiblical Judaism and Medieval Islam* (Chicago, IL and London: University of Chicago Press, 1994), p. 150.

15 Miriam Ma'at-Ka-Re Monges, 'The Queen of Sheba and Solomon', p. 241.

16 'From Sheba a Distant Report', exhibited in a series of hymns (1791), https://hymnary.org/text/from_sheba_a_distant_report, accessed 02.10.23.

20

Wicked Women and an Unexpected Saviour: The Medium of Endor, Jezebel, Athaliah and Jehosheba

KATE BRUCE

Their Stories in the Revised Common Lectionary (Sundays)

The Medium of Endor

Not included.

Jezebel

Year B	Sunday next before Lent (CW)	Second Service 1 Kings 19.1–16 (CW, SS)
Year C	Proper 6 (CW)	1 Kings 21.1–10[11–14] 15–21a (CW, PS)

Athaliah

Not included.

An apparent necromancer and two ruthless murderers – what can we say about these women? Is there anything redeeming in their stories?

The Medium's Words in the Bible

'Surely you know what Saul has done, how he has cut off the mediums and the wizards from the land. Why then are you laying a snare for my life to bring about my death?' (1 Samuel 28.9)

'Whom shall I bring up for you?' (1 Samuel 28.11)

'Why have you deceived me? You are Saul!' (1 Samuel 28.13)

'I see a divine being coming up out of the ground.' (1 Samuel 28.14)

'An old man is coming up; he is wrapped in a robe.' (1 Samuel 28.14)

'Your servant has listened to you; I have taken my life in my hand, and have listened to what you have said to me. Now therefore, you also listen to your servant; let me set a morsel of bread before you. Eat, that you may have strength when you go on your way.' (1 Samuel 28.21–22)

Jezebel's Words in the Bible

'So may the gods do to me, and more also, if I do not make your life like the life of one of them by this time tomorrow.' (1 Kings 19.2)

'Why are you so depressed that you will not eat?' (1 Kings 21.5)

'Do you now govern Israel? Get up, eat some food, and be cheerful; I will give you the vineyard of Naboth the Jezreelite.' (1 Kings 21.7)

She wrote in the letters, 'Proclaim a fast, and seat Naboth at the head of the assembly; seat two scoundrels opposite him, and have them bring a charge against him, saying, "You have cursed God and the king." Then take him out, and stone him to death.' (1 Kings 21.9–10)

'Go, take possession of the vineyard of Naboth the Jezreelite, which he refused to give you for money; for Naboth is not alive, but dead.' (1 Kings 21.15)

'Is it peace, Zimri, murderer of your master?' (2 Kings 9.31)

Athaliah's Words in the Bible

'Treason! Treason!' (2 Kings 11.14; 2 Chronicles 23.13)

The Medium of Endor (1 Samuel 28.3–35)

Necromancer, pythoness, hag, witch, charlatan, ventriloquist, prophetess, medium, healer, shaman, proto-feminist, and psychotherapist – the Woman of Endor has cast her spell across two millennia of history.[1]

Where some see her as a witch, to be justifiably persecuted along with other peripheral women, others see her as a woman of compassion and spirituality.[2] What evidence does the text present to us? Be prepared for ambiguity.

A wicked woman?

She is described as 'ō·wḇ or medium, one able to communicate with the spirits of the dead, a practice roundly condemned in Deuteronomy 18.11–12. Saul had 'expelled the mediums and the wizards from the land' (1 Samuel 28.3), though this expulsion was clearly a superficial matter since he seeks out the help of a medium when God is silent concerning enquiries about his enemies (1 Samuel 28.4–6).

Interestingly, in spite of the ban, Saul's servants knew of her presence (1 Samuel 28.7). Is her existence tolerated as an open secret? When Saul comes to her in disguise, she is wary; her life could be at risk (v. 10). She is aware that she is operating on the wrong side of the tracks. But reassured for her safety, she summons Samuel. When he appears to her, she 'cried out with a loud voice', suggesting fear and anger: 'Why have you deceived me? You are Saul!' (v. 12). Saul asks her what she sees, since he cannot see anything. She describes a 'divine being coming up out of the ground ... an old man ... wrapped in a robe' (vv. 13–14). Saul recognizes this as a description of Samuel and does obeisance (v. 14).

Should we take the narrative at face value? Is she a wicked, disobedient woman, contravening Yahweh's word? The writer of Chronicles certainly sees her in this light:

> Saul died for his transgression which he committed against the LORD, even against the word of the LORD, which he kept not, and *also for asking counsel of one that had* a familiar spirit, *to enquire of it.* (1 Chronicles 10.13 AV).

In this view, she is in league with a spirit who acts on her behalf in dealing with the dead.

That she is the only one able to 'see' Samuel, and hers is the mouth through which he 'speaks', means the story is shot through with ambiguity. Could *she* be speaking prophetically, an intuitive woman who understands more than she lets on about Saul's predicament and through whom Yahweh speaks as she assumes the 'voice' of Samuel concerning Saul's fate (1 Samuel 28.16–19)?

Wicked or inspired, what we can say is that she is spiritually sensitive, and the words that come from her mouth come to pass. In her context, with its male-dominated priestly caste, where could a woman of spiritual sensitivity exercise her vocation? *The Women's Bible Commentary* posits:

'Women could have performed priestly or quasi priestly duties only in the peripheral religious culture, as in the set practices Saul had recently banned in 1 Samuel 28.'[3]

Compassionate and generous

Her compassionate response to Saul's paralysing distress is evident, however. She assumes a position of parity with Saul, bluntly: 'I have listened to you, now you listen to me' (vv. 21–22). She offers Saul a 'morsel' to give him strength to go forward, and then goes on to kill the fatted calf and bake unleavened cakes for him and his entourage (v. 24). The Hebrew verb used to describe her slaughtering of the beast can mean 'to slaughter as a sacrifice'.[4] Is this 'a sacrificial meal prepared as part of her quasi-priestly function in a peripheral and banned religious subsystem'?[5] At the very least she generously offers Saul a last supper. Lynn Japinga writes: 'This banished, marginalized woman is the loving and compassionate presence in the story. She is the role model. She is the one who is concerned for Saul's welfare.'[6] Such an observation jars with our expectation. We might expect to condemn the Witch of Endor, as she is popularly known,[7] but the text isn't so clear-cut. Her hospitality is unexpected, her compassion and generosity render her ambiguous rather than wicked.

Jezebel

... commentators describe her as she-devil, dominating wife, idolator, inhuman wretch, pitiless, morally loose, heartless, treacherous, witch, whore.[8]

While not all these adjectives are accurate since there is no evidence that she is unfaithful to her husband, Jezebel gets a bad press and with very good reason. Her character is presented without ambiguity. The nadir of the apostasy of the kings of the Northern Kingdom is personified in Ahab son of Omri who 'did evil in the sight of the LORD, more than all who were before him' (1 Kings 16.30). On top of this he took as his wife 'Jezebel daughter of King Ethbaal of the Sidonians' (v. 31), whose name means 'Baal is alive'.[9] The marriage secured access to the maritime trade centres of Tyre and Sidon, but opened Israel to the apostatizing influences of their gods, principally Baal. Ahab took on Jezebel's religion, serving Baal himself and encouraging this in the kingdom, setting up spaces for idolatrous worship.

Immediately after this introduction, Elijah enters the narrative. The human characters represent the conflict between Yahweh and Baal, with Elijah and Jezebel pitted against each other.

The Sidonian widow and Jezebel – compare and contrast!

Elijah travels into Jezebel's homeland, commanded by Yahweh against the backdrop of drought (1 Kings 17.1, 8–9). Here he encounters a poor Sidonian widow, who recognizes Yahweh's hand in the provision of oil and meal (v. 16) and the restoration of her son to life (v. 23), stating: 'Now I know that you are a man of God, and that the word of the LORD in your mouth is truth' (v. 24). She stands in stark contrast to Jezebel's implacable opposition to Yahweh. Jezebel tried to kill off the prophets of the Lord (1 Kings 18.4) and fed the prophets of Baal and Asherah at her own table (1 Kings 18.19). Whatever motivates her violent opposition to Yahweh it leads to the showdown on Mount Carmel between her prophets and Elijah. She will have been told about how the ineffective ravings of her prophets (18.28–29), of how Yahweh's fire fell and consumed wood, stone, dust and water causing the people who witnessed it to declare, 'The LORD indeed is God' (1 Kings 18.1–39). Unlike the widow, Jezebel lacks the wisdom to re-evaluate her previous understanding based on new evidence. Yahweh's position as God is clearly demonstrated, yet Jezebel refuses to acknowledge this and remains hell bent on destroying Elijah (1 Kings 19.2).

A fearsome enemy

The first recorded words of Jezebel are to Elijah: 'So may the gods do to me, and more also, if I do not make your life like the life of one of them by this time tomorrow' (1 Kings 19.2). There is fearsome fury in her words. Given Elijah is a man acquainted with violence – he killed the prophets of Baal (1 Kings 18.40; 19.1) – his response to her threat is striking. Although he had defeated Jezebel's agents, the man of God flees in a state of terrible spiritual despair (19.3–5), fearing for his life.

Jezebel is a fearsome enemy, as Naboth discovered. He refuses Ahab's request to purchase his vineyard, because it was his inheritance and not to be sold. (See Numbers 27.5–11 on inheritance law.) This sends Ahab into a resentful strop (1 Kings 21.4). Jezebel demands of him, 'Do you now govern Israel?' (21.7), meaning, 'You are king, take what you want.' The irony is that *she* assumes control and acts in Ahab's name, writing letters on his behalf and sealing them with his seal. She engineers the cruel plot to have Naboth condemned and stoned to death (21.8–14) – an innocent man, murdered to please a childish husband. As soon as Naboth's death is confirmed, Jezebel pushes Ahab to make his move on the vineyard. In this episode she again shows herself to be ruthless, merciless and powerful. Elijah condemns Ahab and predicts his death and that of Jezebel. She is particularly singled out as one who will be desecrated in death; the dogs shall eat her (21.23). Ahab, frightened of the prophecy, repents. Jezebel's silence speaks for itself (21.27).

Putting on war paint

Faced with the threat of impending disaster, we were given insight into Elijah's humanity in the story of his despairing flight into the wilderness (1 Kings 19.3–9). Faced with similar incoming catastrophe we are given no indication of vulnerability or fear in Jezebel. She stands her ground, fierce and seemingly unafraid. Her make-up acts as war paint.

Earlier, Jehu had been anointed as king. He journeys to Jezreel, where Joram, Jezebel's son, is on the throne. Joram rides out to meet Jehu, asking if he comes in peace. Jehu's response is devastating: 'What peace can there be, so long as the many whoredoms and sorceries of your mother Jezebel continue?' (2 Kings 9.22). The reference to whoredom here is less likely to be an indication of Jezebel's sexual behaviour since she appears loyal to Ahab throughout, but an indication of her degrading effect on Israel's faithfulness to Yahweh.

That Jezebel has become associated in the popular imagination with harlotry or sexual indulgence is surely a comment on the images of women in the history of biblical interpretation or on assumptions about female power in our modern culture; the text does not make judgements about Jezebel's sexuality.[10]

Faced with certain death, as Jehu arrives in Jezreel, Jezebel remains unrepentant and boldly sarcastic. She calmly puts on her make-up and headdress and looks out of the window. This is not the act of a woman preparing a seduction, as we can clearly see by what she says to Jehu as she looks down upon him, 'Is it peace, Zimri, murderer of your master?' Here she is making a sarcastic reference to Zimri's murder of King Elah of Israel (1 Kings 16.8–20). Zimri reigned for seven days before death by suicide. The bitterness in her question rather suggests her make-up acts as war paint as she looks down on Jehu from the symbolic high ground she has chosen. She must know this is the end. She is old and Jehu will gain nothing by keeping her alive. The staging of her final scene suggests composure, courage and contempt.

Her high position is finished. Having no loyalty to her, her eunuchs cast her down on Jehu's orders. Her blood spatters on the wall and the horses trample her (2 Kings 9.33–34). This powerful woman has finally fallen, and her end is as ignominious as prophesied: 'But when they went to bury her, they found no more of her than her skull, feet and the palms of her hands' (2 Kings 9.35). The dogs consumed her, and there is no resting place for her body. She is eradicated. No one can say, 'This is Jezebel' (v. 37).

Jezebel: an assessment

In Revelation 2, the name Jezebel is associated with fornication, idolatry and a refusal to repent (Revelation 2.20–21). The Jezebel we meet in both books of Kings does not appear to be unfaithful to Ahab, though she clearly introduces idolatry and refuses to repent when she learns of Yahweh's supremacy.

While she is clearly a wicked woman, we might want to notice a few issues. She is held up as the scapegoat for Israel's apostasy, but all Israel had a choice. They knew first hand Yahweh's faithfulness and yet they embraced other gods. Her death scene implies that Israel's terrible apostasy is wiped out with her memory. It isn't. Ahab is presented as going astray because of Jezebel's influence – but he too had choices. She is presented as a ruthless killer of prophets, a fiery religious individual, but the same description could apply to Elijah.

However wicked she undoubtedly was, the danger of scapegoating is that it lessens the responsibility of the person pointing the finger. If all the evil is 'over there', then there is nothing to see here. That should make us stop and think.

Athaliah (2 Kings 11; 2 Chronicles 22.2)

A wicked queen

Some texts state that Athaliah was daughter of Omri, King of Israel (2 Kings 8.26; 2 Chronicles 22.2), others that she was daughter of his son, Ahab (2 Kings 8.18; 2 Chronicles 21.6). If we take the latter position, it is likely she was Jezebel's daughter, since Ahab had three children, Ahaziah, Jehoram and Athaliah, and there is no mention of Ahab having another wife or consort.

Athaliah, a daughter of Israel, was married to Jehoram of Judah, son of King Jehosophat of Judah (2 Kings 8.18–19; 2 Chronicles 21.6–13). The marriage was a means of alliance between the two kingdoms. Confusingly, there is also a Jehoram of Israel, Athaliah's brother, who reigned in Israel at the same time (2 Kings 8.16). Influenced by Athaliah, we learn that Jehoram (of Judah) walked in the ways of Ahab (2 Kings 8.18), who in turn was influenced by Jezebel. Jehoram (of Judah) reigned for eight years before dying in agony of an unspecified bowel disease (2 Chronicles 21.18–19).

This theme of powerful and wicked women poisoning the rule of the land continues into the reign of Athaliah's son Ahaziah (2 Kings 22.3–4) who is counselled by her wickedness into doing evil in the sight of the Lord (2 Chronicles 22.3–4). The women are blamed for setting an evil course, yet the men had agency and still followed their lead.

Ahaziah came to the throne of Judah and reigned for one year (2 Kings 8.24; 2 Chronicles 22.1–2) before he was overthrown and killed by Jehu, who had been anointed as king over Israel by Elisha with the specific task of overthrowing the house of Ahab (2 Kings 9.1–13). Athaliah's ruthless corruption can be in no doubt. In order to secure the throne, she has her own sons and grandchildren killed, before seizing power for herself.

She is never named in the text as queen, but she does hold this position for six years. Wicked kings get royal titles. Wicked queens are airbrushed out.

Jehosheba: An Unexpected Saviour

Athaliah loses the throne because of the courageous, quick-thinking actions of Jehosheba, a daughter of Jehoram, and possibly of Athaliah. Jehosheba manages to snatch one of the king's sons from Athaliah's killing spree. She hides the boy, Joash, for six years. In his seventh year, her husband, the priest Jehoiada, engineers Joash's coronation and the execution of Athaliah (2 Kings 11.1–20; 2 Chronicles 22.10—23.21). We might pause here to wonder at the ingenuity, skill and courage it must have required to hide a child from a ruthless queen, in a court full of intrigue and gossip. Jehosheba is faithful to God – a small but weighty counterbalance to Athaliah, she ensures that the last remaining boy in the Davidic line is saved. Ponder that. Without Jehosheba, no line of David.

Sermon Suggestion: Jehosheba – a Mighty Woman

A few weeks ago, I went to visit my friend Elaine. She is a resolute atheist so will be amused to feature in a sermon! She was keen to get my opinion on the Lucy Letby case and there ensured a long discussion as we examined the story and pondered it all.[11] There is something horribly compelling about such stories. We can't wrap our heads around the why, or around the incomprehensible suffering of those affected, in this case by the actions of a fresh-faced young woman. There is something utterly baffling about the story. Elaine and I pondered it for a long time.

Stories of wickedness sell papers. Stories of wicked women particularly so – think of all the ink spilled over Myra Hindley, Rose West and Lucy Letby. We are oddly fascinated by evil. Think of how many conversations have been had over these women. We often ponder evil; there is something oddly compelling about trying to understand.

If I asked you to name the wicked women of the Bible, I wonder who might spring to mind. I'm sure Jezebel would be mentioned. She tried to hunt down the prophet Elijah to have him eliminated, among plenty of other terrible acts. Then there was her daughter, or stepdaughter, Athaliah. She had her grandsons 'offed' to make sure she could grasp the throne. Then, as now, we are shocked, baffled that anyone could harm a little one. Athaliah wanted to be queen and the only way to make that happen was to ensure there were no prospective kings about. The Bible states, 'Now when Athaliah, Ahaziah's mother, saw that her son was dead, she set about to destroy all the royal family' (2 Kings 11.1). It doesn't specify her means – probably a good thing. We might ponder her story and think she must have been a psychopath – no feeling, no empathy, no compassion. How could she take this course of action? Her story – in today's context – would sell newspapers, inspire long discussions on social media and in countless conversations. Evil is strangely fascinating, and we often seem to ponder it.

But what about acts of courage and goodness? Why not ponder them? I don't want to give more airtime to the wicked people. Athaliah has had her mention. That's it. I want to focus on the light in her story, on the actions of a female relative who, seeing Athaliah's horrendous intent, did something. I don't think anyone will be able to name this woman, but without her intervention the line of David would have been severed. Ponder that!

But she does have a name. Remember it: Jehosheba. Her name means 'Fullness, or oath, of the Lord'. She is certainly full of courage. Aunt Jehosheba. A mighty woman. At the start of 2 King's 11 we read:

> Now when Athaliah, Ahaziah's mother, saw that her son was dead, she set about to destroy all the royal family. But Jehosheba, King Joram's daughter, Ahaziah's sister, took Joash son of Ahaziah, and stole him away from among the king's children who were about to be killed; she put him and his nurse in a bedroom.

The words that jump out to me are 'but Jehosheba'. Athaliah is on her killing spree but Jehosheba acts, but she does something, but she intervenes. She can't save all the children – but she does what she can, and snatches up the baby, Joash. Ponder that. Jehosheba stands up against ruthless horror. This is dangerous. Capable of murdering her grandsons, Athaliah is not going to have any inhibitions about taking Jehosheba out. Ponder her courage, her quick thinking, her commitment. This is not a one-minute wonder; she hides the child for the first seven years of his life. Ponder that.

How do you hide a baby? First, the baby and nurse are squirreled into a bedroom. As the killing spree occurs, the baby needs to be kept from the agents of death, so silence was essential. Jehosheba and the unnamed nurse must have been terrified: hearts pounding, eyes wincing at every passing sound. Trying to shush the infant. One wail and it's game over.

Joash is moved, at some point, to the Temple where, according to 2 Kings, 'he remained with her for six years, hidden in the house of the Lord, while Athaliah reigned over the land'. How and when was he moved? Not easy in a palace where there are eyes and ears everywhere. And notice, 'he remained with her'. Together with her husband, the priest

Jehoiada, they protect Joash, nurturing him in the Temple for over six years. How? We aren't told. The risk is very high; perhaps they can only hope that the child is seen as someone else's and can hide in plain sight. An opportune moment arises when they enable him to take the crown. This happens in his seventh year when he is crowned and Athaliah executed. It's a brutal story.

What shines out are the actions of the little-known woman Jehosheba, who ensures the continuity of the Davidic line. She prevents the power of evil from having the final word. She should be celebrated with her own day: Jehosheba Day. But she has been forgotten – utterly overlooked. So today we name her – Jehosheba – a foremother of Jesus; a woman of quick-thinking courage who played the long game with forbearance. She could not have known at the time that in saving the child she ensured the continuity of the Messianic line. Her actions had ramifications way beyond her life. Just think of that other baby, generations later, nestling in Mary's arms, in a room near an inn.

Jehosheba – remember her name, and remember all those who have done what they can with the power they have, bringing about change in the face of disproportionately powerful evil. Remember with Jehosheba, Irena Sendler – a Polish social worker – who smuggled many children out of the Warsaw Ghetto, providing false identity papers, and never revealing their whereabouts, even under torture. She worked with others who provided shelter and homes for children caught up in the Holocaust. Ponder her actions – Irena Sendler.

Remember Stanislawa Leszczynska (pronounced Stanislava Lesinska), a Polish midwife who delivered around 3,000 babies in Auschwitz, of whom some few hundred survived. Her courage in bringing comfort to traumatized women, in a vulnerable position, in a place of death, is remarkable. She sourced basic medical necessities, bringing calm in a place of hellish horror. Because of her actions, some survived. Stanislawa Leszczynska, a woman of great humanity and courage. Ponder her decisions – Stanislawa Leszczynska.

Jehosheba, Irena Sendler, Stanislawa Leszczynska – remember their names. Goodness like theirs is fascinating – more so than evil. How did they manage? Where did they draw their strength, courage and resolve? How did they carry on day after day? Ponder this.

Their goodness reminds us of the power of using the resources we have to do what we can. We might think to ourselves, 'These women stood up to the might of the respective empires they faced. I'm just small and ordinary. What can I do?' Start there. Acts of goodness create ripple effects. The ripples spread out and bring positive effect. Remember these names – Jehosheba, Irena Sendler, Stanislawa Leszczynska. Ponder their goodness, and pray for the strength to echo such attitudes in our lives.

God grant to us, just ordinary people, the courage and insight to use the power we have to bring hope, healing, hospitality, light and possibility wherever we find ourselves. Ponder goodness.

Homiletic Points

1 The sermon moves from pondering evil to pondering goodness – beginning with the Letby story and moving to Jezebel and Athaliah. Blending the horizons of the contemporary context and the biblical narrative serves to earth the ancient stories in the here and now.
2 The sermon turns from the focus on evil in the story of Athaliah and shines a light on the actions of Jehosheba. Her name is deliberately repeated through the sermon, because she is so little known.
3 From her story the sermon explores the work of Irena Sendler and Stanislawa Leszczynska, asking the hearer to ponder their goodness and remember their names, linking the three women together.
4 The application comes at the end in a call for the hearer to deliberately enact goodness in whatever ways are possible.
5 The call to ponder is woven through the piece, adding to the structural integrity of the whole.

Collect

God of goodness,
teach us to light a candle
rather than curse the darkness.
Draw us to reflect on agents of your goodness in the world,
and shape us after their pattern,
willing to do what we can, with the power we have,
in the situations we find ourselves.
Amen.

Notes

1 Owen Davies, 'The Witch of Endor in history and folklore', *Folklore*, No. 134 (March 2023), pp. 1–22, https://doi.org/10.1080/0015587X.2022.2152252, accessed 29.11.23.

2 Davies, 'The Witch of Endor', p. 20.

3 Carol A. Newsom, Sharon H. Ringe and Jacqueline E. Lapsley, *The Women's Bible Commentary* (Louisville, KY: Westminster John Knox Press, 1992), p. 58.

4 Newsom et al., *The Women's Bible Commentary*, p. 158.

5 Newsom et al., *The Women's Bible Commentary*, p. 158.

6 Lynn Japinga, *Preaching the Women of the Old Testament* (Louisville, KY: Westminster John Knox Press, 2017), p. 125.

7 Davies, 'The Witch of Endor', p. 20.

8 Japinga, *Preaching*, p. 143

9 Donald J. Wiseman, *1 and 2 Kings*, Tyndale Old Testament Commentaries (Leicester: IVP, 1993), p. 162.

10 Newsom et al., *The Women's Bible Commentary*, p. 174.

11 Lucy Letby is a British nurse who was found guilty of the murder of seven babies and the attempted murder of six others at the Countess of Chester Hospital, between 2015 and 2016. The judged handed down a 'whole life order', meaning she will never be released from prison.

21

Nameless Presences:
The Widow of a Prophet and the
Shunammite Woman

KATE BRUCE

> **Their Stories in the Revised Common Lectionary (Sundays)**
>
> Neither woman features in the lectionary.

The stories of these nameless women come back-to-back in a series of miracle stories centred on Elisha. Both women are nameless, but we can gather much about their characters by looking at their actions. Let's focus the spotlight on them.

The Widow's Words in the Bible

'Your servant my husband is dead; and you know that your servant feared the LORD, but a creditor has come to take my two children as slaves.' (2 Kings 4.1)

'Your servant has nothing in the house, except a jar of oil.' (2 Kings 4.2)

'Bring me another vessel.' (2 Kings 4.6)

The Shunammite Woman' s Words in the Bible

'Look, I am sure that this man who regularly passes our way is a holy man of God. Let us make a small roof chamber with walls, and put there for him a bed, a table, a chair, and a lamp, so that he can stay there whenever he comes to us.' (2 Kings 4.9–10)

'I live among my own people.' (2 Kings 4.13b)

'No, my lord, O man of God; do not deceive your servant.' (2 Kings 4.16b)

'Send me one of the servants and one of the donkeys, so that I may quickly go to the man of God and come back again.' (2 Kings 4.22)

'It will be all right.' (2 Kings 4.23)

'It is all right.' (2 Kings 4.26)

'Did I ask my lord for a son? Did I not say, Do not mislead me?' (2 Kings 4.28)

'As the LORD lives, and as you yourself live, I will not leave without you.' (2 Kings 4.30)

A Widow of Tremendous Strength

The nameless widow (2 Kings 4.1–7) was either the wife of one of the prophets or the wife of one of the prophets' sons. The Hebrew suggests the latter. Either way, her husband died, leaving her with considerable debts. Such was the scale of them, a creditor wanted to take both her sons as slaves. Desperate, she comes to the prophet. Her plea highlights a struggle 'You know that [my husband] feared the LORD, but ...' (4.1). Her husband's faith in God has not prevented disaster knocking on her door. There is a world of pain and confusion in her statement. The rapid escalation of events threatens to leave her traumatized and in poverty. In desperation she reaches out to God, through the agency of the prophet.

Her response to Elisha's question about what she has in her house reveals the dire state of her poverty; all she has is a 'jar of oil' (v. 2). Has she already been cleaned out by other creditors? Elisha instructs her to 'Go outside' and borrow plenty of vessels from her neighbours (v. 3). Put yourself in her shoes. She is dealing with grief, shame, fear and desperation. Facing this, many would choose to stay inside, curled up and alone. But she does as Elisha demands, making herself vulnerable as she reaches out to her community, probably provoking a barrage of curious questions. The miracle occurs in part because the woman risks reaching out, faithfully following Elisha's instructions. Now behind closed doors, the oil continues to flow from the single jar into the many vessels her sons pass to her. There is enough resource for her to pay the debts and live off the remainder.

The single jar replenishing all the empty vessels stands as a metaphor for the grace and provision of God; it also represents the widow – the single jar – who pours herself out to rescue herself and her sons from penury, and slavery. The miracle belongs to God – directed by Elisha, enacted by the widow, supported by her sons and the wider community. The story tends to be known as 'the miraculous provision of oil'; perhaps we should also know it as 'a widow of tremendous strength'.

The Shunammite: A Great Woman

We are never given a name for the Shunammite woman, so named because she comes from the town of Shunem, but we learn a great deal about her from the narrative which 'reveals a woman who is self-reliant, pious and a leader'.[1] She is an *ishah gedolah*,[2] or great woman, in terms of her wealth (4.8) and, as we shall discover, her wisdom. Her husband is presented as a '"hollow man" whose character defects serve to highlight her virtues'.[3] We see she is observant and generous, urging that Elisha receive hospitality at her table, initially for a single meal and later on a regular basis. She discerns that Elisha is 'a holy man of God' (v. 9) and provides a carefully furnished room for his use. She is the active partner in her marriage, leading on the building plans for Elisha's room (vv. 9–10).

Wanting to give the Shunammite woman something in return for her trouble, Elisha directs his servant Gehazi to send for her. Notice that Elisha sends for the woman, not her husband; he recognizes her hand in the provision of hospitality. He asks what may be done for her, offering the influence of king and commander (v. 13). Her response is terse and uncomplicated, 'I live among my own people' (v. 13). Independent and satisfied with her lot, her 'response is one of complete security'.[4]

Undeterred, Elisha asks his servant, 'What then may be done for her' (v. 14). Gehazi's answer is based on the view that the woman, who is childless, with an old husband, necessarily wants a son (v. 14). No one asks her whether that is her desire. Without discussion with her, Elisha announces to her that 'in due time' she will 'embrace a son' (v. 16). Her response is ambiguous. 'No, my lord, O man of God; do not deceive your servant' (v. 17). This could be read as an expression of heart-stopping joy, 'Is this really going to happen?', or simply disbelief from a woman who has come to terms with her lot and doesn't need the upset! We don't know because no one bothers to ask her. Rabbi Gila Colman Ruskin points out:

unlike the other barren women in the Bible (Sarah, Rebecca, Rachel, Hannah, Samson's mother, and Michal), the Shunamite woman had not been praying for a child, nor did her life seem to be incomplete without one.[5]

A Decisive Woman

We get more signals of the passivity of the woman's husband when, later on, the son falls ill in the fields. Rather than carry his son himself, the father orders a servant to 'Carry him to his mother' (v. 19). Again, we see the decisive Shunammite woman driving the action; she nurses her son until noon, when he dies (v. 20). She lays him on Elisha's bed, closes the door and leaves, before asking her husband for a servant and a donkey to go quickly to the man of God (v. 22). The father may not know of his son's death; he seems confused as to why she is going on this particular day, a journey of some 16 miles away.[6] Her brusque response to her husband suggests great faith in Elisha: 'It will be alright' (v. 23). She commands the servant to urge the animal on and not spare her discomfort (v. 24). When Elisha sees her at a distance and perceives something is wrong, he sends his servant Gehazi to question her, but she brushes him off with a repetition of what she said to her husband, 'It is all right' (v. 26). She knows that she needs the master and not the servant, so doesn't waste time explaining the situation to Gehazi. When she sees Elisha, she 'caught hold of his feet' (v. 27). The action suggests entreaty, but her words denote anger: 'Did I ask my lord for a son? Did I not say, Do not mislead me?' (v. 28). No one asked the woman what she wanted, and she certainly did not ask for this.

When Gehazi tries to push her away from Elisha, he admits that while she is in bitter distress, the Lord has hidden the reason from him (v. 27). The man of God seems to be having a crisis of confidence, but the woman is certain Elisha must come with her. Elisha sends his servant off to lay his staff on the boy's face. The woman demands Elisha comes with her, 'As the LORD lives and as you yourself live, I will not leave without you' (v. 30). Her words echo Elisha's as he begged Elijah not to die (2 Kings 2.2, 4, 6). As she sensed, the staff has no effect on the boy's restoration. She knew it would take Elisha's presence and life force to restore him. It does. She falls at Elisha's feet, takes her living child, and leaves (vv. 36–37).

A Woman of Initiative

We next encounter the Shunammite woman when Elisha tells her there will be a seven-year famine and urges her to uproot her household and settle elsewhere (2 Kings 8.1). Notice Elisha deals with her and not her husband. He is not mentioned at all in this passage. He might be dead, but given his passivity in the previous storyline he may simply remain dormant.

She takes the advice of the man of God and resettles her household in the land of the Philistines. At the end of the seven years, she takes the initiative to return home and appeal to the king for the restoration of her land, which has since been claimed by another. She arrives as if by divine appointment, approaching the king just as Gehazi is in the middle of recounting the raising of her son. The King instructs an official to 'Restore all that was hers, together with all the revenue of the fields from the day that she left the land until now' (v. 6). It's a generous recompense, suggesting recognition of her earlier generosity. It happens because she took the initiative.

Sermon Suggestion: God Works with Us

God does not do to us. God works with us.

It takes God to offer a miracle, and humans to complete it. One possible definition of a miracle? Divine providence meets human action. I want to look at two unnamed women whose stories exemplify this idea.

They are found in 2 Kings 4, their stories back-to-back, an unnamed widow and a woman from Shunem. Usually, when we look at their stories, we look at what they tell us about the ministry of Elisha the prophet, the miracle-worker, but I want the spotlight to fall on the two women to see what that might bring.

God does not do to us. God works with us.

Without these two women, there would have been no miracles, less evidence to support Elisha's identity as Elijah's replacement. The initiative, courage and action of these two provide the opportunity for Elisha's fame to spread.

Each woman faces a disaster. In neither case is the situation of her own making.

The widow has to deal with her late husband's massive debt, her grief, and the need to keep the wolf from the door. The creditor is circling. The interest is mounting. The creditor eyes her sons' economic value as slaves. Debt, poverty, possible slavery. What can she do? What would you do?

The woman of Shunem faces a different disaster. The son she never asked for, but loved anyway, is ill, dying, dead. Humanly speaking, it's game over. Time to mourn and weep, bury and grieve. It's done. What can she do? What would you do?

Both women show incredible courage and faith.

Both women act decisively.

Frankly, both women are impressive.

Both women seek God in the way they know how. They turn to the prophet Elisha.

What about you? How do you seek God?

God does not do to us. God works with us.

Neither woman is particularly polite. The widow reminds Elisha, 'Your servant, my husband ... feared the LORD, but ...' To put it another way, 'It's all gone pear-shaped anyway.' She lays her problem before Elisha – naming the death, the debt and the demands.

The Shunammite is also pretty direct: 'Did I ask you for a son? Did I not say, "Don't mislead me?"' She might as well have said, 'You caused all this. I was quite OK, until you came along, and now my son is dead, my heart is broken, and I need you to act.'

We tend to think the miracles in these stories consist of the ways in which the natural laws are broken: the provision of lots of oil from just a little, and the resurrection of a dead child – certainly miraculous, but I think we need to understand the scope of the miraculous more broadly. For the God of all creation, making more matter from matter, or breathing life into dead matter, is probably a walk in the park. But getting human beings, endowed with free will, to engage honestly and with vulnerability is probably a tad more difficult!

The directness of the women is part of the miracle.

Look at how they reach out in fierce faith and expect God to act through Elisha.

God is at work in them.

Look at the willingness of the widow to be vulnerable, to go to her community and ask for flasks and vessels, exposing her grief and need.

See her willingness to follow the prophet's strange instruction.

She could have said 'no' and walked away.

She could have said 'no' and done a midnight flit from the creditor.
She doesn't.

She reaches out in faith and her faith is rewarded.

The loan shark is speared. Her sons are saved. Her future assured.
Miracle.

If the mark of a miracle is divine providence meeting human action,
then these women are part of the miracle.

What about the Shunammite woman? Not only does she metaphoric-
ally kick Elisha's door down, she simply will not be fobbed off. She makes
Elisha accompany her back to the dead child. No half-hearted measures
will cut it. She knows instinctively what is needed, and she goes out and
gets it.

In the Shunammite woman we see some gutsy action. #God is at work
in her and she responds – part of the miracle

God does not do to us. God works with us.

Why does this matter?

Faced with the spin balls of life, we can take a leaf from the pages of
these women's stories.

God is for us, with us and in us – not a distant agent whose arm might
just be twisted if we are good enough, but an engaged friend who does
not do to us but works with us.

So today ask yourself, 'What do I need from God?'

Ask God, 'What do I need from you?'

Name what you discover.

Share it with others you trust.

If you are angry, be angry.

If you are brassed off – say it how it is.

Be as you are. Honestly.

Learn from the widow and the Shunammite. Be open, willing to be
vulnerable, take risks – and trust. You will meet God in the miracles
where divine providence meets human action – and surprising things
happen.

God does not do to us. God works with us.

Homiletic Points

1 The sermon is woven around a chorus as a means of repeating the central theme and giving it structure.
2 The sermon draws out the similarities between the two women and explores their part as co-workers in the respective miracles.
3 The women's troubles are placed side by side, making the point that they are not of their own making, and challenging the hearer, 'What would you do?'
4 The sermon picks up on the textual presentation of both women as bold, direct and not at all pious. They are themselves. The underlying plea is for normality in spiritual engagement.
5 A rhetorical question is set up: is it harder for the Creator to make more from matter/re-enliven matter or to get free-willed humans to engage with God? This is part of the exploration of miracle as involving both the divine transformation of matter and the divine–human partnership.
6 The sermon lands in the 'and so what' – the call to meet God in the miracle of co-operation and surprise.

Collect

Name-knowing God,
thank you for these nameless women
who meet you in the miracle.
Bold, fierce and faithful,
they earth your providence
in the willingness of their action:
vulnerable, courageous and co-operative.
Work in us as you worked in them.
Act for us and within us,
for the good of your creation.
Shape us as people of miracle,
people of hope.
Amen.

Notes

1 Carol A. Newsom, Sharon H. Ringe and Jacqueline E. Lapsley, *The Women's Bible Commentary* (Louisville, KY: Westminster John Knox Press, 1992), p. 175.

2 Rabbi Gila Colman Ruskin, 'The Shunamite woman: a model of radical empathy', https://www.myjewishlearning.com/article/shunamite-woman/, accessed 02.10.23.

3 Richard Nelson, *First and Second Kings*, Interpretation Series (Louisville, KY: Westminster John Knox Press, 1987), p. 172.

4 T. R. Hobbs, *Word Biblical Commentary, Volume 13: 2 Kings* (Waco, TX: Word Books, 1985), p. 51.

5 Ruskin, 'The Shunamite Woman'.

6 Albert McShane, *I & II Kings* (Kilmarnock: John Ritchie Ltd, 2002), p. 206.

22

A Slave in Syria,
but a Servant of God:
Naaman's Wife's Maid

LIZ SHERCLIFF

Naaman's Wife's Maid in the Revised Common Lectionary

Naaman's Wife's Maid in the Revised Common Lectionary

Year C   Proper 23 (OT 28)   2 Kings 5.1–3, 7–15c

The Words of Naaman's Wife's Maid in the Bible

'If only my lord were with the prophet who is in Samaria! He would cure him of his leprosy.' (2 Kings 5.3)

Her Story

The social status of this maid is illustrated by the lengthy 'name' she is given: Naaman's wife's maid, the possession of a possession of someone. She had been taken captive by one of Naaman's raiding parties, and put into the service of Naaman's wife. As the commander of the army, Naaman likely had his pick of the captives, and maybe there was something outstanding about this girl – appearance or ability, perhaps. Whatever the young girl's position in the house, she is not invisible. She knows of Naaman's illness and is able to commend a solution. In the whole story, the girl says one thing: 'If only my lord were with the prophet who is in Samaria! He would cure him of his leprosy.'[1] This knowledge, however, gives her dignity. Philosopher Miranda Fricker argues that when we assume someone knows nothing, we fail to treat them as a human being; conversely, recognizing someone's wisdom, dignifies them.[2] By taking notice of this insignificant captured slave girl, her mistress shows her unusual respect.

In contrast with the girl, Naaman is a great man. He is a 'mighty warrior', holds a high position, and enjoys the patronage of the king. There is, however, a cloud on his horizon – a skin disease, usually interpreted as leprosy. Clarke describes Naaman as 'afflicted with a disorder the most loathsome and the most humiliating that could possibly disgrace a human being'.[3] Notice what happens to knowledge in this story. The slave girl passes it to her mistress, her mistress passes it to her husband, her husband passes it to the king. Is this an early example of a man taking credit for the insights of a woman? The girl, the knower, disappears from the story. Nobody checks with her who the prophet in Samaria might be. The knowledge is subsumed in the assumptions of the powerful. The person who could heal must be the most powerful in the land – the king. The letter goes to the king of Israel: 'I've sent you my servant so you can heal him.' The king of Israel interprets the letter in terms of power – 'he's trying to trick me into a quarrel'.

Then Elisha hears about it. From here on the story inverts hierarchical assumptions. Naaman is to go to Elisha, Elisha doesn't even go out to meet him. Instead, he sends a message, 'Go, wash in the Jordan.' Naaman's bias kicks in: 'He should come to me; anyway, his river is rubbish, we have far better; why should I do what he says?' His servants have the courage to stand up to him: 'You'd have done it if he'd asked you to do something difficult. Why not give it a go?' Wisdom is allotted to the servants; Naaman the brave has to do nothing other than take a dip in a river; Naaman the rich cannot even pay the prophet for healing him. The world is turned upside down.

Notice one more thing. This is not a conversion story. Elisha does not say, 'Let him come to me, that he may learn that there is a god in Israel,' but, 'that he may learn that there is a *prophet* in Israel' (2 Kings 5.8) Why is this important? Power silences those it deems inconvenient, by giving 'the speaker less credibility than [they] otherwise would have given'.[4] Boaventura de Sousa Santos goes further: 'Unequal exchanges ... have always implied the death of the knowledge of the subordinated.'[5] The death of subordinate knowledge results in dominant ways of knowing being presented as the only ways of knowing. We see this happening in our story. The girl offers subordinate knowledge, knowledge that comes from an inferior social position, inferior race and inferior sex. Her knowledge is passed to the men, who appropriate it, misunderstand it and make unwarranted assumptons about its meaning. In feminist theological terms, women's ways of knowing and knowing about life, faith and God are suffocated out of too much debate. Eventually what the girl knew is interpreted as a threat by the king of Israel and only unscrambled when it comes to Elisha's attention. Elisha insists that this knowledge must be understood – others should recognize that there is a prophet in Israel. The main tasks of a prophet are to forthtell and to enact their message. That is precisely what Elisha does; the inferior knowledge sends the great commander to bathe in an inferior river.

The girl's step may be small, her faith may be informed, but let us not ignore the importance of this story in demanding that subordinate knowledge can change things. The story is an encouragement to believe that change might come from the grassroots, from those rarely heard. It is an encouragement for women preachers to speak of women's experiences of God and faith and life. It is even an encouragement to believe that there are men who will support what we say!

Sermon Suggestion: A Nobody Speaks

You might have seen the *Punch* cartoon in which a man addresses what appears to be a board of directors. 'That's a very good suggestion, Miss Triggs,' he says. 'Perhaps one of the men would like to make it.' It's funny because it's recognizable. We are more likely to believe some people than others. Our legal system is more likely to believe white men than anyone else.[6]

In this story we have someone who is bottom of the believability pile. She's so far down that she belongs to somebody who belongs to somebody. Naaman's wife's maid. She was among other loot brought back to Aram from a raid into Israel. There must have been something about her, though, because when she speaks her mistress listens.

The master of the house, Naaman, is powerful, successful, accomplished, in with the in-crowd. He has just one problem, and it's a devastating one. He has leprosy. It isn't curable. The maid, though, is convinced that Elisha not only could, but would, heal him. Imagine the consequences of being wrong for this slave girl. But she knows something her master needs to know. She tells her mistress, her mistress seems to pass on the message accurately, and Naaman even goes into the king and tells him just what the girl said. Clearly, he couldn't have explained it fully, because the king decides that the person in Israel who could heal must also be a king. The king of Israel seems not to think wider than himself either. He sees the request as a way of tricking him into war.

Fortunately, Elisha hears what's going on and contacts the king. 'Send him to me so that he may learn that there is a prophet in Israel.' Notice what he says: 'that he may learn there is a *prophet* in Israel', not a god in Israel. Sometimes people need to go to people, to hear from people first. Elisha's actions show, of course, that there is a prophet in Israel.

But events begin with a prophet in Aram – an insignificant prophet who has just one line to deliver and just enough courage to deliver it. She may not have been believed – she was the wrong class, the wrong race, the wrong sex. The message may have been taken from her to be delivered – wrongly – by one king to another. But what she said changed things for Naaman. He was healed. He wasn't converted. He didn't change his faith. Even as he confessed, 'there is no God in all the earth except in Israel', he also asked that the Lord would pardon him when he went in to worship in the house of Rimmon. This isn't a story about changing the world, it's about the world as it is.

It's a story that begins with a captive, enslaved young girl in the house of a powerful privileged man. She doesn't yield to resentment of the relative status. When she sees a need and a solution, even for one so much above her in society, she speaks. Her life must have witnessed to her integrity, for her brief words reach the ears of the king and trigger events that lead to healing. In the rest of the story, we see the topsy-turvy kin-dom of God, in which another servant takes the prophet's message to Naaman, an important man is told to go and wash in an inferior river, and has his reward refused. The conclusion to the story is not really satisfactory; there is no dramatic conversion, no victory of the girl's religion over Naaman's. All we have is the grace of God working through the prophet in response to a girl's words.

Perhaps where the kin-dom of God is to be found – among the insignificant – perhaps we might be given just one line to deliver, and just enough courage to deliver it, and it might be enough to begin a change.

Homiletic Points

1 The reference to the *Punch* cartoon opens the way into the theme of believability, with the point being made that the servant girl is at the bottom on the 'believability pile'.

2 The sermon is short and memorable, an exploration of the story with the focus on the girl's courage, faith and willingness to risk so that Naaman is able to access a cure for his leprosy.

3 The sermon lands with a focus on the importance of insignificance. Having the courage to act in small ways can enact the grace of God.
4 There is an important theme here about noticing how God works through the outsider, the one with the least power. What might we see if we took this seriously?

Collect

God of the insignificant, the one-liner, the forgettable,
Give us courage to speak from a marginalized faith to those in power over us,
And to listen to those who are on our margins.
Prosper what words we do say, so that we might begin to change the world around us.
In the name of the one who came as Word to change the divisions of the world.
Amen.

Notes

1 Most scholars do not consider the skin disease to have been leprosy. See, for example, https://www.ministrymatters.com/all/entry/2382/naaman, accessed 06.12.2023.

2 Miranda Fricker, *Epistemic Injustice: Power and the Ethics of Knowing* (Oxford: Oxford University Press, 2007), p. 3.

3 See https://www.studylight.org/commentaries/eng/acc/2-kings-5.html, accessed 02.10.23.

4 Fricker, *Epistemic Injustice*, p. 3.

5 Boaventura de Sousa (2014), *Epistemologies of the South: Justice Against Epistemicide* (Abingdon: Routledge, 2014).

6 See, for example, 'Ethnicity and the criminal justice system: what does recent data say on over-representation?', House of Commons Library, https://commonslibrary.parliament.uk/ethnicity-and-the-criminal-justice-system-what-does-recent-data-say/, accessed 07.10.23; 'A view from the Bar: race and the British justice system', Open Access Government, https://www.openaccessgovernment.org/british-justice-system/90897/, accessed 07.10.23.

23

Caught Up in Power Politics:
The Woman of Timnah, Delilah,
Ahinoam Daughter of Ahimaaz,
Ahinoam of Jezreel,
Michal, Abishag and Jeroboam's Wife

KATE BRUCE

Their Stories in the Revised Common Lectionary (Sundays)

Of these women, Michal is the only one whose story features, partially, in the Lectionary:

Year B   Proper 10 (OT 15)   2 Samuel 6.1–5, 12b–19

Their Words in the Bible

The Woman of Timnah

'You hate me; you do not really love me. You have asked a riddle of my people, but you have not explained it to me.' (Judges 14.16)

Delilah

'Please tell me what makes your strength so great, and how you could be bound, so that one could subdue you.' (Judges 16.6)

'The Philistines are upon you, Samson!' (Judges 16.9)

'You have mocked me and told me lies; please tell me how you could be bound.' (Judges 16.10)

'The Philistines are upon you, Samson!' (Judges 16.12)

'Until now you have mocked me and told me lies; tell me how you could be bound.' (Judges 16.13)

'The Philistines are upon you, Samson!' (Judges 16.14)

'How can you say, "I love you", when your heart is not with me? You have mocked me three times now and have not told me what makes your strength so great.' (Judges 16.15)

'This time come up, for he has told his whole secret to me.' (Judges 16.18)

'The Philistines are upon you, Samson!' (Judges 16.20)

Ahinoam Daughter of Ahimaaz, Ahinoam of Jezreel, Abishag, and Jeroboam's Wife

No words are recorded.

This apparently disparate collection of women is united in their connection to powerful men – Samson, Saul, David and Jeroboam. Their lives are caught in the crossfire of power politics, and they suffer the fallout. The woman of Timnah is burned to death; Delilah is given the (unfair) reputation of a conniving seductress; Ahinoam daughter of Ahimaaz is married to the violent and unpredictable King Saul; Ahinoam of Jezreel, along with Abigail, is taken captive in the trauma of war; Abishag's body is treated as the territory of conquest, and Jeroboam's wife bears the consequences of her husband's rap sheet. They each deserve careful reflection.

The Woman of Timnah: Struggle, Fire and Death

The woman of Timnah is a nameless Philistine who unfortunately attracts the eye of Samson. He brings struggle, fire and death into her life. She is caught up in a cycle of violence and vengeance between the Philistines and Samson. Samson is no hero; he is a deeply flawed individual, a Nazirite who touches corpses (Judges 14.8) and holds seven-day parties (14.12), at which it is hard not to see the wine flowing – forbidden for a Nazirite. He desires the woman of Timnah (14.2). His parents counsel against marrying outside Israel, but he is headstrong and entitled: 'Get her for me, because she pleases me.' Literally, she seems good in his eyes. The comment resonates with the more general observation in Judges that 'Every man did that which was right in his own eyes' (17.6; 21.25, AV). Struggle, fire and death come to this woman's door, and beyond it we can trace the backdrop of a spiralling decline into darkness.

Samson poses his riddle as a way of wringing considerable booty out of the wedding guests (Judges 14.12–14). Frustrated, the woman's own people threaten to 'burn you and your father's house with fire' (14.15) if she doesn't get the answer to the riddle out of Samson and pass it on to them. She begs Samson for the answer. The text says she weeps and nags for seven days until he relents (v. 17). McCann describes this as 'a feigned and persistent emotional display', interpreting 'nagged' as 'pressed'.[1] It's no wonder she pressed Samson in what is likely to have been a genuinely emotional plea, given the failure of her mission will result in a fiery death. She passes the riddle's solution to the men of the town and when they present it to Samson he responds with disdain for his wife, 'If you had not ploughed with my heifer' (v. 18). It's a crude image, implying the information has been passed on during pillow talk. There is no evidence for this slur on the woman.

Furious at losing, Samson kills 30 men of Askelon and uses their festal garments to pay the wager. Then 'Samson's wife was given to his companion, who had been his best man' (v. 20). She is passed on like an object, without agency or choice. This does not prevent Samson wanting to enter her room, presumably for intercourse, sometime later. He is blocked by her father because he believed Samson had rejected her (Judges 15.1). Her father offers her younger, prettier sister to Samson (15.2). The girl escapes because Samson doesn't accept the father's offer. Rather, Samson responds with unbelievable cruelty.

He captures three hundred foxes, ties their tails together and attaches a lit torch to the tails. He sends the poor animals into the harvest and burns precious resources – grain, vineyards and olive groves, to say nothing of the foxes. When the Philistines learn who did this and why, they burn to death Samson's wife and her father, as they had earlier threatened. The brutality is breathtaking. Samson brings only suffering, fire and death to this unnamed woman.

Where is God in this Story?

God is active in the background of this story, using the marriage between Samson and the woman of Timnah as a 'pretext to act against the Philistines' (14.4). The text gives no sense of God's care or compassion for this woman taken at Samson's demand, threatened by her own people, treated as an object, and finally burned to death in an act of vengeance in an ongoing cycle of violence between the Philistines and Israelites. God is never mentioned in relation to the woman of Timnah.

In contrast, God is linked directly to Samson four times in Judges 14 and 15: strength is given to him to tear the lion apart (14.6); we read that the 'spirit of the LORD rushed on him', enabling him to kill the men of Askelon (14.19); the spirit of the Lord enables the ropes to melt off his hands (15.14); after all his violent exertion, slaughtering one thousand men with a donkey's jawbone, at his request God brings water from a hollow place to quench Samson's thirst (15.18–19). At the same time the text is clear that Samson is headstrong and disobedient, violent and cruel. God's working through Samson should not be taken as affirmation of his unfaithfulness, more a sign that God works through earthen vessels (2 Corinthians 4.7).

What are we to make of this: the foreign woman abused, and the powerful, flawed man enabled by God? The text of Judges read alone would imply that the woman is just collateral damage in the bigger picture. However, Judges does not present a complete view of God, and certainly not an uncomplicated one. Wisdom guides us to notice the silences, the marginalizing of the woman, and the horrific violence done to her and her father. There are many images of God presented throughout scripture that show divine compassion, care, intervention and love for the powerless outsider. This isn't one of them. Where the text offers no compassion to this woman, surely the reader must.

Delilah: A Straight-Talking Woman

Samson is clearly attracted to foreign women. He has sex with the unnamed prostitute of Gaza, though nothing more is heard of her. 'After this he fell in love with a woman in the valley of Sorek, whose name was Delilah (Judges 16.4). 'Her nationality is not stated, but she was likely either a Philistine or sympathetic to their cause.'[2]

There are close similarities between the story of the woman of Timnah and that of Delilah. Both reside in the valley of Sorek. Did Delilah know of the story of Samson's wife? Both women are told to 'coax' Samson into revealing important information. The woman of Timnah is threatened with immolation if she doesn't provide the riddle's answer. Delilah is offered 'eleven hundred pieces of silver' (16.5) for information about the source of Samson's strength. We are not told if she was ever paid. Could she have turned the assignment down? Look what happened to the woman of Timnah – refusal was not an option. Delilah could not afford to fail in her task. Offers of money and reward can disappear just as quickly as they are made.

Delilah's name is layered with cultural accretion; she is commonly seen as a great beauty, commanding seductive power, a 'vixen, seductress, tramp, tart, conniver, cheat, tease, slut, and whore'.[3] Like the woman of Timnah, Delilah uses the leverage of love to push Samson for an answer – each woman claiming he does not love her (14.16; 16.15). They use what power they have as women caught up in broader power politics. However, the text makes no reference to Delilah's appearance and her questions to Samson could not be more upfront and obvious. Delilah is a straight-talking woman. Four times she directly asks him how he could be subdued and bound (16.6, 10, 13, 16), enacting each suggestion, with a handful of Philistines hiding just around the corner. Each time she declares to him, 'The Philistines are upon you, Samson!', which is a bit of a giveaway (16.9, 12, 14). Astoundingly, Samson tells her the truth about the source of his strength, and this time the Philistines really are upon him (16.20–21). If the information is elicited through seductive cajoling, it is given in blind stupidity. Wisdom is not Samson's strong point! There is a horrible irony in the Philistines' gouging out of his eyes – it symbolizes his deep failure to 'see'.

After Samson's imprisonment, the narrative moves on with him, and we know no more of Delilah.

Ahinoam Daughter of Ahimaaz: What Goes on Behind Closed Doors?

Ahinoam daughter of Ahimaaz is Saul's wife (1 Samuel 14.50). Ahinoam of Jezreel is a wife of David, along with Abigail (1 Samuel 25.43). Levenson argues they are the same person: 'Could it be that David swaggered into Hebron with the wife of a Calebite chieftain on one arm and that of the Israelite king on the other?'[4] Levenson sees this as the fulfilment of Nathan's words to David, 'I gave you your master's house and your master's wives into your bosom' (2 Samuel 12.8). However, is it likely that David stole one of Saul's wives while Saul was still alive, and no mention of this made in the account of their conflict? Also, Ahinoam, wife of Saul, was Michal's mother (1 Samuel 14.49). Michal was David's first wife (1 Samuel 18.27). It seems unlikely that David could have married his mother-in-law without some comment or protest, given the prohibition in Leviticus 18.17.

We can reasonably assume, therefore, that there are two women named Ahinoam. Of the first, little can be said except she was married to Saul, a man known to be unstable and prone to dark moods and violence against David and his family (1 Samuel 16.14–15; 18.10–11; 19.9–10; 20.33). How that affected Ahinoam we can only speculate. It's not easy to tell what goes on behind closed doors.

Ahinoam of Jezreel: Tied to David's Political Fortunes

Ahinoam of Jezreel is mentioned at the end of the story of Abigail and Nabal (1 Samuel 25).[5] David married Abigail and he also married Ahinoam of Jezreel. Both women are tied to David's political fortunes, When David discerns that sooner or later Saul will kill him, he flees to King Achish of Gath (1 Samuel 27.3). Ahinoam and Abigail are among the hundreds who went with David. Such a move would have been disruptive, perhaps exciting, and definitely dangerous. Since David is at risk, so are his household.

This is borne out when the city of Ziklag, which king Achish gave to David (1 Samuel 27.5–6), is burned down in an Amalekite raid. All of David's people, including Ahinoam and Abigail, were taken captive (1 Samuel 30.1–3).

The next mention of these women is when David finds the Amalekites celebrating their spoil and recovers everything taken, including 'his two wives' (1 Samuel 30.16–20). From twilight to the evening of the following day David's forces attack the Amalekites. The traumatic sights and sounds of slaughter would be indelible aspects of the captives' experience. This is the payload of being caught up in violent politics.

Ahinoam and Abigail are next mentioned journeying to Hebron with David, where he is anointed king over Judah (2 Samuel 2.2). The final reference to Ahinoam comes in 2 Samuel 3.2, where she is mentioned as the mother of David's firstborn son, Amnon. She is the crown prince's mother. Whether she lives to witness her son's utter misuse of power – he rapes his half-sister Tamar, and then reviles her (2 Samuel 13.1–17) – we don't know.

Michal: A Woman Spurned

Michal, the youngest of Saul's two daughters (1 Samuel 14.49), is caught up in the political tensions between Saul and David. She loved David (18.20). This is 'the only place in the Hebrew Bible where it is stated that a woman loves a man'.[6] There is no mention that this love is reciprocated. Saul weaponizes Michal's love by stating that the marriage present will be 'a hundred foreskins of the Philistines' in the hope that David, whose popularity and military prowess he fears, will die in the attempt (18.20–25). Michal's feelings are irrelevant to him. Earlier Saul had tried a similar ruse, offering Michal's elder sister Merab in exchange for David's valour in battle (18.17–19). This plan came to nothing and Merab was given to another man.

David presents Saul with the requisite number of foreskins and Saul gives him Michal as a wife. However, the very love he had sought to weaponize becomes a source of fear for Saul. Notice how his perception of God's presence with David is linked with Michal's love for him (18.28–29). She is a sign of God's blessing on David.

Saul is desperate to have David killed. Michal, like her brother Jonathan, disobeys her father, seeking to save David. Saul, again in an evil temper, attempted to pin David to a wall with a spear, so he fled. Saul had his house watched, with a view to sending in hit men the next morning (19.9–11). Michal executes a plan to save her husband, putting herself at considerable risk of her father's wrath. She tells David of the plot to kill him, helps him escape through a window, and dresses up an idol, placing it on the bed, to give an impression of a person lying there. When Saul's henchmen come to take David, she blocks them, declaring, 'He is sick' (19.14). Michal buys David more time to make good his escape as the men return to Saul. Saul makes them return to actually lay eyes on his enemy, and they discover the idol in a wig. Saul is furious at the deception. By way of excuse, Michal claims David threated to kill her (19.11–17). Michal demonstrates she is a courageous woman, prepared to face down armed men in her house, execute a cunning ruse and confront an angry king, all for the man she loves.

The narrative focuses on David's escape and life in exile. Although David encounters Jonathan, Michal's brother, there is no message for the loyal wife who saved his life. Given David had other wives in the wilderness, why is Michal, who loved and saved him, abandoned? The next time we hear mention of her is in the report that 'Saul had given his daughter Michal, David's wife, to Palti son of Laish' (25.44), in a move designed to prevent David claiming the throne through her.[7]

Michal once again becomes useful to David after Saul's suicide (31.4). His position has become stronger, and he has been crowned king of Judah. Now he seeks the throne of Israel. Michal becomes the bargaining chip in David's negotiations with Abner of the house of Saul. He refuses to see Abner unless Michal is brought to him, and he demands Ishbosheth, Saul's son, return 'my wife Michal'. She is taken from Palti, who walks weeping behind her (2 Samuel 3.12–16). We are given no insight into Michal's feelings.

Later, as David dances publicly as the ark of the Lord is brought into Jerusalem, Michal watches from a window and despises David in her heart (2 Samuel 6.16). This is the only part of her story which features in the Lectionary, which skews our understanding of her. This text presents her as 'a mean-spirited woman who did not share David's religious convictions or support him in his time of political and spiritual triumph'.[8] But we know there is more to the story than this. The ark of the Lord is not only a religious symbol but also a political one. David has retrieved Michal from her second husband not out of love but to gain control over Saul's daughter. Now he dances before an Ark that demonstrates his political power.

She upbraids David directly, coming to meet him as he returns to the household. What is driving her anger? Her family has lost the throne of Israel, and Israel's new king is prancing about in public, in little clothing, for every maid to see (2 Samuel 6.20). Michal had loved David. He abandoned her after she had saved him, took other wives, sought her out again only out of political expedience, then ended her marriage to Palti, who seemed genuinely to love her, given the tears expressed when she was taken from him. Now she spectates from a window as David dances wildly for all to see. The constant rejection has turned her love to hatred.

David's only recorded words addressed to Michal are furious and come directly after her words of rebuke. He focuses on God's rejection of her father's house, on how he has been chosen and appointed prince over Israel and he will dance as he chooses before God – and still the maids will honour him. It's a self-centred speech, unworthy of a great king and unkind to a once loyal wife (6.21–22).

The text adds one final detail about her: 'Michal the daughter of Saul had no child to the day of her death' (6.23). She is identified with her father, not her husband – and denied children perhaps in part as political expediency (the house of Saul must end) and perhaps as punishment for expressing her rage. There is some confusion over whether she does actually have children since some manuscripts refer to the 'five sons of Michal, Saul's daughter', which David hands over to the Gibeonites

(2 Samuel 21.8–9). Other manuscripts record that these were the sons of her sister Merab. Either way, David hands her sons, or nephews, over to be murdered. She is truly a wife spurned.

Abishag: Her Body and the Body Politic

The book of Kings opens with an extensive search for a beautiful young virgin to help warm up the old and cold King David. There is nothing coy about the purpose: 'let her lie in your bosom, so that my lord the king may be warm' (1 Kings 1.2). If David can 'rule' over Abishag's body he will have proved he is still fit to govern the body politic. In this way, a connection is made between David's virility and his royal prowess. Abishag serves and attends the king, but he 'did not know her sexually' (1.4). Behind the scenes, Abishag must have been questioned about the nature of her bed warming – and the king's impotence, which she witnesses directly, is known. Straight away David's son, Adonijah, declares that he will be king.

After Solomon has been declared king, Adonijah asks to have Abishag as his wife (1 Kings 2.17). Solomon recognizes this as part of Adonijah's design on the throne (2.22). Abishag's body continues to be treated as contested territory: 'Sex with Abishag had been the test of kingship that David had failed, but Adonijah is ready to pass that test.'[9] Solomon has him killed for his design on the throne (2.25). Notice how this ambition includes designs on Abishag's body. Her life is ruined. A beautiful woman, plucked from obscurity, for ever associated with David's impotence and Adonijah's ambition. What for her now but a life shut away in the royal harem? Another woman caught in the crossfire of power politics.

Jeroboam's Wife: A Silent Presence

Jeroboam's wife is not named and no speech of hers is recorded. Her namelessness draws attention from her, and we easily overlook her humanity and her plight. She is an undeveloped character, caught up in a sea of political intrigue not of her own making.

In short, Jeroboam was head of forced labour in Israel (1 Kings 11.28). The prophet Ahijah tells him he will be given ten of the tribes of Israel, as punishment for Solomon's idolatry. Solomon learns of this and wants him dead, so Jeroboam flees to Egypt (11.29–40). When Rehoboam, Solomon's son, succeeds his father, Jeroboam returns from exile.

Unwisely, Rehoboam does not heed the request of the labourers for a lighter burden and rebellion ensues, leading to Jeroboam being crowned king of Israel (12.4–20). He is a poor king and draws Israel into idol worship (12.28–33). As punishment for his sin, his son Abijah falls sick.

Jeroboam's wife has lived in the background through all this turbulence. Presumably she flees Solomon with her husband, but we aren't given an insight into her life; her story is not a feature of the dominant narrative. Now she is thrust centre stage by necessity, her child is critically ill.

She is tasked with a series of orders from her husband: 'Go, disguise yourself'; 'go to Shiloh; for the prophet Abijah is there'; 'Take with you …'; 'go to him' (14.1–3). Silently, she obeys. Jeroboam does not want the prophet to know he is seeking guidance regarding the child, prob-ably because he knows the prophet will rebuke him for his idolatry. The ruse fails. Although the prophet has poor sight, God tells him who she is (14.5). God sees her.

She is given a disastrous prophecy to bear back to Jeroboam, a proph-ecy that speaks of the death of her son and the ending of her family. Silently she departs. It's hard to imagine her grief as she makes her way home. She carries news of the desecration in death of all Jeroboam's house, except her son; he is the only one who will receive a burial. She too, as one who belongs to Jeroboam, will be consumed, post-mortem, by either the dogs or the birds (14.11). As soon as she arrives back at her house, her child dies; the prophecy is in motion (14.1–18).

Jeroboam's wife is caught up in a situation she has not created, in which she has no apparent power. She is the carrier of a message of doom that affects her directly. We could interpret her silence as passivity, but could it be that her silence is an active choice?[10] She demonstrates self-possession in the face of a bullying husband, and great self-control as she absorbs the prophet's words, which point to a chargesheet of her husband's making, which she too must pay (14.7–16). There is great strength and dignity in her silence.

Sermon Suggestion: Because They Matter

Imagine a picture. A woman is running. The camera captures the terror in her face. Her mouth is an open 'O' of anguish. With her left hand she grasps the hand of a young boy of five or six. He is clutching a single plastic shoe. On her right hip she carries a half-naked baby. Close on her heels is a girl of around ten with a small child glued to her. The camera captures their fear-filled haste. They have nothing. They are running from some unseen horror, but to what?[11] The picture was taken in February 1968, during the Tet Offensive in Hue, South Vietnam. The photographer, Catherine Leroy, a pioneer for women reporting from war zones, captured in that photograph the vulnerability, anguish and shock of women and children caught up in the crossfire of a political firestorm. What happened to them?

Now to a different story of two woman caught up in a violent political situation and its consequences. One is named Ahinoam of Jezreel, the other Abigail. When David is in the wilderness, fleeing Saul's murderous rage, he marries her, along with Abigail, the widow of a man called Nabal, who was an abusive drunk. Ahinoam and Abigail.

Ahinoam and Abigail both experience the fallout of being married to David. When David flees Saul and heads to Gath, these women go along with his troops, every man with his household. There are other unnamed women and children caught up in this move, with all the demands of feeding, finding fresh water, changing, soothing, caring and providing. They find themselves in the city of Ziklag, where they settle. Relief. They are able to establish a pattern of life, routine, shelter, food, water, warmth – the basics of life, a sense of safety. In exchange for the safety of Ziklag, David and his men become hired muscle for Achish, the Philistine leader. The men are often away, engaged in raiding parties against various tribes, among them the Amalekites.

Meanwhile back in Ziklag a semblance of normality has descended in a place to call home. Except ... David has made enemies. One day their peace is shattered by an Amalekite attack on the city. The Bible gives us the headlines:

the Amalekites had made a raid on the Negeb and on Ziklag. They had attacked Ziklag, burned it down, and taken captive the women and all who were in it, both small and great; they killed none of them, but carried them off, and went on their way. (1 Samuel 30.1–2)

Imagine the warning cry. 'Troops are coming. Who are they? What do they want?' Uncertainty descends into panic as the attack begins. Noise. Shouting. Fear. The smell of smoke as fires take hold. The chaos of people in shock; trying to hide or flee; snatching up children; grabbing whatever possessions they can, trying to run – but to where and to what? Their attackers round them up. Shouting. Orders. Pushing and shoving. The wail of children. Fear palpable. They are rounded up and moved out – the women and children, and any men not with David. At this point, is it life or death? The place of safety is no more. They are on an unknown road, to an unknown destination. Vulnerable bodies. But still the demands of feeding, finding fresh water, changing, soothing, caring and providing don't go away. They have to manage. At this point they have no idea if or when they might be rescued, or find a semblance of home, or see their menfolk, or know peace and security again.

A photograph from 1968 and an imagined scene behind a brief biblical description about a city attacked and burned. Questions flow from the connection. What does it mean to be vulnerable in war? What does it mean to have only the clothes on your back? What does it mean to face a rifle butt, or worse? How do you protect the children? Yourself? The questions matter because the answers are part of the lived experience of countless in this present moment. Try it – a search for images of 'Women fleeing from'. Type in Syria, Afghanistan, Ukraine ... The images are haunting. Look at the faces.

For those of us who have never been there, it's easy to skim over the details – a little like the biblical account of the story of the raid on Ziklag. Just brief statements. We have to read with imagination and empathy, to see beyond the headlines. Why? Because those fleeing war today are people created in God's image – their scarred humanity is sacred. They matter.

'Ah but. It is too big, and I am too small. I don't know what to do, how to respond. Is it my business? My problem? I don't want to think about it. It's far away. Distant names of distant places that are nothing to do with me. It's more than I can comprehend.'

We can easily be snared by paralysing guilt and helplessness. We distance ourselves. Close down. Shut out the disturbing questions. Pull up the drawbridges.

God. What do you require of us? What do you call out from those of us far from their front lines? Can we simply say it's their political crossfire, not mine? Nothing to do with me. If we close up and forget them, then we are living a lie. Resting in a false comfort.

A starting point is the acknowledgement that in this moment, when I am comfortable, warm and secure, their reality is bitter. In this acknowledgement we start, even in a small way, to push back the horizons of our immediate experience to acknowledge theirs. We begin to allow our interconnectedness as fellow human beings to shape us, to form our concerns, to enlarge our hearts, to shape our prayers beyond banal intercessions and empty platitudes. If we really want to be instruments of peace then we need to look, see, imagine, empathize and open ourselves to a deeper, active, open-minded, open-hearted concern that will cost.

God, the picture, the biblical text, the contemporary stories are disturbing. Disturb us beyond paralysis – into action, however small, however seemingly insignificant. Draw us down the pathways of your inspired work, step by step.

Open our hearts – in compassion.
Open our minds – to engage.
Open our spirits in prayer.
Open our mouths – to speak out.
Open our wallets – in generosity.
Open our imaginations – to see inside the picture and beneath the headlines, recognizing the suffering and need of our sisters and brothers.

Homiletic Points

1 The photograph and the biblical story of the raid on Ziklag are held together, asking the question of what women in war face then and now.
2 The analysis of the photograph focuses on the small details that capture a sense of the fear in the picture.
3 The imagined detail in the raid on Ziklag seeks to bring alive the lived experience behind the brevity of the biblical text. In both analyses the language is staccato. The sentences short. Snapshots in linguistic form.
4 The invitation to search images relating to women in war points to the contemporary, ongoing experiences of women caught up in conflict.
5 From here the sermon gives voice to the objections we raise as we consider things we would sooner shut down, naming our paralysis.
6 The sermon draws to a close with a prayer for discomfort – and for the inspiration to act.
7 The 'open' riff at the end acts as a foil to the earlier references to closing down. Even where we feel overwhelmed, too small and insignificant, if we are willing to open out then possibility becomes reality.
8 This is an uncomfortable and inadequate sermon. Honest inadequacy is better than acquiescent silence.

Collect

Ever present God,
in our stumbling inadequacy
we hold before you those pinned down by political crossfire:
We remember our sisters and brothers,
traumatized and brutalized,
by siege and raid and war and want,
in destruction and ruin.
Mothers and carers trying to cope,
little ones bewildered,
frightened, shocked.
Lead us out of our banal complacency,
out from the wilderness of wilful ignorance.
Show us what you desire and require from us.
Give to us the courage to love.
Amen.

Notes

1 J. Clinton McCann, *Judges*, Interpretation Series (Louisville, KY: Westminster John Knox Press, 2011), p. 104.

2 Lynn Japinga, *Preaching the Women of the Old Testament* (Louisville, KY: Westminster John Knox Press, 2017), p. 95.

3 Japinga, *Preaching the Women*, p. 94.

4 Jon Douglas Levenson, '1 Samuel 25 as Literature and as History', *The Catholic Biblical Quarterly*, Vol. 40, No. 1 (1978), p. 27.

5 Kate Bruce and Liz Shercliff, *Out of the Shadows: Preaching the Women of the Bible* (London: SCM Press, 2021), pp. 68–80.

6 J. Cheryl Exum, 'Michal: Bible', *The Shalva/Hymen Encyclopaedia of Jewish Women*. https://jwa.org/encyclopedia/article/michal-bible, accessed 23/09/2023; see also Japinga, *Preaching the Women*, p. 114.

7 Exum, 'Michal'.

8 Japinga, *Preaching the Women*, p. 114.

9 Carol A. Newsom, Sharon H. Ringe and Jacqueline E. Lapsley, *The Women's Bible Commentary* (Louisville, KY: Westminster John Knox Press, 1992), p. 168.

10 David T. Adamo, 'The unheard voices in the Hebrew Bible: the nameless and silent wife of Jeroboam (1 Kgs 14:1–18)', *Old Testament Essays*, Vol. 33, No. 3 (2020), pp. 393–407.

11 The picture described is by the war photographer Catherine Leroy, and can be found in Elizabeth Becker, *You Don't Belong Here: How Three Women Rewrote the Story of War* (New York: Public Affairs, 2021), centre pages, not numbered.

24

Prophetic Pictures:
The Prophetess, the Builders, the Image
of Exile, and the Loving Mother

LIZ SHERCLIFF

These Women in the Revised Common Lectionary

Not included.

Prophetic Pictures

This chapter brings together some of the most silent women in our Old Testament. Two suffer abuse, two are skilled manual labourers, one is a prophetess.

The Prophetess

The nameless prophetess is one of five women prophets: Miriam, Deborah, Huldah, Noadiah and ... well, her. While it is clear that Isaiah has sex with her – she bears him a son – it is by no means clear that she is his wife. Perhaps she prefers to maintain her independence in a society where wives are possessions. She suffers the fate of anonymity so many women endure. Her words are unrecorded, her fate is undocumented. Yet Isaiah 8.3 names her a prophetess.

The Builders

Nehemiah also chooses not to afford women the luxury of names. Shallum's daughters labour with him, rebuilding the wall of Jerusalem. Since Nehemiah 4.14–23 tells us that all those working on the walls carried weapons, it seems likely these women were also armed. They do the same work as the men, their contribution is equal, but they are not named.

Lest we fall into the trap of thinking 'that was then', let us remember that to commemorate the first ordinations of women at Bristol Cathedral on 12 March 1994, a plaque was installed that bore the names not of those women but of the men who ordained them. A plaque bearing the names of the women was hung in 2022.

The Image of Exile

And so we come to two much trickier stories. The God of the Old Testament, at first sight, seems to have no compunction about brutalizing women. Frequently, the unfaithful people are compared to whores or adulterous wives. God tells Ezekiel, 'I am sending you to the people of Israel … a nation of rebels … impudent and stubborn' (Ezekiel 2.3–4). Ezekiel's message to the people includes one of the most brutal passages in the Bible (Ezekiel 16). Jerusalem is compared to an abandoned infant, its umbilical cord still intact, lying in blood and placental discharge. God commands her to survive in the hope she will honour this love (Ezekiel 16.4–6). Later, God reconnects with the adolescent girl – the essence of the story is that God marries her (Ezekiel 16.8–13). She is subsequently unfaithful, and God, now her husband, facilitates her public gang rape as punishment (Ezekiel 16.35–42). God's harshness continues. Although Ezekiel does not fail in his mission – the death of his wife does not interrupt his work (Ezekiel 24.18) – God decides to 'take' Ezekiel's wife (Ezekiel 24.16). One conservative website merrily tells us, 'The circumstances of Ezekiel's wife's death were divinely orchestrated, and her death was used by God to teach His people in captivity a lesson.'[1] God, it seems, kills her, despite God's own law forbidding murder (Exodus 20.13). Is she, then, expendable? To be sacrificed for her husband's ministry?

Let's be honest. I have no satisfactory defence of a god who would do such things. I am led, in fact, to conclude that God did not do them. The prophet perhaps uses a lengthy metaphor to make the people realize the gravity of their situation, 'to convince them that they had hit rock bottom, and that only YHWH could save them'.[2]

Prostitute or Promiscuous?

There is, it seems, no way of rescuing Gomer. Although most English Bible translations present her as a prostitute or a whore, Gale Yee tells us that the more accurate description is that she was promiscuous.[3] The difference between prostitution and promiscuity is important here, particularly in a patriarchal society. Prostitutes sell. Wives, by contrast, are sold. When Gomer acts the harlot, then, she takes an independence that is not hers. In a labour-intensive agricultural society, children, particularly boys, were imperative for survival. The importance of wives, as we see throughout the Old Testament, is their fecundity. Society was held together by an honour/shame system. Shame was seen as 'positive concern for one's reputation or honour'.[4] A man's honour was measured by his ability to provide for and defend his household, and his ability to sire children. A woman's shame (positive, remember) was embodied in modesty, meekness and deference to male authority. A man who did not show courage in defending his family, or a woman who was not sexually pure, would be shameless and shamed by the community. To a significant extent, a man's honour was linked with the sexual behaviour of mothers, wives and daughters. To maintain their honour, men kept the women of their households separate from other men, and restricted their social behaviour. If a woman was sexually shameless, her male relatives would be dishonoured. In Yee's words, 'adultery was therefore a first-class offence'. It violated men's rights over their wives' sexuality, and, worse, if she did bear a child, it put his paternity in doubt. Gomer's worst sin, then, is not her promiscuity but the fact that she undermines Hosea's honour. The rules for men are different. They were free to have sex outside of their marriages, unless they were caught, and only if the woman was married or engaged (Deuteronomy 22.23–29). Using prostitutes seems acceptable (Genesis 38.12–23; Joshua 2.1–7; 1 Kings 3.16–27).

For Wilda Gafney, Gomer's biggest sin is that she exercises control over her own sexuality, in a culture where women's sexuality was controlled by men.[5] The idea that promiscuity might be condoned seems problematic, but remember that, at the time, marriage was nothing more than a business transaction and did not relate to modern romantic schema in any way. Gomer's promiscuity challenges the patriarchal honour/shame culture, and demonstrates that men's control of her is illusory. Judging Gomer is a bit like judging the difference between a freedom fighter and a terrorist; it depends which side you are on. As a metaphor for God's relationship with God's people, perhaps Gomer's marriage to Hosea hints at the shame God feels when the people disobey.

Gomer has three children, Jezreel, which means 'God will sow', but is also the site of a bloody battle; Lo-Ruhamah, which means 'not loved' (NIV); and Lo-Ammi, which means 'not my people' (Hosea 1.4–8).[6] The names indicate the progressively worsening relationship between God and the people. Gafney finds the gap between Gomer's second and third child significant. Hosea 1.8 tells us, 'When she had weaned' Not-Loved, Gomer 'conceived and bore a son'. Gomer spent time breastfeeding and weaning her daughter. Despite the name the girl carries, her mother does love her. For Gafney, this is one place where we find the love of God in the story. Yee suggests a different resolution to the story. Chapter 14 *almost* proclaims the faithful love of God: 'I will love them freely, for my anger has turned from them' (Hosea 14.4). It is impossible to forget the wrath meted out to the wife before forgiveness is offered, such behaviour patterns are all too common.

The final verses of the prophecy finally seem to offer hope. They recall, I suggest, my first point, that Gomer's behaviour was challenging to male power in patriarchal culture. God says, 'I am like an evergreen cypress' (Hosea 14.8), and 'the ways of the LORD are right, and the upright walk in them' (14.9). In these verses, Yee argues, God becomes Woman Wisdom, from Proverbs 3.18. She concludes: 'For the wise and discerning, for the abused and the pained, God the husband gives way to the Wisdom of God, Woman Wisdom as the tree of life.'[7] For me, this is not necessarily a sexist point, that female is better than male. The contrast I want to make is between death and life, honour based on oppression and punishment, and life rooted in wisdom.

Sermon Suggestion (Based on Hosea 2.2–12 and 14.8–9): The Way the World Is

If you heard today's text as it was read, or if you have read it previously, and are now sitting back hoping for some good explanation of what it means, you are in the wrong place. If you have ever wondered why the Bible seems so sexist, and are looking for a defence of it, you are in the wrong place. If you are hoping that I am going to explain how to read the Bible in a way that is liberative for women, you are probably still in the wrong place. Maybe we should start with a prayer:

Wise and loving God,
whose incarnation means you share our flesh,
male and female.

give us wisdom and understanding,
faith and integrity
to hear something of you
from the scripture before us.

Let's get orientated.

Marriage at the time of this story had nothing to do with love. It was simply a business transaction – the wife was bought and sold. Unfaithfulness in marriage was very important, though. Because when a wife was unfaithful it showed her husband had lost control of her, and, by implication, of his household. In the minds of his community, this made the man nothing more than a woman.

So when God tells Hosea to marry an unfaithful wife, it is probably less about setting up the prophet for a life of heartbreak and more about setting him up for a life of shame. This, God seems to say, is how God feels when the people go astray. God's response sounds like something from a Jordan Peterson or Andrew Tate podcast: 'I will strip her naked and expose her ... I will punish her' (Hosea 2.3, 13). Is this really what God is like?

Gomer's children don't escape God's wrath either. Their names just get worse. The name of the first is ambivalent – it means 'God sows', but is also the name of a bloody battlefield. The second name is very clear – 'not loved'. And the third is 'not my people'. God seems to be turning away from the people.

What do we have so far? An unfaithful wife and a vindictive God. Not a great story. Perhaps, though, it is a story of the way the world is. What we see is violence and pain, but woven through it, imperceptibly, are strands of love. Black American preacher Wil Gafney notices that Gomer takes time to wean her daughter Not-Loved, caring for a girl whose name declares her unworthy of care.

In the middle of what reads like a text of toxic masculinity, though, I want to tentatively suggest something different. At the end of the prophecy, in chapter 14, God shows a different side of godly character. 'I am like an evergreen cypress; your faithfulness [fruit, ESV] comes from me' (Hosea 14.8). Compare that to the 'tree of life' in Proverbs 3.18. In the Proverbs text, God is Woman Wisdom. I am not making a sexist, pro-women, anti-men point here. The difference, I think, is between death- and life-dominated thinking. Death-dominated thinking calls for violence and punishment to maintain honour. Life calls for gentleness and uprightness to promote flourishing. If we want to live fruitful lives, we will not find it in self-defence, but in openness.

A poem from Martha Postlethwaite speaks movingly about openness. 'Clearing' has a simple yet profound message: stand still, make a space for yourself and wait patiently. Only as you hold space for yourself, a clearing in the 'dense forest' of life, can your song fall into your 'open cupped hands'. You will then know what gifts you might offer to this broken world – 'a world so worthy of rescue'. Standing in a clearing will not change the whole world but, by appreciating yourself, your gifts might help some of the people who receive them.

> ... create
> a clearing
> in the dense forest
> of your life
> and wait there
> patiently
> until the song
> ... falls into your open cupped hands.[8]

Homiletic Points

1 The threefold repetition of 'in the wrong place' emphasizes that the sermon is not simple fodder for those who want to sit back; it won't offer a simple explanation, a defence of biblical sexism or a means of easy liberative reading.
2 The sermon is a plea for the forming of godly character after the image of God rooted in Woman Wisdom flowing into life-focused thought.
3 The final quotation from the poem points to the importance of patience, openness and gentleness in the inner life.

Collect

God of life and love,
God of complexity,
bring us to that place where we wait on you.
To a place where we are open to you and to those around,
that we might live full and fruitful lives.
Amen.

Notes

1 'Why did God kill Ezekiel's wife?', https://www.gotquestions.org/Ezekiel-wife.html, accessed 02.10.23.

2 J. E. Lapsley, 'Ezekiel', in Carol A. Newsom, Sharon H. Ringe and Jacqueline E. Lapsley, *The Women's Bible Commentary* (London: SPCK, 2014), p. 289.

3 G. A. Yee, 'Hosea', in Newsom et al., *The Women's Bible Commentary*, pp. 299–304.

4 Yee, 'Hosea', p. 302.

5 Wil Gafney, 'When Gomer looks more like God', https://www.wilgafney.com/2018/09/24/when-gomer-looks-more-like-god/, accessed 02.10.23.

6 Yee, 'Hosea', p. 305

7 Yee, 'Hosea', p. 307.

8 Martha Postlethwaite, 'Create', in *Addiction and Recovery: A Spiritual Pilgrimage* (Minneapolis, MN: Fortress Press, 2019).

25

Interrupting Power:
Pilate's Wife

LIZ SHERCLIFF

<table>
<tr><td colspan="3">Pilate's Wife in the Revised Common Lectionary</td></tr>
<tr><td>Year A</td><td>Palm Sunday: Liturgy of
the Passion</td><td>Matthew 27.11–54</td></tr>
</table>

The Words of Pilate's Wife in the Bible

'Have nothing to do with that innocent man, for today I have suffered a great deal because of a dream about him.' (Matthew 27.19)

Her Story

Pilate's wife, Claudia Procula, is unnamed by Matthew, but stands in his line of unlikely women heroes. Matthew brackets Jesus' life with a genealogy that includes Tamar, Rahab, Ruth and Bathsheba, and a trial interrupted by Claudia (Matthew 1.1–16). Perhaps this is an indication that although women are few and little is said about them, they are essential to Jesus' story. Like the other women, as we have seen elsewhere in this book and its sister volume, we are free to read Claudia in several ways. In the early church Ambrose condemns Pilate for not taking notice of her, while Hilary of Poitiers absolves him because he *does* listen to her and washes his hands of the situation.[1] In the York medieval mystery plays she serves as a foil against which Pilate demonstrates his ruthless power;[2] for contemporary poet Carol Ann Duffy she is an admirer of the Galilean teacher she met previously on Palm Sunday.[3] For the Greek Orthodox,

Eastern and Ethiopian Churches Claudia Procula (or Proscura) is a saint.[4] Was she her husband's trusted confidante, accustomed to advising him, or did she find him despicable and weak?

Her Role in Matthew

It seems easy to regard this pericope as an unusual interruption to the story of Jesus' trial. We haven't met Pilate's wife previously, and she does not appear in other Gospels. But in Matthew she continues some significant themes. She is part of the Roman governor's household. She would probably have entertained Jewish religious leaders in her home; she must have come across Jesus, or stories about him, before. Her dream continues a Matthean theme: the magi are warned in a dream not to return to Herod (Matthew 2.12); Joseph is warned to flee to Egypt (Matthew 2.13); Joseph is told to return and settle in Galilee (Matthew 2.22). These dreams, like Claudia's, seem aimed at preserving Jesus' life.

Her Role in the Passion Narrative

Claudia stands in solidarity with servant girls and in contrast to powerful men in Matthew's passion narrative. After Jesus' arrest, two servant girls recognize Peter: 'You also were with Jesus' (Matthew 26.69, 71). Pilate's wife recognizes Jesus. Peter denies knowing Jesus, and departs, weeping bitterly (Luke 22.62–64). Pilate perhaps recognizes Jesus but will not intervene on his behalf. The religious leaders of the people recognize Jesus' challenge to their power and determine he must die (Matthew 26.3–4). Claudia recognizes Jesus and seeks to intervene, the sole voice of justice in a febrile situation.

This woman's brief appearance on the scene, and Pilate's response to her intervention, lead us to focus not on individual blame but on systemic corruption. It is not, in the end, the people or the priest or the politicians who are to blame, but the kind of thinking that supports and propagates systems of power – what we might call 'empire-think'. Disruptors are to be ignored or destroyed. The questions of the servant girls could have prompted Peter to courage, to stand by his friend. The intervention of Pilate's wife could have prompted Pilate to justice. But power is dispersed throughout political systems, and its flow is difficult to jam.

Pilate's Wife: Carol Ann Duffy

I enjoy Carol Ann Duffy's poem 'Pilate's Wife' for its portrayal of Jesus and his unexpected interaction with Claudia. The premise of the poem is that she despises her husband. Its themes include women's oppression (despite her position, Pilate's wife has no real influence) and toxic masculinity (Pilate demonstrates his power by having servants bring him grapes, and by washing his hands of Jesus' fate). To escape the boredom of the palace, Pilate's wife sneaks out with her maid into the city at Passover time. And there in 'the frenzied crowd' she looks up and sees Jesus:

> He looked at me. I mean he looked at *me*. My God.
> His eyes were to die for.[5]

The power of Jesus looking at a woman used to being ignored is palpable. It is a reminder for preachers not to ignore these fleeting but influential women.

Sermon Suggestion: The One Who Speaks Up

What follows is not a sermon per se, but a reflection I wrote as part of a Good Friday vigil. I decided to focus the three-hour service on women around the cross. The material was based in scripture, but imaginative and reflective.

> So after they had gathered, Pilate said to them, 'Whom do you want me to release for you, Jesus Barabbas or Jesus who is called the Messiah?' For he realized that it was out of jealousy that they had handed him over. While he was sitting on the judgement seat, his wife sent word to him, 'Have nothing to do with that innocent man, for today I have suffered a great deal because of a dream about him.' (Matthew 27.17–19)

Looking around this bleak hillside, I see Roman soldiers – and women.

The destructive might of empire, and the companionship of loving friends.

Among the faces of the women, looking up to Jesus as he suffers, I think I catch a glimpse of someone who is not Jewish.

Certainly not a Galilean.

In fact, I think she is Roman. By her bearing she is important, and the dress she tries to hide beneath a maid's cloak betrays her aristocratic standing.

She's been seen before. About a week ago. She sneaked into Jerusalem with her maid, just to get away from the oppressive atmosphere of the governor's palace, to experience the life of the city. As she wandered its streets she heard shouting, a great crowd by the sound of it. She followed the noise and came across some Galileans waving palm branches and celebrating a local hero of some sort – a Galilean too. He was riding a donkey, as though he was an emperor. As a Roman woman the sight shook her. But then she caught his eye, and the look he gave her saw into her soul. She was known. Not by Roman spies sent to keep an eye on her. Not by her maids ready to jump to fulfil her every wish. Known by this Galilean man, 'Son of David', in a way she did not understand.

I think she is here because of a dream. Last night she dreamt of this man on the cross. She saw skewered hands and blood; she saw the crown of thorns, the whips and the mockery. She sent a note to her husband, just then entertaining chief priests and scribes, lording it over some insignificant itinerant preacher they wanted to be rid of.

Leave him alone, she wrote.

But Pilate called for water, rolled up his sleeves, and washed his hands. He would not be guilty of this innocent death. He would not come near it either.

But I think I see Pilate's wife here among the women at the foot of the cross.

The only person to try to intervene in this miscarriage of justice. The only person to try to stop Pilate from condemning Jesus to death.

I think she is here.

Was this man God? I think Pilate's wife believes he was.

Homiletic Points

1 The piece is an imaginative reflection which places Pilate's wife at the foot of the cross. It's an exploration of where her dream and insight might have taken her.
2 The preacher imagines the root of her dream in an actual encounter with Christ – who truly sees her.
3 The point is made that she is the only person who intervenes to try to stop the unfolding events that lead to Jesus' death.
4 The imagined idea of Pilate's wife at the cross implicitly asks us to consider Jesus' effect on people. She experienced the dream – what else happened for her? Christ affects people across cultural boundaries and affiliations.

Collect

Loving God, Lord Jesus,
as we remember Pilate's wife,
the one who sought to protect you
from the ruthless religious, the politically perceptive,
the corrupted crowd:
help us to be like her,
to defend the oppressed,
and seek justice for the persecuted,
in spite of the risks.
In the name of the one who had courage
even to die.
Amen.

Notes

1 R. Van der Bergh, 'The reception of Matthew 27:19b (Pilate's wife's dream) in the Early Church', *Journal of Early Christian History*, Vol. 2 (2012), pp. 70–85.

2 K. Fonzo, 'Procula's civic body and Pilate's masculinity crisis in the York Cycle's Christ before Pilate 1: the dream of Pilate's wife', *Early Theatre* (2013), pp. 11–32.

3 Carol Ann Duffy, 'Pilate's wife', in *The World's Wife*, new edn (London: Picador, 2017).

4 See https://www.oca.org/saints/lives/2014/10/27/103070-saint-claudia-procula, accessed 07.10.23.

5 Duffy, 'Pilate's wife'.

26

Daughters of Dysfunction:
Herodias and Salome

KATE BRUCE

Herodias and Salome in the Revised Common Lectionary (Sundays)		
Year C	Proper 9 (CW)	Mark 6.7–29 (CW, SS)
Year B	Proper 10 (CW)	Mark 6.14–29 (CW, PS)

The Words of Herodias and Salome in the Bible

She [Salome] went out and said to her mother, 'What should I ask for?' She [Herodias] replied, 'The head of John the baptizer.' Immediately she rushed back to the king and requested, 'I want you to give me at once the head of John the Baptist on a platter.' (Mark 6.24–25)

Prompted by her mother, she said, 'Give me the head of John the Baptist here on a platter.' (Matthew 14.8)

Background to the Story

'The family tree of the Herods is extraordinarily complex, and full of incestuous relationships',[1] not to mention murders. They were a dysfunctional lot! Understanding their family history is not helped by their fondness for naming offspring 'Herod'.

Herod the Great, the same Herod whom the magi approached concerning the whereabouts of the King of the Jews (Matthew 2.1–15), had ten wives and multiple offspring. The Herodian dynastic propensity for violence is clear in him:

When Herod saw that he had been tricked by the wise men, he was infuriated, and he sent and killed all the children in and around Bethlehem who were two years old or under, according to the time that he had learned from the wise men.' (Matthew 2.16)

He murdered his wife, Mariamne I (Herodias' grandmother), in 28 BC, out of jealousy and fear of her family. He also had three of his sons executed, driven by rivalry.[2] He placed a Roman eagle above the Temple gate, understandably offending the Jews, and then had those who pulled it down put to death. Wanting to ensure that he would be mourned at his passing, as he lay dying he filled the Jericho stadium with influential and loved people who were to be executed at the moment of his death.[3] Thankfully, his wishes were not carried out, but the plan chimes with all we know of the man. A glance at the wider family confirms the proverb that the apple doesn't fall far from the tree.

Three of Herod the Great's sons are relevant to the background of this story. Aristobulus, Herod Antipas (also known as Herod the Tetrach) and Herod Philip I were half-brothers. Aristobulus had a daughter, Herodias. She was married to her half-uncle, Herod Philip I, and they had a daughter, Salome. Salome married Philip II (also known as Philip the Tetrarch – see Luke 3.1). All very confusing!

Herod Antipas was married to the daughter of Aretus, King of Arabia. On a visit to his half-brother Philip, Herod and Herodias began an affair. Half-uncle and half-niece schemed to divorce their respective spouses and marry. Herod's wife got wind of the plan and told her father. Furious at Herod's behaviour, he declared war on Herod and destroyed his army.[4] Meanwhile, Herod and Herodias married, which did not go down well with the Jewish community – disapproval voiced publicly by John the Baptist.

Mark's Account: The Cost of Speaking Truth to Power

Mark frames his account of the death of John the Baptist with the sending out of the Twelve and their return. This gives a sense of time passing, and highlights the potential cost of discipleship. John speaks truth to power and the consequences are grim.

Above the great west door of Westminster Abbey are statues memorializing ten modern martyrs who also died for speaking truth to power. Many of the names are well known, such as Dietrich Bonhoeffer, Oscar Romero and Janani Luwum. Among them is a lesser-known figure,

Manche Masemola, a young woman of the Pedi tribe, in the Transvaal, born around 1913. She was determined to pursue her Christian education. Her parents, fearing she would refuse to marry, or leave them, tried to prevent this by regularly beating her. Finally, they murdered her in 1928. In each of the stories of these martyrs the same thread emerges – speaking truth to power is costly.[5]

Mark's account takes the form of a flashback. Herod, on hearing Jesus was performing powerful deeds and influencing his disciples to do the same, fears that Jesus is John the Baptist, whom he had beheaded, raised from the dead. This is the first the reader knows of John's fate at Herod's hands. The flashback fills in the missing details. We learn that Herod imprisoned John because he 'had been telling (*elegen*) Herod, "It is not lawful for you to have your brother's wife"' (Mark 6.18). The verb *elegen* is continuous; John had raised the matter with Herod many times. In marrying his brother's wife, Herod Antipas contravened Jewish law (see Leviticus 18.16; 20.21). Herodias was particularly affronted by John's criticism and, like Jezebel with Elijah, she was fixed on revenge (1 Kings 19.1–2), but was unable to enact it:

> for Herod feared John, knowing that he was a righteous and holy man, and he protected him. When he heard him, he was greatly perplexed; and yet he liked to listen to him.' (Mark 6.19–20)

Like Pilate with Jesus (Matthew 27.11–14; Mark 15.2–5), Herod is troubled and fascinated by John. It is likely that John was a source of conflict between Herod and Herodias. If Herod listened to John, Herodias' position would be in jeopardy. Under the same roof, Salome must have been aware of this tension. Maybe Herodias confided her fears and her desire to be rid of John to her daughter. By imprisoning John, Herod prevents the fulfilment of Herodias' murderous intent – until the birthday banquet.

Disturbing Dancing and a Blunt Demand

Notice that Herod's birthday banquet is a male gathering consisting of influential Galilean leaders (Mark 6.21). Even Herodias is not directly present, but in another room. Herod has his stepdaughter (also his half-niece) brought in to delight the male gaze. Salome's dance is a disturbing matter. She pleased Herod and his guests. In what way? Given the context, it is unlikely to have been the dance of a small child, watched by kindly adults. Rita Hayworth in *Salome* (1954) performed the dance as a strip tease. It may have been some form of belly dance. Whether or not she had any choice in the matter, Salome is able to dance in such a way as to gain influence over Herod. 'She pleased Herod and his guests' (6.22) and he twice offers her gifts in return: '"Ask me for whatever you wish, and I will give it."' And he solemnly swore to her, "Whatever you ask me, I will give you, even half of my kingdom"' (vv. 22–23).

But Herod is not a king. Mark is mistaken in this, or perhaps uses the title 'king' because that is local custom. However, Herod is Tetrarch, a governor subordinate to Rome. He has no kingdom to give away. His oath is probably a sign of drunken largesse on show for the influential gathering.

Salome consults her mother, who sees the opportunity to finish John. The demand for his head is brutal, vicious and cunning. It will send a powerful message to all who try to stand in the way of Herod: don't criticize the powers if you want to keep your head. To behead John is to dishonour him, and inflict deep pain on his friends and followers. In Mark's narrative it looks as though Salome herself adds the detail of demanding the head 'on a platter' (v. 25). It seems both mother and daughter are profoundly dysfunctional people.

Despite being grieved by the request (v. 26), Herod complies, not wishing to lose face. He is spineless – unable to act against his wife's desire for revenge. He dispatches a soldier immediately to behead John and bring his severed head on a platter for Salome. The casual violence is breathtaking. The picture is sickening. Without comment Salome hands the platter her mother (v. 29).

Mark's account ends with the line, 'When his disciples heard about it, they came and took his body, and laid it in a tomb.' John's head is never accounted for. The reference to his body being laid in a tomb points us ahead to Jesus' fate.

Differences in Matthew's Account: Position in the Narrative

John's murder is in a different place in Matthew's narrative. In the immediate run-up Matthew places the parable of the sower and various parables of the kingdom, and then Jesus stating that 'Prophets are not without honour except in their own country and in their own house' (Matthew 13.18–57). These passages affect our interpretation of the subsequent story. The seeds John scatters in Herod's life fall on shallow and thorny ground (13.5–7). The kingdom of heaven is something valuable to be treasured (13.44–45), but the 'kingdom' of Herod is a toxic, brutal place where John the Baptist is certainly shown no honour. Matthew follows the account with Jesus withdrawing on hearing of John's death, before healing and feeding those who sought him (13.13–21). In grief, Jesus makes space for himself to mourn, before providing for others.

Differences Within the Narrative

The portrait of Herod we are offered by Matthew has no redeeming features. There is no reference to Herod protecting John from the scheming Herodias. Matthew tells us Herod wants John dead but was afraid of the crowd because they saw John as a prophet (14.5). Josephus makes the same point.[6] Given Herod wanted John dead it is hard to see why he was grieved when Salome asked for John's head (14.9), unless the grief is linked to fear for his own position should John's followers rise up. The Romans wouldn't be impressed!

Matthew gives us no sense of Herod fearing John or being interested in him (cf. Mark 6.20). We are not told who the company at the party are (cf. Mark 6.21), nor do we get the narrative tension of the offer of a gift being made twice to Salome, nor the reference to half the kingdom, although Herod does swear an oath in both accounts (Matthew 14.7; Mark 6.22–23). In Matthew the demand for the head being on a platter is made by Herodias not Salome (cf. Matthew 14.8; Mark 6.24–25).

Matthew's account doesn't feature in the Sunday lectionary, possibly because Mark's has more detail and pace.

Sermon Suggestion: Evil Does Not Have the Last Word

The murder of John the Baptist is not the most obvious passage for an uplifting sermon! Here is a gruesome tale of dysfunctional relationships and casual violence. It comes in the middle of a section of Mark's Gospel chock full of miraculous stories. The days painted by Mark seem to pulse with energy, life and amazing possibility. Jesus calms the storm, heals a deeply disturbed man in the region of the Gerasene, restores the woman who had haemorrhaged for 12 years, and raises Jairus' daughter from death, The Twelve are sent out and perform miraculous healing. Energy, life and amazing possibility seem to leap off the pages of the Gospel. After the account of John's death, we read of the feeding of the 5,000 and of Jesus walking on water and of more healings in the area of Gennesaret.

Slap bang in the middle of all that life and amazing possibility there is this hideous smear of brutality bleeding across the page; a story of dysfunction writ large.

What is it doing here?

Let's look more closely.

Picture a cinema screen.

The film rolls.

The silhouette of a man is central.

The soundtrack plays. Voices:

'Who is this man?'

'He heals.'

'He has authority.'

'Who is this man?'

'It's John the Baptist raised from death.'

'No, it's Elijah.'

'He's one of the prophets of old.'

Voices demanding: 'Who is he? Who is he? Who is he?'

A new voice cuts in. Herod Antipas:

'It's John the Baptizer. I had him beheaded. But he's come back from death.'

Fade to black.

Words come up on the screen: 'Sometime earlier' …

A party. We hear music, laughter, the raucous conversation of the hopelessly wine sodden. We see men eating, drinking, laughing and leering at a young girl who dances before them. Not just any girl. This is Herod's step-daughter dancing at his birthday party – an all-male affair. The context suggests this is not the dance of a small child, watched by kindly adults.

The camera focuses in on Herod, his face reddened with over-indulgence. He licks greasy fingers and surveys with satisfaction the success of his birthday celebration. Another man nudges him and tips his head at the girl. Herod nods. All eyes on the girl.

Herod gulps his drink, wipes his mouth, and gestures to the young woman who sashays over to him, all smiles and sinuous movement. Desperate to please. The camera zooms in on Herod. He throws back his head, wine drenched and delighted with her performance:

'Girl, whatever you want, ask, it's yours.'

The men lean in, hungry.

'Anything,' he gestures expansively, winking to the gathered crowd, 'up to half my kingdom. It's yours.'

The man to Herod's left splutters and coughs, spraying half-eaten food across the table ...

The girl rushes from the room.

The camera follows. Menacing music builds.

Close up: two women. Head-to-head. A hushed conversation. The older woman throws back her head in triumph, 'Herod dare not back down; not in the presence of those guests. I want the Baptist's head.'

Cut to black.

What are we to make of this terrible story? What's it doing here?

Goodness and evil sit cheek by jowl in Mark's narrative, reflecting a wider truth. Evil lurks nearby. We see it all the time. Just cast your mind to the latest world news – images of war, accounts of abuse, corruption in high office ... We might easily feel utterly dejected by this, but the account of John the Baptist's death in the context of Mark's narrative reminds us that while darkness lurks and has its effect, the light always has the final word. John's death and burial point us on to the death and burial of Jesus – that burial becomes a doorway to the truth that death is ultimately defeated. 'The light shines in the darkness, and the darkness did not overcome it' (John 1.5). However, we must beware an unseemly dash for Easter hope since this will mute the cry of suffering. The account of John's murder takes the reality of evil, in all its guises, seriously.

There is an uncomfortable undertone here. The step-daughter of an influential man performs a dance for a male-only group of powerful leaders and is offered gifts for her services. In our context this should have safeguarding alarm bells ringing. What is going on here? The dance raises questions of power, choice and consent. What's happening for Salome? The hints are all there.

Salome could go to town with Herod's offer of a gift, lining her pockets. She doesn't. She goes to consult her mother: 'What should I ask for?' There is a bond here – though not a particularly healthy one. Salome doesn't baulk at her mother's demand for the head of John the Baptist. There is no sense of shock, revulsion or resistance. She simply complies, taking the message to Herod, adding in her own detail – she wants the head 'on a platter' (Mark 6.24–25). Perhaps Salome complies because she is loyal and wants to protect her mother from John the Baptist, who has condemned her marriage to Herod? Perhaps she adds in the platter detail in a twisted attempt to please her mother? Salome's perception and judgement are distorted. Evil insinuates itself into the fractures in human relationships. Given Salome's family history this is hardly surprising.

Theirs is a deeply dysfunctional dynasty. Herodias hated John because he spoke against her marriage. Herod should not have taken his brother's wife. Throw into the mix that Herod is also Herodias' half-uncle and she left a different half-uncle to be with Herod and we start to get a flavour of this family. Herodias' grandfather, Herod the Great, was the same Herod who decreed that all the Jewish male babies under two should be killed in an attempt to wipe out the infant Jesus. He also had Herodias' grandmother killed, and bumped off two of his sons. Toxic dysfunction runs through this family – incest, rivalry and violence, an unholy trinity which leads directly to the brutal death of John, Jesus' cousin, because he spoke truth to power.

There is no reflection or self-awareness in any of these characters. No humility.

Herodias ruminates, feeding her grudge, stoking the fire of her hatred of John. John's truth-telling threatens her position and uncovers her guilt. Herod grieves Herodias' request – but he still complies, too arrogant to stand down. He dispatches a soldier there and then to murder John. Evil sets a swift and unreflective pace. Salome rushes between her mother and step-father (Mark 6.25) – perhaps simultaneously trying to please Herod and protect her mother? No one protects Salome.

Salome requests John's head on a platter. No one intervenes. No one expresses horror. As a popular quote says, 'For evil to flourish, it only requires good people to do nothing.' The goodness of John the Baptist is snuffed out on a whim and no one objects. Salome is presented with a dismembered head on a plate. Not one guest intervenes. Evil silences through fear. Does Salome present the platter to her mother as a gift, or give it away as soon as she can? We can only guess. Salome's family environment has normalized brutality. Salome, and Herodias before her, and Herod too, have grown up in the unhealthy context of an incestuous and violent family. It is toxic, dysfunctional and deeply unsafe.

What are we to make of this story? What is it doing here?

It raises the question, does such abhorrent evil have the last word? We need to read the gospel as a whole to see the answer is no, but on the journey to that final answer there is much to mourn. What does Jesus do when he hears news of John's death? He withdraws. This is most explicit in Matthew's account, for when Jesus heard the news of John 'he withdrew from there in a boat to a deserted place by himself' (14.13). This time away offers him space to reflect, pray and begin to mourn.

There is so much to mourn in the story of John the Baptist's murder. Principally, John's life has been cut short in a vicious, cunning and unjust attack. A man of God cut down by evil forces. His death comes as a direct result of intergenerational, toxic dysfunctionality. But there is more still to mourn.

Look – there is Herod – who had recognized the holiness in John but failed to respond. Although grieved by Herodias' desire for John's life, he fails to intervene – he simply goes along with it. He had the opportunity to attend to John's words but, ultimately, he stopped John's tongue. What might have been, had he actively listened?

Look – there is Herodias scrabbling for power, fully aware of the fate of her grandmother, murdered at her grandfather's hand. She has learned no compassion, but been shaped by the sins of her forebears, capable of vengeful, vicious acts. The dysfunctionality trickles down through the generations. What if someone had helped Herodias change the script?

Look – there is Salome, using the power she has to try to influence. She is a young woman paraded before a room full of men, probably not for the first time, groomed with praise and gift. A young woman bounced between the adults in her life, trying to please, copying the patterns she has been taught. What if someone had offered her a different way?

As Jesus mourns his cousin's murder, he faces into the consequences of the sin that has run rife through Herod's dynasty, handed down from generation to generation. He is caught up in the cost of dysfunctionality, not immune to it. He is inside the pain of the world – a man of sorrows and compassion. He understands.

The circumstances of John's death foreshadow Jesus' own. He too will be caught up in a web of toxicity – betrayed by the kiss of a friend, arrested, interrogated and bounced about by the powers of the day before dying a horrifying death (Mark 14.45—15.39). However, the difference is clear. John's body remains in the tomb, but as the young man in white tells the terrified women at the end of Mark's Gospel:

'Do not be alarmed; you are looking for Jesus of Nazareth, who was crucified. He has been raised; he is not here. Look, there is the place they laid him. But go, tell his disciples and Peter that he is going ahead of you to Galilee; there you will see him, just as he told you.' (Mark 16.6–7)

Whatever we face, like the women, we must seek Jesus who is waiting to be found, waiting to minister to the dysfunction, abuse and pain of the world. Like the women at the end of Mark, we might be afraid, but that changes nothing.

The presence of the account of the death of John the Baptist at the hands of Herod and his dysfunctional dynasty does two things.

1 It tells us that Jesus knows the reality of evil in his own personal life. He is a man of sorrows and compassion.

2 It points us forward to his overcoming of that evil in resurrection. He is the source of all hope.

> Picture a cinema screen. The silhouette of a man is central.
> The soundtrack plays. Voices:
> 'Who is this man?'
> 'He heals.'
> 'He has authority.'
> 'Who is this man?'
> 'It's John the Baptist raised from death.'
> 'No, it's Elijah.'
> 'He's one of the prophets of old.'
> Voices demanding: 'Who is he? Who is he? Who is he?'
> New voices cut in:
> 'It's Jesus our brother.'
> 'He breaks the cycle of dysfunction.'
> 'Comforter of the abused.'
> 'Companion in the IT unit.'
> 'The silent embrace at the graveside.'
> 'Light in the darkness.'
> 'Hope in the present.'
> 'Hope for the future.'
> 'The transforming power of God with us.'
> 'Messiah, Risen One.'
> Fade to white.

Homiletic Points

1 Narrative flow: the sermon begins by looking at the presence of the account of John's death in the narrative flow in Mark, noting the contrast between the mood of that story and the themes of the surrounding material. This leads into the question, 'What is this story doing?' This is the driving question behind the sermon.

2 Appeal to imagination: once this question has been established the sermon is framed by imagining the events unfold on a cinema screen. This allows the preacher to recap some of the key issues in the passage at the outset, as well as handle the flashback in the narrative and widen the vision of the sermon at the end. Notice the actual murder of John is not included in the cinematic phase. This is deliberate – to avoid being unnecessarily explicit.

3 Pastoral awareness: the sermon explores the nature of evil as portrayed in the passage, mentioning intergenerational dysfunctionality, violence and abuse. The latter theme is handled gently, exploring in broad terms the issues of consent and grooming, without being too explicit – aware of the triggering nature of the topic. However, the sermon does not shy away from the abusive undertones of the passage. These need naming.

4 The sermon imagines Jesus as he withdraws after hearing the news of John's death, making the point that Jesus, while mourning John, is affected by the dysfunctionality of this family. This points to a man of sorrows and compassion, acquainted with suffering.

5 The question underpinning the sermon, concerning the purpose of the story, is answered explicitly, in a way that is pastorally rich and theologically grounded in hope.

Collect

Jesus, man of sorrows, we pray for all who grieve,
who know the cost of violence, injustice or abuse.
May those who suffer, know your compassion,
your understanding and your deep love.
Grant to those trapped in dysfunctional situations,
wise and caring intervention and the offer of new pathways.
Give to all who despair a new vision of your resurrection hope,
overcoming darkness with goodness and light.
Amen.

Notes

1 Morna Hooker, *The Gospel According to St Mark* (London: A&C Black Ltd, 1991), p. 160.

2 See https://www.notablebiographies.com/He-Ho/Herod-the-Great.html, accessed 28.04.22.

3 See https://www.thattheworldmayknow.com/herods-family, accessed 24.04.22.

4 Josephus, *Antiquities* XVIII, 5.2. *The Antiquities of the Jews*, by Flavius Josephus, gutenberg.org, accessed 24.04.22.

5 See https://www.westminster-abbey.org/about-the-abbey/history/modern-martyrs, accessed 29.02.22.

6 Now when [many] others came in crowds about him [John], for they were very greatly moved [or pleased] by hearing his words, Herod, who feared lest the great influence John had over the people might put it into his power and inclination to

raise a rebellion, [for they seemed ready to do anything he should advise,] thought it best, by putting him to death, to prevent any mischief he might cause, and not bring himself into difficulties, by sparing a man who might make him repent of it when it would be too late. Josephus, *Antiquities* XVIII, 5.2.

27

She Answered Back:
The Syrophoenician Woman

LIZ SHERCLIFF

The Syrophoenician Woman in the Revised Common Lectionary

NB Matthew refers to this woman as a Canaanite, while Mark calls her a Syrophoenician.

| Year A | Proper 15 (OT 20) | Matthew 15.10–28 |
| Year B | Proper 18 (OT 23) | Mark 7.24–37 |

The Syrophoenician Woman's Words in the Bible

'Have mercy on me, Lord, Son of David; my daughter is tormented by a demon.' (Matthew 15.22)

'Lord, help me.' (Matthew 15.25)

'Yes, Lord, yet even the dogs eat the crumbs that fall from their masters' table.' (Matthew 15.27)

'Sir, even the dogs under the table eat the children's crumbs.' (Mark 7.28)

The Syrophoenician Woman's Story

Where was she from?

Mark (7.26) says the woman was from Syria Phoenicia. Phoenicians were city dwellers who lived around the Mediterranean. One population centre was in Tyre, a coastal town in present-day Lebanon. They were an ancient Semitic people related to the Canaanites.[1] Mark underlines the woman's non-Jewish nationality by introducing her as a Gentile (7.26). Matthew uses an older, and perhaps more deprecatory, term. To him she was a Canaanite, of a nationality traditionally regarded as anti-Israel (15.22). Mark, then, locates her more specifically, and racially, while Matthew identifies her simply as 'not one of us'.

What does she do?

Both Gospel writers tell us that Jesus has gone to an area somewhere near Tyre. They tell the rest of the story slightly differently:

Matthew 15.10–28	Mark 7.24–37
A Canaanite woman from the region comes and starts shouting (15.22).	Jesus is in need of a break (he goes away); he doesn't 'want anyone to know' where he is (7.24).
Jesus apparently ignores her (15.23).	
His disciples tell him to get rid of her (15.23).	Nevertheless, the woman notices (apparently enters the house) and bows at Jesus' feet (7.25).
Jesus attempts to do so: 'I was sent only to the lost sheep of the house of Israel' (15.24).	She begs Jesus to cast the demons out of her daughter (7.26).
The woman comes before Jesus, kneels and asks for help: 'Lord, help me' (15.25).	Jesus rebuffs her: 'Let the children be fed [first],[2] for it is not fair to take the children's food and throw it to the dogs' (7.27).
Jesus again rebuffs her: 'It is not fair to take the children's food and throw it to the dogs' (15.26).	She responds 'Sir, even the dogs under the table eat the children's crumbs' (7.28).
She responds: 'Yes, Lord, yet even the dogs eat the crumbs that fall from their masters' table' (15.27).	Jesus answers: 'For saying that, you may go – the demon has left your daughter' (7.29).
Jesus answers: 'Woman, great is your faith! Let it be done for you as you wish' (15.28).	And when she went home, she found the child lying on the bed and the demon gone.
The daughter is healed from that moment.	

Whatever the detail, the basic story seems to be that Jesus goes into the region of Tyre. A woman of the area finds him and asks him to heal her daughter. Jesus initially rebuffs her and insults her. She argues back and Jesus changes his mind. What are we to make of this story?

Romanticized Versions

Of all the tricky stories in the Gospels, this one seems to throw up some unique problems. An online search of sermons on either passage shows a tendency among preachers to divert our attention away from the main problem. 'Jesus already knew what he was going to do, he just wanted to test (take your pick from) the disciples/the woman/both.' The problem with this exegetical move is that it removes the woman's agency. She is incidental to the story. If Jesus is just using her to teach his disciples, he fails to treat her as a real person with a real problem. Another tactic is to make the woman an example of a persistent, prayerful mother. Again, her personhood is obscured and she becomes simply a motif. I read the passage with a group of women ordinands, who desperately wanted to rescue Jesus from the mess he seems to have got himself in. But there really is no avoiding the impression that in this story, with this woman, Jesus is both rude and racist! How else can we read it?

The Outsider Helps Jesus Clarify His Mission

To mine the riches of this story we need to broaden our focus. How do we understand not just Jesus but the woman too? How do we interpret the interaction between them? Ben Witherington suggests that Jesus has gone to the region near Tyre to escape the Pharisees, having just dismissed the most important aspect of Jewish law, purity.[3] The woman is an intrusion. Worse, bowing down, included in both Gospels, is only a sign of respect, according to Myers,[4] when one man bows to another. This impure, Gentile woman brings disgrace on Jesus immediately after his argument about purity. Perhaps Jesus' own sense of mission is challenged here. Hisako Kinukawa suggests the incident offers Jesus an opportunity to change his mind,[5] perhaps based on his own arguments in the earlier incident. The brief exchange about dogs shows cultural difference between Jesus and the woman. Francis Dufton writes: 'The Jews were not pet-lovers. To them dogs were the dirty, unpleasant and savage animals which roamed the streets in packs.[6] It was, therefore, an appropriate word for Jews to use of outsiders. However, the woman switches what Jesus says to refer to house dogs – in his culture, bread would have to be thrown from the window because the dogs were on the street, not under the table, where house dogs dwell. The word used in the story, is not dogs, however, but puppies. Vincent Taylor suggests that this not only softens what Jesus says, but also betrays the fact that he is in two minds 'about the scope of his ministry ... he is speaking to himself as well as to the woman ... Her reply shows that she is quick to perceive this.'[7] Alec Burkill, too, credits the woman with insight and foresight, understanding Jesus as Lord of the Gentiles as well as the Jews.[8] This woman, then, aids Jesus in the further understanding of his mission. In the end, he resists patriarchal and racial dominance to engage with a woman on the periphery.[9]

Reading from Underneath

Perhaps the best understanding of this story comes from those who can empathize with the woman. 'The story of the Syrophoenician woman is disturbing to me ... seeing how Jesus attributes secondary-ness to someone,' writes Surekh Nelavala, a Dalit theologian. 'Several aspects of my identity as a person from the third world, a Dalit, a Christian from India, and a woman, shape the questions, fears and hope prompted by this story.'[10] Nelavala contrasts Dalit women with the Syrophoenician woman. Both are unclean, one through caste and birth, the other through nationality. Both approach the men politely, both are humiliated and rejected. Hope comes because, in the end, the Syrophoenician woman gets what she asks for. Nelavala, like Kinukawa, reads the story of the Syrophoenician woman as a moment of transformation in Jesus' ministry. His argument with the Pharisees seems like a stepping-stone on the way from narrow exclusivism to including even the lowest and most despised. 'The evangelizer ultimately was evangelized.'[11] Who is this woman who changes Jesus' mind, or at last affirms his inclusive ministry? A Gentile, a woman and a social outcast;[12] a forerunner of Gentile Christian women.[13] At her insistence, Jesus moves from the patriarchal centre to the margins, where he realizes that his mission is to the whole world.[14]

Dalits have declared loudly and clearly over the years that they are not impure and that they are equal to others,[15] but without the oppressors' willingness to change, the protests of the oppressed are in vain. Jesus' readiness to listen to the Syrophoenician woman, weigh her argument and change his position is crucial to his offer of justice. One significance of the story for Nelavala is that Jesus shows those of us who are privileged or powerful exactly how we should behave when our prejudice is confronted by those who are its victims.

Sermon Suggestion: Embarrassing Jesus

This is awkward, isn't it? I really wanted him to make a good impression. I want people to like him, to listen to him. He says so many good things. Like, 'It's from the heart that evil comes,' and, 'Unwashed hands don't make you as dirty as your attitudes.' I can relate to that, I like it when Jesus takes down the hypocrites. When he challenges them, the Pharisees in particular, the ordinary people, like me and you, warm to him. So it's a bit awkward that just as we are beginning to like him, this situation arises.

A foreigner, a woman, a Gentile, a mother, a nobody finds out where Jesus is, and comes to see him. She even has the audacity to behave like a man, bowing before him as though she has any social position that could offer respect to a Jewish man. Very awkward.

Immediately, Jesus does the right thing. He gives her the brush-off. 'I haven't come for you lot,' he says. 'I've come for the children, not the dogs.' His disciples breathe a sigh of relief. No big debate is brewing. This won't be like the showdown with the Pharisees. The woman is an embarrassment, but that's all. Anyway, why would a Jewish man, a rabbi at that, listen to her, a nobody?

But the woman doesn't go. She argues back! 'Even the dogs get fed, though,' she says.

Jesus stops in his tracks. His face clouds for a moment. He is pensive. Is he remembering his recent debate about purity with the Pharisees? Is he thinking about his mission? Wondering whether he could be sent to Gentiles – and women – as well as the house of Israel? We can never know that, of course. A moment later he is resolved. He speaks to the woman, commends her insight, promises that her daughter is released: 'For saying that, you may go – the demon has left your daughter.'

I did, I do, want you to love Jesus. Not because you approve of him, or accept him, though. He's awkward. He doesn't do what we expect.

I didn't want you to like the woman. Not really. She's rude, she isn't one of us, and her arguing with Jesus complicates things for us. Does he really insult her? Can he genuinely have repeated racist slurs? That's awkward.

I didn't want you to like the woman. But I do hope you agree with her.

I don't know whether she heard about Jesus' argument with the

Pharisees or not. But it looks as though consciously or unconsciously she gives Jesus the opportunity of putting into practice what he's just said. 'It's the things that come from inside a person that defile them,' he said. 'It isn't their race or their gender or their social status, it's what's inside.' His natural, in-built, human instinct is to recoil from this woman – a foreign female, with a demon-possessed daughter, multipli unclean. But her challenge to him makes him pause and reflect.

This is an awkward Gospel reading. Many have tried to make sense of it. I wonder whether the best understanding might come from those who share in the woman's experiences. We want to rescue Jesus from an embarrassing situation. But for those on the margins, along with this woman, the story is filled with hope. Because the person in power here, the man Jesus, breaks through the 'us' and 'them' dynamic of societies then and now, and offers justice.

How ready are we, I wonder, to hear the cries of the outcasts, the oppressed, the poor and the needy. It may be awkward, but Jesus has modelled it for us.

Homiletic Points

1 The sermon wrestles honestly with the awkwardness of the passage. The problem is named at the outset, which creates tension and interest; how will the preacher address this?

2 The opening move is framed with the word 'awkward' – which sums up this tricky passage.

3 Jesus' initial interaction with the woman and her response are placed together, before the preacher offers us a linguistic close-up on Jesus' face at the point where his thinking begins to change, as he connects his earlier purity teaching with his interaction with her.

4 The sermon lands with a reiteration of the awkward nature of the reading and the observation that for those who are oppressed and marginalized, the reading is a source of hope because Jesus, the person with power, connects with the woman who argues back.

5 The specific example is broadened out to point to the God who reaches out and offers justice and the call for us to do likewise.

Collect

God of the awkward,
we give thanks for the words of this Syrophoenician woman,
so ready to question the prejudices of her day –
even when apparently expressed by Jesus:
give us courage to challenge injustice,
and humility to hear the cries of the oppressed.
Convict us and the whole church
so that we are willing to hear
and to act for justice.
Amen.

Notes

1 C. Setzer, 'The Syrophoenician woman', https://www.bibleodyssey.org/arti
cles/the-syrophoenician-woman/, accessed 23.05.22.

2 Some commentators, e.g. T. A. Burkill ('The historical development of the
story of the Syrophoenician woman' (*Novum Testamentun*, Vol. 9 (1967), p. 109)
and Bultmann (*The History of the Synoptic Tradition*, Oxford: Blackwell, 1963)
argue that Mark added the word 'first' because he was writing to a church of both
Jews and Gentiles. Bultmann argues that by using the word, Jesus would have been
weakening his argument.

3 B. Witherington III, *Women in the Ministry of Jesus* (Cambridge: Cambridge
University Press, 1987), pp. 63–4.

4 C. Myers, *Binding the Strong Man: a Political Reading of Mark's Story of
Jesus*, 20th anniversary edn (Maryknoll, NY: Orbis Books, 2008), p. 203.

5 H. Kinukawa, *Women and Jesus in Mark: A Japanese Feminist Perspective*
(Eugene, OR: Wipf and Stock, 2003), pp. 51–65.

6 F. Dufton, 'The Syrophoenician woman and her dogs', *The Expository Times*,
Vol. 100 (1989), p. 417.

7 V. Taylor, *The Gospel According to Saint Mark* (London: MacMillan, 1953),
p. 350.

8 Burkill, 'The historical development of the story of the Syrophoenician
woman', pp. 112–13.

9 E. M. Wainwright, 'A voice from the margin: reading Matthew 15.21–28 in
an Australian feminist key', in F. F. Segovia and M. A. Tolbert (eds), *Reading from
this Place* (Minneapolis, MN: Fortress Press, 1995), pp. 150–3.

10 S. Nelavala, 'Smart Syrophoenician woman: a dalit feminist reading of Mark
7:24–31', *The Expository Times*, Vol. 118 (2006), pp. 65–6.

11 S. Nelavala, 'Smart Syrophoenician woman', p. 69.

12 S. H. Ringe, 'A Gentile woman's story, revisited: rereading Mark 7.24–31a',
in A.-J. Levine (ed.), *A Feminist Companion to Mark* (Sheffield: Sheffield Academic
Press, 2001), pp. 91–2.

13 E. Schüssler Fiorenza, *But She Said* (Boston, MA: Beacon Press, 1992), p. 97.

14 Wainwright, 'A voice from the margin', pp. 150–3.

15 Nelavala, 'Smart Syrophoenician woman', p. 66.

28

Seen by Jesus:
The Widow with the Two Coins

KATE BRUCE

The Widow with the Two Coins in the Revised Common Lectionary (Sundays)

The unnamed widow does not feature in the Church of England *Common Worship* Lectionary. The relevant verses in Luke's account (21.1–4) are cut from the Year C lection for the Second Sunday before Advent, which begins at the fifth verse. She is airbrushed out.

The absence in the Lectionary of her story from Mark's Gospel is puzzling. The *Common Worship* Lectionary published by the Church of England for Year B, Fourth Sunday before Advent, has the reading as Mark 12.28–34, which means we don't get to her. We would expect the Gospel lectionary reading for the following Sunday to move on to her story; instead we jump back to the calling of the first disciples (Mark 1.14–20). The next Sunday jumps ahead to Mark 13.1–8. Again, she is passed over.

However, the Revised Common Lectionary, as published by Vanderbilt University (their free online service),[1] does include her for the Twenty-fifth Sunday after Pentecost (Year B, Proper 27, OT 32, Mark 12.38–44), which is odd since both lectionaries are usually the same.

Her Words in the Bible

None.

Background: Her Story in Mark

It's helpful to locate her story in the narrative flow of each of the Gospels in which she features. In Mark, Jesus' observation of the widow comes at the climax of a series of five dialogues between Jesus and various religious groups: scribes, chief priests, Sadducees, Pharisees and Herodians. These last three were not natural allies. Sadducees, an extreme conservative group,[2] maintained that only the written law was binding and denied the oral tradition. The Pharisees accepted both.[3] Pharisees were deeply loyal to Judaism, whereas the Herodians were a political group supportive of Herod the Roman puppet-king. All are welded together in mutual opposition to Jesus (11.27—12.44). Four of these exchanges are clearly hostile. The setting throughout is the Temple, where we see attempts to trap Jesus over questions relating to his authority (11.27–33), paying taxes to Caesar (12.13–17), and marriage in the resurrection (12.19–27). Meanwhile, Jesus seeks to expose their hypocrisy (12.1–12, 38–40). The mood is tense. The fifth dialogue differs – the scribe questioning Jesus is open and respectful. He asks about the greatest commandment. Jesus answers:

> Jesus answered, 'The first is, "Hear, O Israel: the Lord our God, the Lord is one; you shall love the Lord your God with all your heart, and with all your soul, and with all your mind, and with all your strength." The second is this, "You shall love your neighbour as yourself." There is no other commandment greater than these.' (Mark 12.29–31)

The scribe is commended as being not far from the kingdom, showing that not all scribes were guilty of the hypocrisy Jesus subsequently condemns, in the verses immediately before the scene with the widow:

> As he taught, he said, 'Beware of the scribes, who like to walk around in long robes, and to be greeted with respect in the market-places, and to have the best seats in the synagogues and places of honour at banquets! They devour widows' houses and for the sake of appearance say long prayers. They will receive the greater condemnation.' (Mark 12.38–40)

Jesus calls out the hypocrisy of the scribes, condemning their posturing piety and spiritual superficiality. The odd phrase 'they devour widows' houses' (12.40) reveals the greedy hoovering up of the resources of the vulnerable. Malachi specifically condemns the oppression of the widow (Malachi 3.5). Being a widow in that society 'virtually guaranteed a life of extreme poverty'.[4] They were not permitted to manage their late husband's estate and so were reliant on trustees,[5] not all of whom were scrupulous. The implication of Jesus' criticism is that some of these so-called guardians won trust through elaborate shows of religiosity. Using religious power to manipulate another for personal gain is straightforward abuse. Such behaviour shows an utter lack of love of God and of neighbour.

Mark follows the story of the widow's offering with a section concerned with huge themes: the end of the Temple, war, famine, disunity, false prophets, and the need to hold firm. After the literary camera has focused in on the widow and her two little coins, it pans out and takes a panoramic view of tribulation, in which the poor are more vulnerable than ever (Mark 13.1–37).

Background: Her Story in Luke

As in Mark's Gospel, Luke places the widow's story after the series of hostile exchanges between the religious authorities and Jesus (Luke 19.45—21.4). However, the question about the greatest commandment is placed in a different part of Luke's Gospel (10.25). This makes the mood in this section of Luke unremittingly tense; there is no relief from a redeeming scribe! Luke edits Mark's account of the widow into a more concise form, but the details are the same. Like Mark, Luke follows the account of the widow with a vision of tribulation (Luke 21.5–36).

Enter the Widow

Jesus is in the Temple watching as people make their offerings. He is probably in the Court of Women, around which were 13 chests placed for the reception of money. The top of these where trumpet-shaped bronze funnels.[6] Like the ostentatious scribes condemned in earlier verses, the rich could trumpet their generosity by throwing in large sums, their largesse literally ringing out. The detail about the trumpet shape of the chests adds another layer to Jesus' admonition in Matthew's Gospel: 'whenever you give alms, do not sound a trumpet before you ...' (Matthew 6.2).

It is moving to observe that Jesus notices the widow as she puts in her two little coins. Her gift is economically infinitesimal. A *lepta* was the smallest coin in circulation, worth less than one-sixty-fourth of the amount a labourer would earn in a day.[7] However, given her poverty, it is a staggeringly generous offering.

Jesus sees her and uses the scene as a teaching opportunity for his disciples:

> 'Truly I tell you, this poor widow has put in more than all those who are contributing to the treasury. For all of them have contributed out of their abundance; but she out of her poverty has put in everything she had, all she had to live on.' (Mark 12.43–44)

What does Jesus want his disciples to learn through reflecting on the widow's situation? Does he hold her up as an example of unstinting generosity or as a victim whose house has been devoured?

An Example of Unstinting Generosity?

Looked at this way, her actions epitomize a desire to love God and neighbour with everything and she stands as a foil to those who seek to accrue wealth and draw attention to themselves in a form of self-worship. The sermon flowing from this would focus on the need to give with unstinting generosity. This is a common interpretation, as an online search on sermons on this passage reveals – the widow's example often being used to encourage generous stewardship. Such generosity *is* a key virtue to be cultivated, but is this really what *this* text is about?

If we link the widow's situation to the previous verse – the condemnation of scribes for 'devouring widows' houses' (Mark 14.40; Luke 20.47) in a rapacious failure to love God or neighbour – we get a radically different reading and thus a very different sermon.

An Example of a House Devoured?

That she is noticed by Jesus speaks volumes about his focus and concern. Who else sees her at all? Caring for the widow is a key theme in the Bible (see Exodus 22.22–23; Deuteronomy 24.17–21; 14.28–29; Acts 6.1; James 1.27). However, no one except Jesus seems to know or care that this woman has 'put in everything she had, all she had to live on', making herself utterly destitute. *Why* has she only got two small coins to her name? Surely, she should be a beneficiary of the Temple treasury with its wealthy benefactors. Where has she imbibed the message that giving to the Temple is more important than feeding herself?

Notice how her story comes at the end of a section of discord between

Jesus and the Temple authorities. Her story is another expression of that conflict. The institution stands accused of not caring for the poor. On the contrary, it bleeds them dry. Not only has the Temple devoured this widow's house, it has swallowed up her final meagre resources in an example of rampant economic injustice. The irony is that immediately following this vignette Jesus predicts the destruction of the Temple: 'Not one stone will be left here upon another; all will be thrown down' (Mark 13.2; Luke 21.6). The widow's story is bookended by Jesus' condemnation of the Temple. Rather than the widow being praised for giving her mite, the institution stands accused for taking it.[8]

Sermon Suggestion: 'They devour women's houses'

The widow's mite. Perhaps you think you know what the story means. Perhaps you think the point of the story is that the widow is a model of self-sacrificial stewardship. But is the story really saying that giving to the church should render us all insolvent? Let's look again.

It helps to interpret the meaning by looking at the wider context. The widow's story is bookended by Jesus condemning the corruption of the religious institution and predicting its demise. It's a story of Jesus' condemnation of the Temple and his compassion for the widow.

Picture the scene

We are in the Temple, in the court of women. Around the sides of the court stand 13 trumpet-shaped receptacles into which people throw money for the Temple treasury. The top part of these receptacles is made of bronze. Listen to the coins of the rich trumpeting as they are lobbed in by left and right hands – a ringing, clinking sound. In contrast, the widow's last two tiny coins slide in with no more noise than a moth's breath. She turns to slip away, just another widow on just another day.

To be a widow in this context is to be vulnerable. Widows weren't allowed to manage their late husband's estate. They were deemed to need a guardian to do that. Sadly, there were unscrupulous scribes around who would step into this role, on the make. Just before the passage about the widow Jesus says to beware of the scribes. The language of the Authorized Version is particularly striking: 'For ye devour widows' houses' (Matthew 23.14, AV).

Imagine for a moment that we could overhear Jesus' tone of voice as he spoke the words, 'They devour widows' houses'. I think he is spitting mad: 'They devour *widows' houses.' They dine out on resources not their own. They use their status as religious experts, with long prayers, to disguise themselves as they set about savaging the lambs. Jesus is not best pleased.* You've got to ask yourself, what kind of a religious system communicates the message to the most vulnerable that if you want God's blessing you have to give your last coin? That's just corrupt.

Meanwhile back in the scene, the widow turns away from the treasury receptacle, purse empty. She has nothing left. Except this – Jesus sees her, he sees the rich, he sees the system, and he sees a teaching opportunity:

> 'Truly I tell you, this poor widow has put in more than all those who are contributing to the treasury. For all of them have contributed out of their abundance; but she out of her poverty has put in everything she had, all she had to live on.' (Mark 12.43–44)

What does he want his disciples to learn – then and now? See, the rich give without much dent in their abundance. They can afford to be part of this system. See, the widow can't afford it. See, the system that has left her destitute, her 'house devoured'. Jesus sees her, understands her situation, and names it. The widow, as generous as she is, is not being held up as an example of right stewardship. Of course, each of us needs to consider our giving and be generous, as Paul writes, 'God loves a cheerful giver.' However, this is not what this passage is about. The widow is a victim of institutional greed when she should be the recipient of institutional blessing. The system – which has fed her the lie that to be acceptable she must render herself destitute – stands condemned.

Meanwhile, back in the scene the widow walks away with nothing. Where does she go? What will she eat? How will she survive? The pittance she had to live on has slipped into the hungry mouth of the trumpet-shaped cash box. Meanwhile, the wealthy stroll away, feeling righteous, still with fat wallets. She is trampled and pushed aside.

I once heard of a university student who was persuaded through some heavy-pressure preaching on tithing to give her entire grant cheque to the church she was attending, creating multiple problems for herself, and probably for her parents. Her giving was generous, but it was not wise and it was heavily manipulated. Paul writes: 'Each of you must give as you have made up your mind, not reluctantly or under compulsion' (2 Corinthians 9.7).

How had the widow in the text, and the young student I just referred to, come to believe that you have to give your last cent to receive God's blessing? When you consider that this text is bookended by Jesus condemning the scribes for 'devouring widows' houses' and predicting that 'not one stone' of the Temple 'will be left here upon another' (Mark 13.1) it becomes clear what the widow's story signifies – the condemnation of corruption that rips off the poor and vulnerable in the name of God. What kind of god is the system portraying? Not the God of abundant blessing who sees and loves the poor, but a deity that requires the poor and vulnerable to be bled dry.

The widow is left without a crust. The student was left with no means, other than credit cards and parental back-up. This is the corruption Jesus exposes and condemns: she 'put in everything she had, all she had to live on'. The institution has swallowed up her last crust. In what world is this something to be praised?

The widow's mite calls us to beware the greed that crushes the poor; to beware the idea that the vulnerable must give their last coin to receive God's blessing.

In what ways is the income of the church a blessing to the poor? In what ways can those with more quietly ensure that those with less are blessed and not devoured? In what ways do we protect people by calling out those unscrupulous examples of religious institutions or organizations that rip people off, selling 'God's blessings' through heavy-pressure tactics and expectations. Those who have abundance can afford to bless those with little, not savaging, but building up their houses. Seeing them, as Jesus does.

How wonderful if the next frame of the scene showed a scribe running after the woman, stopping her, thanking her for her generosity, but reminding her that God seeks to protect her, and she needs her two coins and more besides to make her way in the world.

How wonderful if the scribe really saw her and gave her resources – a measure pressed down and running over, enabling her to live secure.

How wonderful when the church really sees the poor and vulnerable and gives resources – gifts of food, money, community and belonging. Let's be that church.

Homiletic Points

1 The sermon begins by challenging the common textual interpretation, asking the congregation to look again, which acts as a hook, creating tension. Where will this go?

2 The sermon shape consists of two strands interwoven like a helix. One strand (indicated by italics) takes the hearer into the Temple, to experience the vignette as it develops. The other strand consists of commentary on the unfolding scene.

3 The take-home of the sermon is focused on generosity (as is the more usual interpretation) but the journey to that point takes a different route, asking us to consider the corrupt nature of religious institutions that drain the meagre resources of the poor, rather than protecting and helping. It asks the church to see as Jesus sees.

4 The interpretation pays close attention to the context of the passage.

5 At points, the language implicitly connects to other biblical texts, offering a depth of resonance for some, while not impeding those who don't pick up on the reference. For example:

- 'coins of the rich trumpet themselves as they are lobbed in by left and right hands' (Matthew 6.2–3 – reference to not trumpeting giving, and in giving alms not letting left and right hand know what they are doing);
- 'savaging the lambs' (Matthew 5.15 – reference to ravenous wolves in sheep's clothing);
- 'She is trampled and pushed aside' (reference to Amos 5.10b, 12 – which speaks of the poor being trampled and the needy pushed aside at the gate);
- 'not savaging, but building up their houses' (Mark 12.40 – where Jesus condemns scribes for 'devouring widows' houses').

Collect

God of blessing, rich and generous,
you who see and care for the vulnerable;
help your church to see and care for the poor,
to notice those who are struggling
and to be a blessing and not a drain on meagre resources.
Give the wealthy the courage
to contribute generously and quietly

from the gift of abundance,
and save us from the fear that
grasps resource to self and institution.
Amen.

Notes

1 See https://lectionary.library.vanderbilt.edu/, accessed 25.02.22.

2 Bonnie Bowman Thurston, *Preaching Mark* (Minneapolis, MN: Fortress Press, 2001), p. 135.

3 Morna D. Hooker, *The Gospel According to St Mark* (London: A&C Black, 1991), p. 282.

4 John MacArthur, *Twelve Extraordinary Women* (Nashville, TN: Thomas Nelson, 2005), p. 136.

5 Dawn Ottoni Wilhelm, *Preaching the Gospel of Mark* (Louisville, KY: Westminster John Knox Press, 2008), p. 218.

6 Thurston, *Preaching Mark*, p. 141; see also Ritmeyer Archaeological Design, https://www.ritmeyer.com/2015/05/, accessed 19.03.22.

7 Hooker, *St Mark*, p. 296.

8 Addison G. Wright, 'The widow's mites: praise or lament? – a matter of context', *The Catholic Biblical Quarterly*, Vol. 44, No. 2 (April 1982), pp. 256–65, https://www.jstor.org/stable/43709756, accessed 26.02.22.

29

A Faithful Prophet:
Anna

KATE BRUCE

Anna in the Revised Common Lectionary (Sundays)		
Years A B C	Candlemas	Luke 2.22–40

Anna's Words in the Bible

None.

Anna's Story: Background

Anna features once in the Bible. At first glance her role looks like a minor walk-on part, just three verses at the end of the account of the presentation of the infant Jesus in the Temple in accordance with the Law of Moses. This related to Mary's purification after childbirth and the redemption of Jesus, as the firstborn male (Leviticus 12.2–8; Exodus 13.13; Numbers 18.15–16).

Anna enters the scene after Simeon's momentous prayer, in which he states that his eyes have seen 'your salvation' while cradling the child Jesus, naming him as 'a light for revelation to the Gentiles' and 'the glory of your people Israel' (Luke 2.30–32). Following on from this, Anna's part, though brief, is profoundly significant.

Her presence alongside Simeon mirrors the female–male pairing of Elizabeth and Zechariah, and Mary and Joseph, earlier in Luke's Gospel. Just as Elizabeth confirms Zechariah's naming of John, in solidarity with Gabriel's command (Luke 1.13, 60), so Anna's presence and words confirm and amplify Simeon's prayer, as she speaks about the child 'to all who were looking for the redemption of Jerusalem' (Luke 2.38). Luke shows us women and men working together as part of the divine purpose. Luke's account implicitly picks up the promise of Joel 2.28, later referenced explicitly in Acts 2.17–18:

> Then afterwards
>   I will pour out my spirit on all flesh;
> your sons and your daughters shall prophesy,
>   your old men shall dream dreams,
>   and your young men shall see visions. (Joel 2.28)

Luke describes Anna as 'a prophet … the daughter of Phanuel'. She exemplifies the prophesying daughter promised in Joel, pointing us towards the outpouring of the Spirit at Pentecost. In Anna we see a woman at the pivotal point between Old Testament prophecy and its fulfilment. She demonstrates the significant role of women in discerning, confirming and expressing the true significance of Jesus.

Her Background

> There was also a prophet, Anna the daughter of Phanuel, of the tribe of Asher. She was of a great age, having lived with her husband for seven years after her marriage, then as a widow to the age of eighty-four. (Luke 2.36–37)

Asher was one of the ten tribes of the Northern Kingdom, which fell to Assyria in 722 BC. They were known as the 'lost tribes' and were probably largely assimilated or wiped out in the Exile. However, the fact that Anna can trace her lineage to this tribe suggests that a remnant survived, a thread who remained faithful to God. Anna clearly isn't lost! In blessing the tribe of Asher, Moses said:

> Most blessed of sons be Asher;
>   may he be the favourite of his brothers,
>   and may he dip his foot in oil.
> Your bars are iron and bronze;
>   and as your days, so is your strength.
> (Deuteronomy 33.24–25)

The name 'Asher' means happy, with connotations of blessed. Anna's life expresses much of Moses' blessing. The reference to oil picks up inferences of joy – Psalm 45.7 speaks of the 'oil of joy'. Isaiah 61.3 mentions the 'oil of gladness' associated with the proclamation of the year of the Lord's favour. The image of a foot dipped in oil suggests walking in the way of joy and blessing. While Anna has known grief, she has not been consumed by it. She has walked the path of commitment and found blessing. She looks outward, alert to the great significance of this child revealed at that particular moment.

Moses' blessing connects longevity with strength, and we see this strength in Anna. Luke writes that she was of a 'great age'. Depending how we read it she is either an 84-year-old widow, or she has been widowed for 84 years. In the latter reckoning she really would have achieved Luke's 'great age' since she would probably have married at 14, been widowed at 21, and was present with Jesus some 84 years later, making her the grand age of 105! She happens upon the scene at precisely the right moment, suggesting her physical mobility and strength; Anna is certainly of Asher's tribe, a woman of blessing.

Her Life

Given that she is named as the 'daughter of Phanuel' rather than as someone's wife it seems highly unlikely that she remarried after her early widowhood. There is no mention of her having children. Anna lived in a culture where marriage and child-rearing were the primary source of identity and security for women. We see this in the elderly Elizabeth's response to her conception as removing the 'disgrace' she has 'endured among my people' (Luke 1.25). In a similar vein, Hannah was 'deeply distressed' and 'wept bitterly', describing herself as 'deeply troubled' because of her lack of a child (1 Samuel 1.10, 15). Anna shares the same name as Hannah, meaning 'grace' or 'favour'. Hannah finds favour in her son Samuel; the grace in Anna's life takes a different form.

Anna's expectation of a family life, with its identity and security, was dashed. Her grief might have led her to bitterness, resignation and stagnation. However, her life is one of dedication and focus. The first thing Luke tells us about her is that she is a prophet; this is her primary identity. Before we encounter the best-known New Testament prophet, John the Baptist, we find Anna. How had she developed into a woman of such insight and boldness? Luke writes: 'She never left the temple but worshipped there with fasting and prayer night and day' (Luke 2.37).

Here is a woman with her head up, not bowed down, a woman actively cooperating with God. Her grief has contributed to the formation of a sensitive and searching spirit, focused on worshipping God in spirit and truth.

Her Insight

How are we to understand the idea of her never leaving the Temple? Is it a figurative expression suggesting the absolute dedication of her devotion, or are we to take this literally? People did sleep in the Temple environs. The Temple in Anna's time was run by 15 men, responsible for a variety of oversight tasks. One area of responsibility refers to the priestly guard, a group who slept in a part of the Temple regarded as secular, as opposed to the sacred Temple courts where people were not permitted to sleep.[1] Perhaps Anna found a quarter in one of the secular spaces off the sacred Court of Women. Here were storerooms for oil, wine, wood and musical instruments. Maybe she lived in one of these spaces? Alternatively, she may have lived near the Temple precincts. While we don't know for certain, we do know that her identity is absolutely bound up with her presence there, pointing to her devotion in worship and fasting, night and day. Her freedom from family life allows her this kind of single-minded focus.

Rembrandt's painting *Old Woman Reading*, which is thought to be the prophetess Anna,[2] captures this sense of her focus, depicting her poring over a book. The light from an unknown source comes from behind, bathing her and illuminating the page where her wrinkled right hand traces the words. The suggestion is of a woman intent upon scripture, focused on God.

In her long years, Anna must have seen many, many people bring infants to the Temple for the required rites. Such ceremonies must have taken place in the Court of Women, the place in the Temple where men and women could be together since women were not permitted to go beyond into the Court of Men. What did Anna see in *this* ceremony to draw her in? Luke writes that 'At that moment she came' (Luke 2.32). As we picture the scene, it's hard to say at just what point Anna arrived. Did she see from a distance the amazement on Mary and Joseph's faces and did that attract her attention? Did Anna see Simeon cradle the child and hear his profound words about him, as well as his ominous warning to Mary? We don't know. What we can plainly see is that she arrives at the divinely appointed moment. She sees, knows and speaks of the significance of Jesus: 'At that moment she came, and began to praise God and to speak about the child to all who were looking for the redemption of Jerusalem' (Luke 2.38).

Anna is bold. She praises God publicly and teaches about Jesus. Notice she addresses 'all who were looking for the redemption of Jerusalem'. How did she know who they were? Behind this intriguing snippet we can discern something of Anna's life in the Temple – sharing, worshipping and reflecting with those who were expectantly looking for the renewal of Israel's spiritual life through the coming of the Messiah. Luke paints us a picture of this elderly woman preaching to a gathered group with a shared interest: Messianic expectation, which was at an all-time high in the early first century.[3] Anna is part of a community of people associated with the Temple.

Her Example

Anna's life is an embodiment of the principles expressed in the Methodist Covenant Prayer, which centres the focus of life on God alone:

I am no longer my own but yours.
Put me to what you will,
rank me with whom you will;
put me to doing,
put me to suffering;
let me be employed for you,
or laid aside for you,
exalted for you,
or brought low for you;
let me be full,
let me be empty,
let me have all things,
let me have nothing:
I freely and wholeheartedly yield all things
to your pleasure and disposal.
And now, glorious and blessed God,
Father, Son and Holy Spirit,
you are mine and I am yours. So be it.
And the covenant now made on earth, let it be ratified in heaven.[4]

Here is a woman who will have known the suffering of bereavement, of being laid aside in terms of motherhood and family life, alongside the fullness of finding a place in the Temple and the richness of her dedication to God. No wonder she is venerated as a saint in the Eastern Orthodox Church, the feast day of Anna the Prophetess falling on 3 February.

Sermon Suggestion: Anna the Prophetess Meets Eleanor Rigby

The Beatles' haunting song 'Eleanor Rigby' asks where all the lonely people come from and where they belong. The first verse focuses on a woman in a church, clearing up the confetti from a wedding. She stands outside the circle of celebration, just a bit part in someone else's story. The lyric presents a picture of aching loneliness; Eleanor putting on a face as she goes out of the door, presenting a different reality to the outside world. The song then focuses on Father McKenzie working on a sermon no congregation will hear and darning his socks alone. He is the only person present at the burial of Eleanor Rigby. It's a singularly moving song which speaks of chronic loneliness.[5]

Loneliness is not a topic we often speak about. Perhaps it's regarded as something shameful or a mark of failure? Loneliness is an aspect of the human experience everyone faces from time to time. It's more than a feeling of being alone; it's a state of spiritual isolation which can become chronic. The 2018 Age UK research into loneliness estimates that by 2026 there will be 2 million over-50s in England who feel lonely. They add: 'The risk of being often lonely is dramatically higher among those people who are widowed or who do not have someone to open up to.'[6] This research was before the trauma and isolation of the pandemic, so it is likely that the figure may be much higher. The cure for loneliness is the experience of meaningful conversation, belonging to community and having significance.

Luke only offers us a small snippet about Anna, yet it communicates much about her experience of meaningful conversation, her membership of a community and her significance. We can see much in the life of this elderly widow to help us as we reflect on loneliness, its causes and its remedies.

Anna was widowed after just seven years of marriage. If we estimate she was married at 14, that makes her widowed by 21. How did she experience and handle the loneliness of her grief as a young widow? How did she come to terms with hopes unfulfilled, after a marriage of just seven years? By the time we meet her she is anywhere from 84 to 105 years old, depending on how you read Luke's account. It's unlikely she remarried, given that she is named as the 'daughter of Phanuel' rather than someone's wife. There is no mention of children. Anna stands outside the societal norms of marriage and family life in her cultural context.

Superficially, Eleanor Rigby and Anna are similar. Both are single women. Both are connected to places of worship. But the similarity ends there. Eleanor Rigby embodies profound loneliness. Where are her meaningful conversations, her community, her significance? There's just an empty space.

In contrast, we see Anna invested in profound conversation and embedded in community – human and divine. She begins to speak about the child to all who were 'looking for the redemption of Jerusalem'. She doesn't speak randomly, but with specific intent to a particular audience. How did she know what they were looking for? It's not too great a stretch to infer that she knew her audience and they knew her: a community waiting with longing for the Messiah. Anna is deeply connected to God, conversing in praise and worship. Luke confirms Anna's significance when the first thing he tells us about her is that she is 'a prophet'. She was a woman of discernment and insight, operating publicly at a point when the prophet John the Baptist is still in swaddling clothes.

The spectre of loneliness, which might have been a consuming feature of Anna's life, is thwarted by key factors. She knows her roots, she is 'of the tribe of Asher'. She has rich conversation. She is in community with God and others. Her role as a prophet gives meaning to her life. This meaning is crystallized as she gazes on and speaks about Jesus.

How do we combat loneliness, whether in ourselves or in others? Loneliness is amplified when people's experience of church is just a gathering of individuals who sit siloed in cold pews for an hour a week. The genuine community of faith is a messy place where conversation needs to embrace and move beyond the superficial. It's a place where people come together and find meaning, companionship and belonging. It's a place where gifts are discovered, named and known, and people are seen. Such communities vanquish the shadows of chronic loneliness – and the hope that Anna saw in Christ is born.

Homiletic Points

1 The first two moves of the sermon come from beyond the horizon of the biblical text (a well-known song and reference to Age UK research),

before moving into an exploration of Anna's life. This works to bring the horizons of text and context together.

2 Comparing Anna with Eleanor Rigby offers a quirky connection between the world of the text and the contemporary world, allowing the sermon to explore the situation of these women in terms of loneliness.

3 The biblical text does not explicitly speak of loneliness, yet implicitly the theme is present – both potentially in Anna's situation and in the more existential sense of the loneliness of a world in need of redemption.

4 The analysis of Anna's life reveals the themes of conversation, community and significance which give her life shape and meaning, ultimately fulfilled in her recognition of Jesus. Herein lies the antidote to chronic loneliness faced by so many, with a call to the church to be a place of warmth, welcome and connection.

Collect

God of life,
we give you thanks for Anna,
this elderly widow full of life and light.
Thank you for her focus,
her witness to the value of age and wisdom.
In her story we see the importance
of deep conversation, community, and significance conferred.
Enable your church to offer this warmth
to all seeking shelter from the chill of loneliness.
Amen.

Notes

1 Joseph Jacobs, Judah David Eisenstein, 'Temple, administration and service of', in the *Jewish Encyclopaedia 1906*, https://www.jewishencyclopedia.com/articles/14303-temple-administration-and-service-of, accessed 30.09.22.

2 See https://www.rijksmuseum.nl/en/search/objects?q=the+prophetess+anna&p=1&ps=12&ondisplay=True&st=Objects&ii=0#/SK-A-3066,0, accessed 30.09.22.

3 John MacArthur, *Twelve Extraordinary Women* (Nashville, TN: Thomas Nelson, 2005), p. 129.

4 'A covenant with God', https://www.methodist.org.uk/, accessed 30.09.22.

5 The Beatles – Eleanor Rigby Lyrics | Genius Lyrics.

6 Age UK, *All the Lonely People: Loneliness in Later Life* (September 2018), https://www.ageuk.org.uk/globalassets/age-uk/documents/reports-and-publications/reports-and-briefings/loneliness/loneliness-report_final_2409.pdf, accessed 30.09.22.

30

Touched by Christ's Compassion: Widow of Nain

LIZ SHERCLIFF

The Widow of Nain in the Revised Common Lectionary		
Year C	Proper 5 (OT 10)	Luke 7.11–17

The Widow of Nain's Words in the Bible

None.

Her Story

The story of the widow of Nain and her son is unique to Luke. He tells it succinctly, perhaps little explanation is needed, for the story is so paradigmatic for women in a patriarchal society that it requires little explanation. The woman has no husband and now no son. Women usually passed from father to husband to son, dependent on their care for survival. This woman is not only grieving, but probably fearful for her future – collateral damage in a fiercely patriarchal society. So when Luke writes, 'When the Lord *saw* her', he probably chose the word deliberately. Jesus saw the invisible. He neither ignores her problem nor glosses over her pain. He comforts her and restores her son to her. In this action, Jesus does not overthrow the oppressive patriarchal system, but he does rescue one of its victims and reverse her fate.

Sermon Suggestion: The Powerful Touch of Compassion

Back in 1971 a composer called Gavin Bryars was listening to some discarded audio clips. He had been part of a project filming the lives of homeless people. Some of them broke into song as they were filmed – bits of opera, or old ballads. But one had sung a kind of hymn. Ultimately this clip did not make the cut, so Bryars took it to his lab, thinking he might compose some music around it. He made a continuous loop of it and left it playing as he went to make himself a coffee. When he returned, the usually busy lab was eerily silent. Some people, he noticed, even had tears in their eyes. The homeless man had been singing 'Jesus' blood never failed me yet'. No hymn with that lyric could be found. But hearing the man sing had moved Bryars' laboratory colleagues away from their busyness to compassion.[1]

Jesus and his friends arrived in Nain on the back of some exciting events. Dramatic healing, revolutionary teaching and religious confrontation. In the prosperous city of Capernaum Jewish elders had asked Jesus to heal the slave of a Roman centurion: religious authority and political power petitioning the Healer they would ultimately collaborate to kill. Jesus' followers had seen him heal by word alone, without even visiting the slave in the privileged centurion's home. Before the miracle, Jesus had taught outside the city Luke's equivalent of the beatitudes: 'Blessed are you who are poor … Blessed are you who are hungry … Blessed are you who weep.' He had challenged the status quo and proclaimed God's preference for the poor.

Powerful in word and deed, Jesus was gaining a following. Perhaps others walked with them as they approached Nain, deep in discussion: 'Is this the Messiah, the one to restore Israel? Might he put the Jews back in charge, and kick out the Romans? Would the new Jerusalem be as great as David's city?' They were busy and buzzing.

But now, they approach humble little Nain.

From the village comes a funeral procession. In the way of Jewish funerals they may even have heard it approaching before they saw it. In these parts funerals were common. Jesus could have easily stood aside and let it pass. Compared to the wealth of Capernaum it was a poor affair, so insignificant that the other Gospel writers do not mention it. But in this funeral procession, outside an insignificant village, among the unimportant and the powerless, Jesus sees, and Jesus is moved with compassion.

Being moved to compassion, Jesus brings together everything he has recently said and done.

'Blessed are the poor, and the hungry, those who weep,' he'd said. Here is a poor, hungry, weeping woman. A grieving woman, with no means of income, no reliable supply of food other than the charity of those around. Jesus is moved to compassion, to feeling with the woman. Compassion is visceral. It is so visceral that sometimes we even talk of having 'compassion fatigue', as though there is a valid reason for turning aside, as though Jesus might have simply allowed this funeral procession to pass.

Instead, compassion is what makes Jesus' teaching live. In posh Capernaum, Jesus had healed the slave by saying the word. He didn't even visit. Here he touches the dead. Earlier he had argued with the religious about purity and holiness. Now he touches a corpse. Previously he taught God's preferential care for the poor, now he takes time to care for one of them.

This woman calls out Jesus' compassion.

Compassion doesn't first make you get out your credit card and pledge money to a television appeal. Compassion isn't what makes you put some loose change in the plastic cup of a homeless person. Compassion doesn't make you give, or volunteer, or protest. Not initially.

Compassion first makes you hurt.

Jesus doesn't see in this woman an opportunity to demonstrate his authority. He feels with her. He is so compassionate he aches. He hurts to the core of his being. That's compassion. Compassion prompts Jesus to radical action. He ignores the insignificance of the place, the poverty of the funeral, the fact that touching a body breaks rules about holiness; he pays no heed to the post-Capernaum triumphalism of his followers. He enters into the lonely, grinding poverty of this woman, and he heals her son.

As followers of Jesus we are called to compassion. To hurt when the world hurts; to share the pain of others; to intervene despite what others might think or say. Ours is not to decide who is worthy of help. Ours is not to judge those whose life choices mean they need help.

Ours is first to share their pain. Only when we have done that are we able to act.

Homiletic Points

1 The reaction of people overhearing the recording of the homeless man singing 'Jesus' blood never failed me yet' is used to introduce the theme of compassion. This could be further enhanced through playing the recording.

2 The story of the widow is located in the flow of Luke's Gospel, using examples of earlier key events – particularly reference to 'Blessed are

you who are poor ... Blessed are you who are hungry ... Blessed are you who weep.' This connects us directly to the experience of the grieving woman of Nain – an insignificant woman outside an insignificant place.

3 The sermon focuses on how Jesus touches the corpse; compassion overrides issues of purity.

4 In the threefold negative riff about what compassion is not we are offered instances of actions that are not the first move of compassion. The first move of compassion is to hurt with the other; actions flow from that empathy.

5 The sermon focuses in on Jesus' compassion, which is 'to feel' 'to ache', 'to hurt' with her, entering 'the lonely, grinding poverty of this woman'. It causes him to act, touching and healing the son.

6 The sermon moves then to the 'and so what' for the followers of Jesus. The first move is to share pain – this then feeds into action. The sermon stresses the importance of being with and entering into another's pain.

Collect

Loving God, whose Son Jesus entered into the pain of a grieving widow,
Give us compassion for others,
Compassion that hurts.
Compassion that moves us to action.
Amen.

Note

1 The piece can be found here: https://youtu.be/E1lnSi7QWY8, accessed 13.11.2023.

31

A Daughter of Abraham:
Woman Bent Over for Eighteen Years

KATE BRUCE

Her Story in the Revised Common Lectionary (Sundays)

Year B	Proper 16 (CW)	Luke 13.10–17 (CW, SS)
Year C	Proper 16 (OT 21)	Luke 13.10–17

Her Words in the Bible

None.

Background: Synagogue Controversies

The healing of the 'daughter of Abraham' (Luke 13.16) is only recorded in Luke. The setting, on the sabbath in a synagogue, should alert Luke's attentive reader to previous synagogue controversies. At the outset of his ministry, in the synagogue in Nazareth, Jesus declares the words of Isaiah, 'He has sent me to proclaim release to the captives', adding, 'Today this scripture has been fulfilled in your hearing' (Luke 4.18b, 21). Initially, all spoke well of him, but when he points out that those outside the covenant – the widow of Zarephath and Naaman the Syrian – find God's blessing, the mood turns ugly and they try to 'hurl him' off a cliff (4.22, 29).

Two chapters later and Luke records another synagogue controversy between the scribes and the Pharisees and Jesus. The religious leaders are looking for reason to accuse Jesus; hawk-like they watch to see if he will heal on the sabbath (Luke 6.7). Knowing what they are thinking, he challenges them by healing a man with a withered right hand (Luke 6.6–11).

Jesus will not permit a principle of sabbath-keeping to be placed above goodness, healing and restoration. Ideas of religious conformity cannot be placed above the relief of this man's debilitating suffering. The controversy boils down to the power of those who control synagogue practice and the power of Jesus; a controversy set to boil over sooner or later.

Fast forward to Luke 13 and we find ourselves witnessing another example of the tension ratcheting up.

Consider the Text

It's the sabbath and Jesus, every inch a Jewish teacher, is in the synagogue – 'the heart of Judaism in its most prevalent ... and strongest form'.[1] Into this scene steps a woman who has suffered profoundly for 18 years – a fact mentioned twice (Luke 13.10, 18). Physically, spiritually and socially, she is bound. She is bent over, 'quite unable to stand up straight' (v. 11). Imagine her pain and frustration as she attempts daily tasks. Imagine the strain on her neck as she peers up, trying to avoid bumping into things. Her plight is attributed to a 'spirit' (v. 11) and to Satan (v. 16). She is seen as being on the receiving end of malign spiritual forces, marking her out as different from the norm. Her affliction would have limited her social as well as her physical standing, pushing her into the status of outsider, unable easily to meet another's eye. People who look down on her physically may also look down on her as a person, imagining that they are somehow better, that she has done something to deserve her situation. She is a captive who needs to be set free – physically, spiritually and socially.

If we pick up on the reference to her 18 years of suffering, we will be reminded of Luke's other reference to the number eighteen (13.4) referring to the number of people who perished when the tower of Siloam fell on them. Jesus is clear that this is not because they were 'worse sinners' than others (13.2). Similarly, there is no sense here that the woman's long years of suffering are due to any specific personal fault.

When Jesus sees her, he acts immediately, calling her over and speaking words of healing, 'you are set free from your ailment' (v. 12) Having interrupted his teaching for the sake of this woman, Jesus goes further. He 'laid his hands on her' (v. 13). His touch signals inclusion, acceptance and love to her personally and to all onlookers. It's an act of solidarity, intimate and affirming. It is in response to this touch that 'immediately she stood up straight' (v. 13). Jesus' voice announces the fact of her healing, but it is his touch that communicates the reality of this to her such that she is able to respond physically. In word and action Jesus fulfils his earlier words: 'He has sent me to declare release to the captives' (Luke 4.18b). As she stands up straight for the first time in 18 years, imagine her changed perspective. Instead of being able to see only the ground, now she can take in her surroundings and look people in the eye. Immediately, she begins praising God; she has grasped that through Jesus' words and actions God is at work (v. 13). She is unbound.

The Leader and the Lord

The text contrasts the leader of the synagogue (v. 14) with 'the Lord' (v. 15). The leader, or *Archisynagōgos*, is the director of synagogue services, responsible for good order. We also see a contrast between the response of the woman who 'immediately' praises God and that of the leader who is 'indignant because Jesus had cured on the sabbath' (v. 14). The Greek *aganaktōn*, translated as 'indignant', in the NRSV can be rendered 'incensed'. He is furious about Jesus' sabbath rule-breaking. Interestingly, he directs his rage at the crowd: 'There are six days on which work ought to be done; come on those days and be cured, and not on the sabbath day' (v. 14). Is there an element of cowardice on the leader's part? Why does he not take Jesus on directly? The implication is that the woman, and any like her, are to blame because they have come seeking help on the sabbath – as though God takes a day off from the desire to love, heal and help! The leader's response lacks any compassion for those suffering. 'Clear off and come on another day,' seems to be his attitude.

That aside, there is no evidence that the woman was seeking healing from Jesus. Jesus reaches out to her, not the other way around. The Lord sees and acts with compassion.

The leader justifies his anger with reference to scripture. Exodus prohibits work on the sabbath, which is to be a holy day of rest (Exodus 20.10; 35.2). He uses scripture to bolster his position, rather than to open the door to the woman's freedom. 'Never mind that the woman suffers today. Today is the sabbath; healing can wait until tomorrow.' He places a principle above both pragmatism and compassion, and seems more driven by ensuring that in his sphere of influence the letter of the law is upheld. He doesn't care about the woman. He cares about his control of the synagogue. His response is in defence of his power.

Luke begins Jesus' speech by naming Jesus as *ho Kyrios*, meaning 'The Lord' (v. 15). This is not simply another teacher addressing the synagogue leader, but the Lord – the Supreme authority who can interpret the Torah accurately. Jesus begins with the exclamation, '*Hypokritai*' (hypocrites). Note the accusation is plural; there are others present who agree with the judgement of the synagogue leader. Earlier Jesus had warned his disciples to 'Beware of the yeast of the Pharisees, that is, their hypocrisy' (12.1). The hypocrite is one who dissembles, consciously or unconsciously, presenting a face to the audience with a heart that lies elsewhere. Such hypocrisy will work through the community like yeast through flour. This yeast will spoil the bread.

Jesus unmasks their hypocrisy with ruthless logic. He refers to a common and accepted sabbath practice which everyone (*hekastos*) does (v. 15) – unbinding an animal to lead it to water. By extension, if the relief of a donkey on the sabbath is acceptable then 'ought not this woman, a daughter of Abraham whom Satan bound for eighteen long years, be set free from this bondage on the sabbath day?' (v. 16). Jesus' irrefutable logic and compassion exposes their cruelty and they are 'put to shame'. The Greek *kateschynonto* carries connotations of blushing (v. 17). No wonder! As Jesus predicted, their attitudes which had been covered up are now exposed to the light (12.2–3). Their argument elevates their power, control and sense of right order above this suffering woman's restoration. Jesus names her as a 'daughter of Abraham'. She stands with the sons of Abraham, a daughter of the covenant, with every right to be a full member of the community. She is not some untouchable no-mark to be set aside for the niceties of religious law. Jesus will not permit her to suffer for another day.

In contrast to the synagogue leader, the 'entire crowd was rejoicing at all the wonderful (*endoxois*) things that the Lord was doing (v. 17). The Greek *endoxois* can also be translated as 'glorious', which really highlights the synagogue leader's petty attitude. Jesus has just restored this woman to wholeness after years of suffering, and the synagogue leader is put out that a 'rule' has been broken. He fails to see that 'the sabbath was made for humankind, and not humankind for the sabbath' (Mark 2.27). Even if a sabbath rule had technically been broken, the leader is unable to see that this is irrelevant since the healer 'is lord even of the sabbath' (Matthew 12.8; Mark 2.28; Luke 6.5).

Parables of the Kingdom: Mustard Seeds and Yeast

Luke follows the story of the healing of this woman with two parables of the kingdom, which help us to see that the healing of the woman is a sign of the kingdom, a picture of restoration and hope. In this case the kingdom comes unlooked for. The woman is in the synagogue, but there is no sense that she has specifically come seeking healing. After 18 years perhaps she had given up any hope of change and was just struggling on, managing as best she could. Yet, it is on this day that the healing she had probably stopped believing could happen breaks in.

How many people really noticed the woman? For many, she is like a mustard seed – easily overlooked, unseen and insignificant. A woman, described in the text as 'crippled'; she is a woman sidelined. But Jesus sees her. He sees her pain and her potential. With word and touch he draws her to God and she immediately responds with worship. Sowed like a mustard seed in the garden, how did the story of Jesus' intervention in her life grow? Who did it inspire and draw to God? We don't know, but we can be sure that it did and that her family, friends and community were affected by her restoration after 18 years of suffering. Her healing is a glorious thing. It is like yeast – it will work through her life and community and have tangible effect. It is the leaven of the kingdom.

Sermon Suggestion: Let the Story Shape You

Movement 1: questions for the woman about her situation

If we could sit down and have a brew with the woman Jesus healed on that sabbath day in the synagogue, what questions would you like to ask her?

[Note – depending on the context, the preacher could get people to discuss this and feed back their questions, shaping the sermon 'on the hoof'. In more traditional services the preacher can ask this in a rhetorical sense and offer something on the following lines.]

I'd want to ask her about the *physical side* of her disability: 'How have you coped for 18 years with your back bent over? It must make everything such an effort! How do you manage the pain?'

I'd want to find out something of her perspective on her *religious practice*: 'Do you come to the synagogue every sabbath? Why? What do you see when you come to the synagogue? How do people treat you? What has your physical condition taught you about your community and people in general?'

I'd like to know about her *theology*: 'How do you make sense of your 18-year struggle in the light of the goodness of God? Does the fact of your suffering make it harder to turn to God or easier? Do you ever get angry with God about your physical limitations? Do you pray for healing?'

Obviously, we can only guess at the answers she might give, but there is much we can infer from her story if we explore with imagination on high alert.

Searching for answers: textual focus and inference

She has been unable to straighten up for 18 years. She must have been in varying degrees of pain over that time. Not being able to 'fully straighten' must have caused her difficulty on a moment-by-moment basis. She would need to find adaptive methods for achieving daily chores and ask for help. My guess is she would have known some pretty bleak days. Constant pain is exhausting, to say nothing of dealing with the intrusive stares and comments of others.

Her suffering does not keep her from the synagogue on the sabbath. No one remarks that her presence is unusual, implying she is a familiar sight. Her physical difficulty forces her to look down much of the time. I wonder if this has sharpened her hearing. Perhaps she sees a great deal with her ears? Sensitive to her own difficulty is she more attuned to the suffering of others?

A travelling rabbi stops his teaching and calls her over (Luke 13.12). I wonder what she was thinking. 'Who's calling? Are they talking to me?' She must have had to twist her body to be able to look up and make eye contact with Jesus before she could fully comprehend that she is the subject of his invitation. She could have ignored him, backed away, reluctant to be the centre of attention as Jesus' listeners turn their focus on her. Yet, she makes her way across the room to him. That takes some courage. All eyes on her as she walks, head bowed down, towards them. What was she thinking? 'Who is this man? What does he want with me? What have I done?' Maybe she had heard about Jesus and was curious?

Movement 2: questions for the woman about her healing

When Jesus says, 'You are set free from your ailment' (v. 12), what went through her mind? In her shoes what might you have thought as he speaks the words of healing?

[*Note – depending on the context, the preacher could get people to discuss this and feed back their thoughts. In more traditional services the preacher can ask this in a rhetorical sense and offer something on the following lines.*]

Perhaps you'd feel honoured at being noticed?

Perhaps you'd feel embarrassed, even shy – everyone staring at you?

'What does he mean? Can I actually straighten up? Is he making fun of me? Is he really a healer?'

Maybe you'd be annoyed, feeling patronized? 'Why has he picked on me? Don't I have enough to put up with? I never asked for help.'

Maybe you'd feel cynical. 'I've managed for 18 years, thanks all the same. Where have you been for the last 17 years and 364 days?'

Any of these responses would be understandable, and perhaps a mixture of lots of them went through her mind.

Searching for answers: textual focus and inference

After he has announced that she is set free from her ailment, the next verse reads, 'When he laid his hands on her, immediately she stood up straight and began praising God' (v. 13). Jesus' touch confirms to her that she is healed: 'immediately she stood up straight'. There is no hesitation. She knows her body can now move in a different way. The limitations are removed.

Notice that his words alone do not communicate healing to her – it is his touch. Is this what shifts any internal fears and hesitation? Given that people have put her physical limitation down to the work of Satan, it is likely that many have shunned her and she has become familiar with isolation and a lack of human contact. The warmth of Jesus' hand upon her restores her physically, spiritually and socially. His touch brings life.

She recognizes that God is acting through this rabbi and without hesitation she 'began praising God' (v. 13). A simplistic reading of the text concludes – a woman with physical limitation gets healed and praises God, which might imply a sense that she has not been worshipping God in the previous 18 years. A more nuanced approach recognizes a suffering woman comes to the synagogue to worship. She does this faithfully and is not an unfamiliar figure in the synagogue. After 18 years of affliction, Jesus heals her and, because her heart is tuned to God, she is fully aware of the source of her healing and the appropriate response – to continue in praise.

Movement 3: questions for the woman about her response to the synagogue leader

I imagine her flexing her back and her neck, rolling her shoulders and stretching, when she becomes aware of the indignation of the leader of the synagogue and listens in to the exchange between him and Jesus. I wonder what she might say to, or think about, the leader of the synagogue as he declares his indignation over her healing.

[Note – depending on the context, the preacher could get people to discuss this and feed back their thoughts. In more traditional services the preacher can ask this in a rhetorical sense and offer something on the following lines.]

She might say, or think 'Is my healing, after 18 years of painful struggle, nothing to you?'

'Am I just "work" – not a person who matters?'

'Why is your precious religious principle more important than me? Am I less to you than the donkey you lead to water on the sabbath?'

'Why can't you, a religious professional, see God at work right in front of you? You miss the elephant with your straining after a gnat.'

Movement 4: questions for the woman about her response to Jesus

We don't know what she said to Jesus. If you were her, what might you have said?

[Note – depending on the context, the preacher could get people to discuss this and feed back their thoughts. In more traditional services the preacher can ask this in a rhetorical sense and offer something on the following lines.]

'Thank you. Today you saw me. You knew what I needed. I didn't have to say. You knew. You called me over and made them all see me. When you healed me, they all saw. When you touched me, they all saw. Your words and actions restored me to myself and my community. My future is changed. I can look others in the eye. I can look upwards and move freely. I don't know why it took 18 years, but you did find me – and you have opened up possibilities I stopped hoping for a lifetime ago. I was bent out of shape. My world shrunk to a small patch of ground before me. You have opened up to me the fullness of life and I can stand tall. Thank you.

Movement 5: questions for the congregation about their response to the story

How does this story affect you? What are the 'and so whats' for you?

[Note – *depending on the context, the preacher could get people to discuss this and feed back their thoughts. In more traditional services the preacher can ask this in a rhetorical sense and offer something on the following lines.*]

Maybe like me you wrestle with why the woman suffered for so long, and that leads you to ponder the question of human suffering. Important theme – but important too not to miss the sign of hope in this passage. For the woman – a mustard seed in the eyes of many – the kingdom does come. Hope is not disappointed, even after so many years of struggle, not being seen, and suffering on the sidelines.

We might reflect on what the woman learned in those 18 years. This is not to dismiss her pain, but to acknowledge that suffering can school us in empathy and insight. There are seams of wisdom to be mined in the hard places.

Maybe the story reminds you of the restorative power of appropriate touch – bringing warmth, acceptance and healing. It's important to hold on to that when so many stories in church and wider society are about the destructive power of abusive touch.

Perhaps you are struck by the fact that Jesus sees this woman and will not allow her to suffer for one more day – such is his compassion for her.

Maybe you are left wondering why the religious professional cannot see the work of God right in front of him, and instead gets annoyed that a religious principle has been broken. Yet the cost of keeping the rule is allowing the woman to suffer. How is that right? When does religion get in the way of healing?

What will you take from this story – and how will it shape you?

Homiletic Points

1 The sermon consists of five movements. The first movement focuses on questions for the woman, looking through physical, religious and theological lenses. The next three movements focus on questions for the woman at key stages in the narrative. The final movement focuses on congregational response.
2 In a more informal context, each movement allows for congregational discussion and feedback. This approach requires the preacher to be script free and able to draw on their preparation to shape a sermon 'on the hoof'. The same sermon structure works in a more formal context – with the preacher posing the questions in a rhetorical sense and offering a range of responses, as suggested in the script above.
3 The sermon runs with the grain of the unfolding narrative, combining close attention to textual detail with an imaginative exploration of what lies behind the gaps and silences.
4 There are implicit theological threads running through the sermon relating to suffering and what we can learn in it, the goodness of God, and the possibility of kingdom hope.

Collect

Healing God,
We pray for those whose struggle is relentless
and whose suffering all encompassing;
for those bent out of shape by the burdens of life,
oppressed in body, mind and soul.
We pray for your kingdom to come,
to burst into the everyday with healing hope.
When we are cynical and tired,
and feel only the endless trudge –
remind us of this woman,
who praised you freely
after her long years of suffering ended
with your word and affirming touch.
Amen.

Note

1 Fred B. Craddock, *Luke*, Interpretation Series (Louisville, KY: Westminster John Knox Press, 1990), p. 170.

32

'Rejoice with me':
The Woman with the Lost Coin

LIZ SHERCLIFF

The Woman with the Lost Coin in the Revised Common Lectionary

Year C   Proper 19 (OT 24)   Luke 15.1–10

Her Words in the Bible

'Rejoice with me, for I have found the coin that I had lost.' (Luke 15.9)

Her Story

The story is clear and brief: a woman has lost a coin, she lights a lamp, sweeps her house, searches carefully, finds the coin and has a party. At first sight it's a simple tale used to bridge the stories of the lost sheep and the lost son, or possibly to demonstrate Luke's inclusive credentials. Diving deeper into the story, however, reveals that there is more to it than a cursory glance might suggest. The woman has lost a drachma, the equivalent of two days' wages for a woman, one day's wage for a man.[1] It is one of ten such coins that she has. Finding the coin was both economic necessity and cultural expectation. It was a woman's role to safeguard the money earned by men,[2] her identity and status were tied up with managing the household and its income. Losing a tenth of the family earnings was, therefore, a significant failure of duty. If this was a single woman the impact of the loss could be more significant. It would take two days' labour to replace the money, and work for women may not have been easily found. Linda Maloney supports the view that this woman was poor.[3] Apparently, she lives in a home with few windows;

searching for the coin requires an oil lamp to be lit, not for day to break. Lighting a lamp would have caused even greater anxiety, because lamp oil was costly. Amy-Jill Levine, on the other hand, argues that the woman in the parable is 'by no means marginal, outcast or poor. She's not only relatively well-off; she has her own home and her own set of friends.'[4]

Seeking the lost coin has become a feminist metaphor for discovering biblical texts about women,[5] so what can we find in these few verses? The story is the centre point of a trilogy: the lost sheep, the lost coin, the lost son. The shepherd and the father in the first and third parables are traditionally read as representing God, and so 'it is only fair to regard the woman with her coin as divine as well'.[6] Perhaps Luke is not only includ-ing a woman, but also the femininity of God. The celebration with her women neighbours parallels the men's celebration when the lost sheep is found – there is joy in heaven/the presence of the angels 'over one sinner who repents' (Luke 15.7, 10). Perhaps Luke is saying that the traditional domestic world of women is just as important as the public world of men. Finally, there is a significant difference between the shepherd who lost a sheep and the woman who lost a coin: the woman admits responsibility. She invites her neighbours to celebrate finding 'the coin that I had lost'. They come together to celebrate her restoration as responsible keeper of the household, as well as the finding of the coin.

Perhaps it says more about our contemporary society than about this story that we focus on the coin, however. Heidemarie Langer invites us to contemplate what the woman has, rather than what she lacks.[7] Most women, she argues, have been trained to suppress their inner wealth, and rediscovering our talents and abilities can be costly; it requires the 'deep and directing wisdom of our intuition'.[8] Communities of women are essential to the emergence of women's experiences as authentic. Sharing women's realities in community allows their voices to emerge as authori-tative so that women begin 'to value our experience, to trust our ability to reason and reflect, and accept ourselves as we really are'.[9] Whether the woman in the parable is rich or poor, then, matters little. What is significant is the importance of her woman's community as mutually sup-portive and empowering, a place where the woman who lost a coin can come to terms with herself.

Sermon Suggestion: Rejoice with Me

I was talking with a group of students about the three parables in Luke 15. They confidently told me that the shepherd was God, and the father was God in the first and third parables. I asked them about the woman in the second parable. 'Think about it. It's a set of three stories. In the first one, the main character is God, in the third one a main character is God, so in the second parable the main character must be ...?' They just couldn't get it. The logic, to me at least, is that if the shepherd is God and the father is God, the woman also is God.

But I think the story is about more than that.

There isn't much to it. If we were to act it out, we'd need a woman, a coin, a broom, a lamp and some neighbours. What can we say about it?

I wonder whether the story is not so much about a lost coin but about some found neighbours. We might use our imagination a little here. The woman runs the home. She is responsible for budget and for safeguarding the money that comes in. She has lost a drachma. If her father, husband or son had earned it, it was a day's wages. If she'd earned it, it was two days' wages. It was significant. She gets a lamp, gets a broom and starts to search. What does she not get? Help. Friends. Neighbours.

Some time ago I visited Uganda. I was taken to a women's project in a barracks. The women told me how at one time they had been isolated, each in her own home alone when her husband was at work. It was tiring and lonely. Perhaps like the woman in Jesus' parable. One day one of the Ugandan women met up with a neighbour. They began to work together – one would mind all the children while the other did the housework for both families. More women joined in. They began to realize that they weren't all needed for childcare and housework, so some of them began to make and sell beads. Then another business grew. The women were no longer lonely, no longer exhausted, and what's more they grew a series of small cooperative businesses. Just because the first two women confessed their needs to each other. Look what is possible when we are honest with ourselves and others about our needs.

I wonder whether there is something of the same spirit in Jesus' story. When the woman loses the coin she is alone, but when she finds it she tells her neighbours what happened and they begin to form a community. That makes this story different from the one before it, by the way. The shepherd, who manages to lose a sheep, does not claim responsibility. The sheep is simply 'lost'. In this story the woman is honest – 'I lost it.'

It's normal in our culture to focus on individuals, so we focus on the woman; or on money, so we think about the coin and ponder its value. But suppose the most important message of the story for us today is the message of neighbourliness. Loneliness is as bad for health as smoking 15 cigarettes a day and worse for your health than obesity.[10] It affects women more than men.[11] Since the pandemic it has got worse.[12] If Jesus were to talk about the importance of community, particularly using a woman and her female neighbours as an example, it would make absolute sense. We know the neighbours are women, by the way, because Luke uses a feminine noun.

Did you spot how this story differs from the one that follows it? The return of the younger son results in complaints and jealousy on the part of his older brother. Not everyone joins in celebrating his return. In this story, the joy is unalloyed. Everyone takes part.

The Arab Spring of the early 2010s seems a long time ago now. It was a time of hope, when authoritarian regimes were confronted, and women played a key part in all the countries involved.[13] They did so by acting in community, just as they did against tyrannical regimes in Argentina and Nicaragua decades earlier. Communities of women change things, just as in the Ugandan barracks I visited. Perhaps that is what Jesus is saying.

Let's retell the story another way:

A woman loses a coin. It is important. She has no one to share her anxiety with, or to help her find the coin. She lights a lamp, gets a broom and searches for the coin. As she does so, she ponders what is happening. Surely other women in nearby houses lose things. They must feel equally anxious and equally alone. Could something be done? When she finds the coin she decides to hold a party. She invites her neighbours to come and celebrate with her. But really, she is investing in community. She tells her story: 'I lost it; it was my fault. I felt so lonely looking for it. Has anything like that happened to you? Let's get together, then, and make sure it doesn't happen again.'

Homiletic Points

1 The sermon offers an imaginative interpretation of the parable, shining the spotlight on the theme of found neighbours – and offering an insightful interpretation.
2 This is developed with the illustration given from a project in Uganda of the power of neighbours working together.
3 This leads into an exploration of the effects of loneliness, earthed in the contemporary context.
4 The connection is made with the contrasting reactions of the elder brother and the community in this parable, using the near neighbours of this text to help in the interpretation.
5 This interpretation feeds into an imaginative retelling of the passage, opening out the focus on community.

Collect

God, our community-builder:
Give us hearts for each other,
Openness to share our own needs,
Willingness to empower others;
May we together build communities
Where no one need be alone,
No one need suffer in silence,
And where your love is known
In and through all.
Amen.

Notes

1 Mary Ann Beavis (ed.), *The Lost Coin: Parables of Women, Work and Wisdom* (New York: Sheffield Academic Press, 2002).

2 Carol LaHurd, 'Rediscovering the lost women in Luke 15', *Biblical Theological Bulletin*, Vol. 24, No. 2 (1994), pp. 66–76.

3 Linda Maloney, 'Swept under the rug: feminist homiletical reflections on the parable of the lost coin (Luke 15:8–9)', in Beavis (ed.), *The Lost Coin*, pp. 34–8.

4 Amy-Jill Levine, *Short Stories by Jesus: The Enigmatic Parables of a Controversial Rabbi* (New York: HarperCollins, 2014), p. 42.

5 Maloney, 'Swept under the rug', pp. 34–8; Levine, *Short Stories*, pp. 45–6.

6 Levine, *Short Stories*, p. 44.

7 Heidemarie, Langer, 'Letting ourselves be found', *Ecumenical Review*, Vol. 38, No. 1 (1986), pp. 23–8.

8 Langer, 'Letting ourselves be found', p. 24.

9 M. D. Turner and M. L. Hudson, *Saved from Silence: Finding Women's Voice in Preaching* (St Louis, MO: Chalice Press, 1999), p. 12.

10 J. Holt-Lunstad, T. B. Smith and J. B. Layton, 'Social relationships and mortality risk: a meta-analytic review', *PLoS Med*, Vol. 7, No. 7 (2010), p. 27, Jul:e1000316. doi: 10.1371/journal.pmed.1000316. PMID: 20668659; PMCID: PMC2910600, accessed 07.10.23.

11 See https://www.ons.gov.uk/peoplepopulationandcommunity/wellbeing/articles/lonelinesswhatcharacteristicsandcircumstancesareassociatedwithfeelinglonely/2018-04-10, accessed 07.10.23.

12 See https://www.redcross.org.uk/about-us/what-we-do/we-speak-up-for-change/life-after-lockdown-tackling-loneliness#:~:text=The%20Covid%2D19%20crisis%20has,be%20eased%2C%20loneliness%20will%20remain, accessed 07.10.23.

13 T. Karman, 'Women and the Arab Spring', *UN Chronicle*, Vol. 53 (February 2017), pp 21–2, United Nations, published online at https://doi.org/10.18356/4d9b3edf-en, accessed 09.10.23.

33

The Power of Her Testimony:
The Woman at the Well

LIZ SHERCLIFF

The Woman at the Well in the Revised Common Lectionary

Year A   Third Sunday in Lent   John 4.5–42

Her Words in the Bible

'How is it that you, a Jew, ask a drink of me, a woman of Samaria?' (John 4.9)

'Sir, you have no bucket, and the well is deep. Where do you get that living water? Are you greater than our ancestor Jacob, who gave us the well, and with his sons and his flocks drank from it?' (John 4.11–12)

'Sir, give me this water, so that I may never be thirsty or have to keep coming here to draw water.' (John 4.15)

'I have no husband.' (John 4.17)

'Sir, I see that you are a prophet. Our ancestors worshipped on this mountain, but you say that the place where people must worship is in Jerusalem.' (John 4.19)

'I know that Messiah is coming ... When he comes, he will proclaim all things to us.' (John 4.25)

'Come and see a man who told me everything I have ever done! He cannot be the Messiah, can he?' (John 4.29)

The Inquisitive Woman Commissioned by Jesus

The story is commonly told of a woman meeting Jesus at a well at midday. She is there at the hottest part of the day, we are told, because she has a shady past and wants to avoid her neighbours. Her shady past involves liaisons with a number of men, and Jesus reminds her that the one she is currently with is not her husband. Rather than address the issue at hand, the woman begins a theological discussion with Jesus. When his disciples return they are shocked to find him speaking with a woman, and a Samaritan woman at that. One example of this type of sermon was given by well-known preacher John Piper, who describes the woman in a 2011 sermon as 'a worldly, sensually-minded, unspiritual harlot'.[1] The woman is clearly rendered a sinner in the eyes of those who tell it: a loose woman with whom Jesus deigns to spend time.

There are several problems with this interpretation of the tale. It assumes that the woman always goes to the well at midday, whereas all we know is that 'she came to draw water' at that time on this occasion. Many women with domestic responsibilities know how often things go wrong, and delay daily chores. It assumes that the woman was free to divorce and to remarry. Women in first-century Palestine could not initiate divorce, unlike men, who could do so for trivial reasons. If, then, she had been divorced this was not at her instigation. She has had the misfortune to marry five feckless husbands, rather than the temerity to divorce them. Divorce is not the most likely scenario. Marriage itself is unlikely. According to Roman laws of the time, only the free-born could marry. Freed slaves, of whom there were millions, were precluded from marriage, and freed women had to become concubines. The word Jesus uses (*anēr*) simply means man, rather than husband as most English translations render it. Society of the time virtually precluded single women. Daughters were the property of fathers, wives the property of husbands. When a husband died, the woman was passed to his next of kin. This woman is unlikely to have been an adulteress. She may have been barren, and so unwanted,[2] divorced,[3] or the victim of levirate marriage like Tamar, with the last man refusing to marry her, as described by the Sadducees in Mark 12.18–27.[4] Finally, the common interpretation takes no account of the fact that in much biblical interpretation, men who have more than one wife are seen as great, whereas a woman who might have had more than one husband is condemned. The common reading of the story does not do justice to it.

Representative of the Despised

Catholic scholar Sandra Schneiders interprets this incident as a 'type story',[5] similar to the Hebrew Bible stories of Abraham's servant meeting Rebecca, Jacob meeting Rachel, and Moses meeting Zipporah at wells. The theme might also hint at Jesus as the bridegroom (John 3.29) and the launch of his ministry at a wedding (John 2). 'The pattern or paradigm is the story recounting the meeting of future spouses who then play a central role in salvation history,'[6] Schneiders says. Jesus, the true bridegroom, 'comes to claim Samaria as an integral part of the New Israel'.[7] In this telling of the story, the five husbands represent infidelity to the Mosaic covenant. The theological discussion that ensues is not a diversionary tactic, but genuine dialogue. Schneiders concludes that we

> cannot fail to be affected by the fact that the recipient of Jesus' universal invitation to inclusion is a woman, universal representative of the despised and excluded 'other' not only in ancient Israel but throughout history and all over the world. Not only is she included, but she is engaged with respect, even asked for a gift (water) that she might receive a greater gift (living water).[8]

Traditionally, this woman has been multiply despised – because of her gender, her race and her wrongly attributed sexual sin. Yet it is with her that Jesus holds his longest conversation.

Contrasting Conversations

Jesus' theological discussion with the Samaritan woman in John 4 contrasts starkly with an earlier debate, in John 3. Nicodemus comes to Jesus by night, while this woman comes in broad daylight. When Jesus asks her for water, she points out his impropriety. Nicodemus, on the other hand, begins with his own understanding of who Jesus is (John 3.2) and Jesus points out that it is flawed. The woman asks the right question – 'Are you greater ...?' – whereas Nicodemus raises objections. Jesus tells the woman everything she's ever done (John 4.29, 39), but tells Nicodemus what he does not understand (John 3.10). Both conversations are life-giving – Jesus affirms to Nicodemus that he has come that the world might be saved (John 3.17). Nicodemus, however, remains on the margins throughout the gospel, while this woman becomes an apostle, spreading the gospel in her village. Where Jesus highlights Nicodemus' weak theology, the Samaritan woman demonstrates knowledge and insight. John thus contrasts a powerful Jewish man with an anonymous Samaritan woman.

Luminous Apostle

Meeting Jesus turned this woman into an effective evangelist. In John 4 we see her grow from questioning Jesus to becoming a credible witness – because of her story, many from that city believed in Jesus (John 4.39). In 'seeing' herself (4.19) and inviting others to 'come and see', she repeats a key theme of John's Gospel – seeing. Her name in the Eastern Orthodox tradition reinforces the theme; she is Photini, which means enlightened one. In thus naming her the Eastern Orthodox tradition respects her as equal to the apostles. In this tradition her mission spreads well beyond her Samaritan village, all the way to Rome, to stand before the Emperor Nero. One tradition has it that through Photini, Nero's daughter became a follower of Jesus. Eventually Photini was martyred by being thrown into a dry well – an ironic detail given that she had met the 'living water' at a well. This is hagiography, rather than history, but it does at least bear greater resemblance to the woman we meet in John's Gospel than does the Western counterfeit.[9]

Preaching the Woman at the Well

Treating the story of the woman at the well seriously in preaching means dropping popular misapprehensions about her moral status, and dealing with her as an intelligent seeker after truth, which is how Jesus treats her. Her story might encourage our listeners to become engaged questioners rather than passive hearers. Her realization that Jesus is a prophet leads her to ask the pressing theological question of her time, one that has led to the marginalization of her people. According to 2 Kings 17.24–41, the Samaritans may have been regarded as descendants of pagan tribes. Certainly, the Jews did not accept them as part of the same covenant with God that they had. This Samaritan woman questions the exclusivity of Jewish interpretation. Jesus reframes her question – we worship in spirit and truth, not on mountains. The woman professes her faith that a Messiah will come, and Jesus reveals his identity to her. Theological engagement leads to new revelation.

The woman doesn't wait for Jesus' instruction to go and tell. In the diversion caused by the arrival of Jesus' puzzled disciples, she seizes the opportunity, leaves her water jar behind – another indication of apostleship, for Peter, James and John leave their nets – and takes an invitation to her neighbours: 'Come and see a man who told me everything I have ever done! He cannot be the Messiah, can he?' (John 4.29). Notice she doesn't begin with Jesus' identity, but her own. Might the implication be that Jesus has, somewhere in the unreported conversation, appreciated her story, her pain and loss? This would be consistent with John's inclusiveness, and with the Jesus portrayed by Matthew, Mark and Luke, who listens as the haemorrhaging woman tells him her whole story (Matthew 9.20–22; Mark 5.25–34; Luke 8.43–48). Because the townsfolk seem to respect her word, they go off to see for themselves. She is a credible witness to the good news.

Finally, we should point out that for this conversation to take place it is Jesus, not the woman, who breaks the rules. A man greeted a foreign woman, and a Jew asked a Samaritan for water.[10] Rightly understood, this is a story that addresses multiple oppressions by demonstrating that Jesus overrules social codes.

Sermon Suggestion: A Luminous Witness

It was a pleasant early summer day. A gentle breeze blew along the valley, cooling her skin. What a morning it had been! One of the goats had got caught in a bush and it had taken her some time to free it. A neighbour had dropped in to ask her advice about something, and delayed her chores. Still, her daily walk to the well to get water for the household was pleasant and gave her time to think. Her heart warmed as she remembered her first husband. He had loved discussing their religious ideas together. His death had led to her being passed along a string of men, unwanted because of her inability to bear children. Finally, she had arrived in the house where she now lived – passed off onto her present protector by being included in a deal for a piece of land. He accused her of thinking too much for a woman; 'It's none of your business,' he would say when she asked what had been said at worship that day, or how the town meeting had gone.

As she approached the well, she could see someone sitting there. A man, Jewish by the look of it. Unless he was up to no good, he wouldn't disturb her afternoon. Jewish men don't talk to Samaritan women. This man breaks all the rules, though. He speaks to her. He asks her for something. He even engages her in theological discussion. And then, he gets personal. He looks in her eyes and sees the pain of rejection, of being passed on – second-hand, useless to men.

Here we have a meeting between a wise but rejected teacher and a woman who breaks the social rules by questioning him.

Jesus breaks the rules. He speaks to a woman. He speaks to a Samaritan. He asks for something from her. He shocks his disciples. She asks pertinent questions. She understands who Jesus is. She goes off to tell her friends and neighbours.

Let us not misjudge this woman.

Centuries of being despised cannot hide the fact that Jesus respects her.

Centuries of representing the neglected, unloved and unpopular cannot hide the fact that Jesus accepts her.

None of it can hide the fact that when she goes to tell people about Jesus they listen to her and follow her.

She is a remarkable woman. Her testimony is not that Jesus recognized her sin and forgave her. It is that Jesus knew everything. The pain, the rejection, the injustice she had experienced, and he refused to treat her that way. To him, she was precious. Just as Jesus sees her for who she is, so she also sees Jesus for who he is, and spreads the word.

In the Eastern Orthodox tradition, this nameless, shameful woman is Photini, the Luminous One, an apostle whose testimony reaches all the way into the Emperor Nero's court, and leads to the conversion of his daughter. A brave, wise insightful woman who met Jesus by chance at midday by a well.

Perhaps the traditional woman at the well is not one of us. We can look down on the immoral woman who has gone through five husbands, who goes to the well in the heat of the day out of shame. But we dare not look down on a woman who understands the issues of her day and discusses them with Jesus. We dare not despise an apostle who witnesses to Jesus not just before local crowds but before powerful emperors too. If someone we have disdained for centuries is such a powerful witness, perhaps there is no one we can malign.

Homiletic Points

1 The imaginative opening draws us into a different way of interpreting this story. She visits the well at midday simply because she is having a busy day, rather than because she is ashamed and avowing people. Her marital status is explained through the lens of levirate marriage.

2 The sermon traces the details of the text, pointing to Jesus' interaction with her and her faithful response.

3 The sermon ends with a positive interpretation of her, and the question, 'If we have been wrong in disdaining her, then is it right to malign anyone?'

Collect

God of the Luminous Woman,
Who showed others the light and truth of Jesus:
May we not misjudge others;
Help us to look for you in everyone we meet,
To see their potential, and know that you love them.
In the name of the one who sat by a well
in the heat of the day
To meet a rejected woman.
Amen.

Notes

1 Reported in *Huffington Post*, 21 March 2011.

2 M. M. Barker, *King of the Jews: Temple Theology in John's Gospel* (London: SPCK, 2014), pp. 364–5.

3 N. Duff, 'The ordination of women: biblical perspectives', *Theology Today*, Vol. 73, No. 2 (2016), pp. 94–104.

4 R. Habermann, 'Gospel of John', in L. Schottroff and M.-T. Wacker (eds), *Feminist Biblical Interpretation: A Compendium of Critical Commentary on the Books of the Bible and Related Literature* (Grand Rapids, MI and Cambridge: Eerdmans, 2012), pp. 662–79. G. O'Day, 'John', in C. A. Newsom, S. H. Ringe and J. E. Lapsley, *The Women's Bible Commentary* (Louisville, KY: Westminster John Knox Press, 2014).

5 S. M. Schneiders, *The Revelatory Text: Interpreting the New Testament as Sacred Scripture* (Collegeville, MN: The Liturgical Press, 1999), p. 186.

6 Schneiders, *The Revelatory Text*, p. 187.

7 Schneiders, *The Revelatory Text*, p. 187.

8 Schneiders, *The Revelatory Text*, pp. 196–7.

9 There are several sources of information on Photini, for example: https://knowyourmothers.com/photini-mother-of-evangelists/; https://ocl.org/orthodox-christian-laity/st-photini-patron-saint-of-ocl/; http://womensordinationcampaign.org/blog-working-for-womens-equality-and-ordination-in-the-catholic-church/2020/2/26/olxuekybneo4kr4naxadczjcgejdag, accessed 13.11.23.

10 Habermann, 'Gospel of John', p. 532.

34

'Some Women' Encounter God: Peter's Mother-in-Law, Women of Jerusalem, Sapphira, Drusilla and Bernice

LIZ SHERCLIFF

The phrase 'some women' is taken from Luke 8.2. This chapter focuses on some women who appear in Luke–Acts:

> Peter's mother-in-law (Luke 4.38–39; also found in Matthew 8.14–15; Mark 1.30–31)
> Women of Jerusalem (Luke 23.28–30)
> Sapphira (Acts 5.1–11)
> Drusilla (Acts 24.24)
> Bernice (Acts 25.13—26.32)

Luke's Women in the Revised Common Lectionary

It was tempting to call this chapter 'absent women' because although they appear in Luke and Acts they are nowhere to be found in the Lectionary.

Their Words in the Bible

Peter's mother-in-law

None.

Women of Jerusalem

Jesus says that at some point in the future the women of Jerusalem will say,

> '"Blessed are the barren, and the wombs that never bore, and the breasts that never nursed." Then they will begin to say to the mountains, "Fall on us"; and to the hills, "Cover us".' (Luke 23.29–30)

Sapphira

> 'Yes, that was the price.' (Acts 5.8)

Drusilla

None.

Bernice (words said with King Agrippa and others):

> 'This man is doing nothing to deserve death or imprisonment.' (Acts 26.31)

Who are These Women and Why are They Important?

Peter's mother-in-law – 'healed just in time for supper'[1]

At best, Simon Peter's mother-in-law seems to be a bit-part player in all three Synoptic Gospels. She's ill, she's healed, she makes the supper! The focus of the story has usually turned to Jesus, as the healer, or to the woman as a servant – conveniently reinforcing the idea that a woman's place is in the kitchen. For some commentators, the privilege of serving Jesus is regarded as a utopian moment, even though it seems to slot her back into her patriarchally assigned gender role.[2] A hermeneutic of suspicion will serve us well here. First, what is the word used by the Gospel writers that is now interpreted 'serve'; second, what is the wider context of women in the Gospels – here I will focus on Luke's Gospel.

The word used for serving, in all three gospels, is *diakoneo*. It is also used, in Matthew and Mark, of the angels who minister to Jesus after his trials in the wilderness (Matthew 4.11; Mark 1.13). In Luke, it is used of other women disciples (8.1–3) and of Martha of Bethany (10.38–42). Although the English translation seems specific, the original sense is much broader. From Luke 8 onwards, women journey with Jesus. They journey not just in the sense that they accompany him, rather they pursue a journey of their own, to inclusion in the people of God. They are called from the margins to the centre, as the haemorrhaging woman in Luke 8; they are called into the covenant, as the woman bent double in Luke 13 is named 'daughter of Abraham' by Jesus. Peter's mother-in-law, then, may be healed for a greater purpose than making the supper. She may be a precursor of the women leaders and disciples who are to follow.

Women of Jerusalem

'A great number of the people' (Luke 23.27) followed Jesus as he was led away to be crucified; 'among them were women who were beating their breasts and wailing'. Perhaps these were professional mourners, paid to play their part in death and dying, but no more significant than that. Since Jesus addresses them as 'daughters of Jerusalem' we know that these are not the women who have followed him on his journey to this moment, or who have supported his ministry – they were from Galilee, not Jerusalem. From many perspectives, these women were unimportant. Yet Jesus speaks directly to them. In contrast to their perhaps insincere mourning for him, they will weep for themselves and their daughters, he tells them. Forty years later, their city, Jerusalem, was completely destroyed by Roman forces. The words Jesus ascribes to them accurately reflect the experiences of women in times of war even to the present day. United Nations Security Council briefing SC/7908 says 'women and girls suffer disproportionately during and after war'.[3] Could it be that even as he is headed to his own death Jesus is reassuring the women that God shares with them, and him, in suffering? For the world's Western powers, the assumption that God is on our side, or, as Anthony Reddie puts it, 'a world in which notions of manifest destiny and White exceptionalism have given rise to a toxic reality built on White supremacy',[4] is undermined by an assertion that God is to be found alongside the conquered and oppressed.

Sapphira

If the daughters of Jerusalem were insincere, Sapphira is dishonest. She agrees with her husband that they will sell a piece of land, give some of the money to the apostles, pretending they were giving it all, and keep some for themselves. It does not seem to be their sale of the land that is judged, but their lie. Peter says that Satan has filled Ananias' heart, though he does not say the same of Sapphira. Perhaps here is an important point: Sapphira knows what is planned and is complicit. While her heart may not have been filled by Satan in the same way, she allows wrong to take place and is therefore guilty.

Drusilla

Drusilla, like Sapphira, is on the edge of the story. When her husband Felix calls for Paul to speak before him, she is there. Whether or not she too becomes frightened, like her husband (Acts 24.25), is not recorded. Like many women, she was a pawn of power. Her father, Agrippa, betrothed her to Gaius Julius Antiochus Epiphanes, but the marriage had not been contracted when her father died. On his death, allegations of incest came to light that so provoked the locals, 'so many of them as were then soldiers, which were a great number, went to his house, and hastily carried off the … daughters … into the brothels … they abused them to the utmost of their power.[5] Such abuse sounds unimaginably cruel, and perhaps it was to rescue Drusilla that her brother, Herod Agrippa II, who took over the tetrarchy of Herod Philip I, broke off her engagement and gave her to Gaius Julius Azizus. Felix had met Drusilla previously, and persuaded her to dissolve her marriage.[6]

Bernice

Bernice is Drusilla's sister, a client queen of the Roman Empire. In this story she is with her brother, King Agrippa, with whom it was thought she had an incestuous relationship.[7] The final part of this story is perhaps the most significant from Bernice's point of view: 'Then the king got up, and with him the governor and Bernice and those who had been seated with them; and as they were leaving they said to one another, "This man is doing nothing to deserve death or imprisonment"' (Acts 26.30–31).

Sermon Suggestion: What Would Happen if We Took Incarnation Seriously?

(If appropriate to the setting, you might get members of the congregation to read a synopsis of the stories of each of these women.)

When I began writing this chapter, I'd just been to hear Robert Beckford, an academic and BAFTA-winning film-maker, speak about decolonizing gospel music. During his lecture Beckford trailed a YouTube video called 'Incarnation'.[8] It asks a challenging and fundamental question. *What would happen if we took incarnation seriously?*

As a theological educator, I'm used to trying to explain *the* incarnation, the problem of how one person, Jesus, was both God and human. The more I've taught it, the more I've concluded that anyone who thinks they understand it must be wrong. It's a complex set of ideas. But that evening, the question was phrased differently. *What would happen if we took incarnation seriously?*

Phrased as a doctrine it's confusing and – to be honest – unhelpful. It raises the age-old question articulated by Rosemary Radford Ruether: 'Can a male saviour save women?' Surely that question is provoked every time we make statements of faith that include God becoming 'man' in Jesus, rather than God becoming flesh. Privileged, white-skinned men often find no problem at all with *the* incarnation; after all, it means Jesus looked like them. If you doubt that, have a look at most stained-glass windows depicting Jesus. Or consider his skin tone in most Western Euro-American religious art. Don't many depictions of Jesus, blonde and blue-eyed, make him look something like a woman with a beard? *What would happen if we took incarnation seriously, though?*

The Word did not become man. God did not become male. While it is true that the Word expressed humanity in a male body, the things that the Word does are distinctly feminine: 'All things came into being through ...' Life was in ... Giving life, giving birth are not well-known masculine accomplishments.

The Word became Flesh.
All flesh.
Faithful Flesh.
Weak Flesh.
Women's Flesh.

The church over the centuries has had little problem in discerning God in men of faith – Luke, whose stories of women we are going to look at in a moment, recalls that King David was called a 'man after [God's] heart' (Acts 13.22) even though he was a rapist and a murderer. So let us not dismiss women in Luke's writing because of their wrongdoings.

These apparently bit-part women are influential, deceitful, insincere. In short, they are human. Sometimes they do what they can: Bernice spoke up for Paul, apparently; sometimes they do not, Sapphira was complicit in her husband's deceit. Perhaps the women of Jerusalem wailed because they were paid to, or perhaps, familiar with death as they were, they realized that this one was different. Perhaps Drusilla was just getting by the best she could, an abused woman, in a patriarchal world.

Incarnation means God became Flesh and God becomes known in Flesh, as real people, real women, gather in real community, with all our faults and failings.

Let's finish with Peter's mother-in-law. There's a quip that says Jesus healed her in time to make supper, because once healed she gets up and serves them. The word used is *diakoneo*, which is used by Luke of other women who minister to Jesus. In Luke 8 these women enable Jesus' mission; in Luke 10 Martha offers Jesus hospitality as he goes round teaching. When women minister to Jesus it is not insignificant. It facilitates Jesus' mission and ministry. The role of women is not just to minister to others, but to minister to Jesus himself.

What happens when we take incarnation seriously? Women are taken seriously too.

Homiletic Points

1 The sermon focuses on a doctrine instead of one biblical text. It raises questions about traditional interpretations by repeating the question, 'What would happen if we took incarnation seriously?'
2 The question, 'What would happen if we took incarnation seriously?' causes the congregation to wonder rather than wait for the answer to be given to them by the preacher.
3 Mentioning King David is relevant because Luke mentions him in Acts (2.25–36; 13.22). This also serves to remind us that venerated men failed too.

Collect

God who became Flesh and becomes Flesh,
we give you thanks for the women who have gone before us.
Thank you for the times they enabled your ministry,
for the times they spoke up.
Lead us to emulate their ministries,
to speak for justice,
to see opportunities to enable your work in our communities.
Amen.

Notes

1 D. Krause, 'Simon Peter's mother-in-law – disciple or domestic servant? Feminist biblical hermeneutics and the interpretation of Mark 1.29–31', in Amy-Jill Levine (ed.), *A Feminist Companion to Mark* (Sheffield: Sheffield Academic Press, 2001), pp. 37–53, 39.

2 See, for example, the commentary on Mark in C. A. Newsom and S. H. Ringe (eds), *The Women's Bible Commentary* (London: SPCK, 2014), p. 481.

3 See https://www.un.org/press/en/2003/sc7908.doc.htm, accessed 03.10.23.

4 A. Reddie, 'Reassessing the inculcation of an anti-racist ethic for Christian ministry: from racism awareness to deconstructing whiteness', *Religions*, Vol. 11, No. 10 (2020) p. 6, https://www.mdpi.com/2077-1444/11/10/497, accessed 13.1123.

5 Josephus, *Antiquities of the Jews*, XIX, 9.1 and XX, 7.1, https://www.gutenberg.org/files/2848/2848-h/2848-h.htm, accessed 07.10.23.

6 Josephus, *Antiquities of the Jews*, XX, 7.2.

7 Josephus, *Antiquities of the Jews*, XX, 7.3.

8 See https://youtu.be/CSLcypE5CUA, accessed 03.10.22.

Appendix

Sermon Series Suggestions

International Women's Day – March

Any chapter

Holy Week/Good Friday

Pilate's Wife
Mary, Jesus' Mother
Mary Magdalene

Windrush Day – 22 June

Naaman's maid

Refugee Week – June

Lot's wife
Naomi

Carer's Week – June

Jehosheba

Black History Month – October

Hagar
Queen of Sheba
Zipporah

All Souls/All Saints

Rizpah

Elimination of Violence against Women Day – November

Dinah
Tamar
Levite's Concubine
Bathsheba
Rizpah and Merab

Bibliography

Ackerman, Susan, 'Why is Miriam among the prophets? (And is Zipporah among the priests?), *Journal of Biblical Literature*, Vol. 121, No. 1 (2002), pp. 47–80.

Adamo, David T., 'The unheard voices in the Hebrew Bible: the nameless and silent wife of Jeroboam (1 Kgs 14:1–18)', *Old Testament Essays*, Vol. 33, No. 3 (2020), pp. 393–407.

Agarwal, Pragya, *Hyster!cal (sic): Exploding the Myth of Gendered Emotions* (Edinburgh: Canongate, 2023).

Akhmatova, Anna, *Poems of Akhmatova*, trans. S. Kunitz and M. Hayward (London: Little, Brown and Co., 1973).

Alter, Robert, *The Five Books of Moses: A Translation with Commentary* (New York and London: W. W. Norton and Co., 2004).

Bacon, Brenda, 'The daughters of Zelophehad and the struggle for justice for women', https://schechter.edu/the-daughters-of-zelophehad-and-the-struggle-for-justice-for-women/, accessed 19.12.23.

Baidāwī, Commentary on Surah 12 of the Qur'an, in A. F. L. Beston, *Baidāwī's Commentary on Sūrah 12 of the Qu'rān* (Oxford: Clarendon Press, 1963).

Bailey, Randall C., *David in Love and War: The Pursuit of Power in 2 Samuel 10–12* (Sheffield: JSOT, 1990).

Barker, Margaret, *King of the Jews: Temple Theology in John's Gospel* (London: SPCK, 2014).

Beattie, Tina, *God's Mother, Eve's Advocate* (London: Continuum, Bloomsbury, 2002).

Beavis, Mary Ann, *The Lost Coin: Parables of Women, Work and Wisdom* (New York: Sheffield Academic Press, 2002).

Becker, Elizabeth, *You Don't Belong Here: How Three Women Rewrote the Story of War* (New York: Public Affairs, 2021).

Biale, David, 'The God with breasts: El Shaddai in the Bible', *History of Religions*, Vol. 21, No. 3 (February 1982), pp. 240–56.

Bliss, Shepherd, 'Revisioning masculinity: a report on the growing men's movement', *Gender*, IC#16 (Spring 1987), https://www.context.org/iclib/ic16/bliss/, accessed 19.12.23.

Boer, R., '1 and 2 Chronicles', in Deryn Guest, Robert Goss, Mona West and Thomas Bohache (eds), *The Queer Bible Commentary* (London: SCM Press, 2006).

Bowman Thurston, Bonnie, *Preaching Mark* (Minneapolis, MN: Fortress Press, 2001).

Brenner, A., *A Feminist Companion to Judges* (Sheffield: Sheffield Academic Press, 1993).

Brooks Thistlethwaite, S., 'Every two minutes', in J. Plaskow and C. P. Christ (eds), *Weaving the Visions: New Patterns in Feminist Spirituality* (New York: Harper-Collins, 1989).

Bruce, Kate and L. Shercliff, *Out of the Shadows* (London: SCM Press, 2021).

Brueggemann, Walter, *First and Second Samuel*, Interpretation Series (Louisville, KY: Westminster John Knox Press, 1990).

Burkill, T. A., 'The historical development of the story of the Syrophoenician woman', *Novum Testamentum* (1967), pp. 112–13.

Buttry, Sharon A. and Daniel L. Buttry, *Daughters of Rizpah: Nonviolence and the Transformation of Trauma* (Eugene, OR: Cascade Books, 2020).

Calvin, John, https://www.bibliaplus.org/en/commentaries/3/john-calvins-bible-commentary/genesis/34/1, accessed 19.12.23.

Carden, M., 'Homophobia and rape in Sodom and Gibeah: a response to Ken Stone', *Journal for the Study of the Old Testament*, Vol. 82 (1999), pp. 83–96.

Casey, K. L., 'Surviving abuse: shame, anger, forgiveness', *Pastoral Psychology*, Vol. 46 (1998), p. 225.

Chankin-Gould, J. D'or, Derek Hutchinson, David Hilton Jackson, Tyler D. Mayfield, Leah Rediger Schulte, Tammi J. Schneider and E. Winkelman, 'The sanctified "adulteress" and her circumstantial clause: Bathsheba's bath and self-consecration in 2 Samuel 11', *Journal for the Study of the Old Testament*, Vol. 32, No. 3 (2008), pp. 339–52.

Craddock, Fred B., *Luke*, Interpretation Series (Louisville, KY: Westminster John Knox Press, 1990).

Criado-Perez, Caroline, *Invisible Women: Exposing Data Bias in a World Designed for Men* (London: Vintage, 2020).

Davidson, Richard M., 'Did King David rape Bathsheba? A case study in narrative theology', *Journal of the Adventist Theological Society*, Vol. 17, No. 2 (Autumn 2006).

Davies, Owen, 'The Witch of Endor in history and folklore', *Folklore* Vol. 134 (March 2023), pp. 1–22, https://www.tandfonline.com/doi/full/10.1080/0015587X.2022.2152252, accessed 19.12.23.

Dennis, Trevor, *Sarah Laughed: Women's Voices in the Old Testament*, 3rd edn (London: SPCK, 2010).

Duff, N., 'The ordination of women: biblical perspectives', *Theology Today*, Vol. 73, No. 2 (2016).

Duffy, Carol Ann, 'Pilate's wife', in *The World's Wife: New Edition* (London: Picador, 2017).

Dufton, F., 'The Syrophoenician woman and her dogs', *The Expository Times* (1989).

Durken, Daniel, *New Collegeville Bible Commentary* (Collegeville, MN: Liturgical Press, 2015).

Engelberg, Abba, 'Lessons from the story of Zelophehad's daughters', https://blogs.timesofisrael.com/lessons-from-the-story-of-zelophehads-daughters/, accessed 25.06.22.

Esquivel, Julia, 'Liberation, theology, and women', in John S. Pobee and Bärbel von Wartenburg-Potter (eds), *New Eyes for Reading: Biblical and Theological Reflections by Women from the Third World* (Oak Park, IL: Meyer-Stone Books, 1987).

Exum, Cheryl J., 'Michal: Bible', *The Shalva/Hymen Encyclopaedia of Jewish Women*, https://jwa.org/encyclopedia/article/michal-bible, accessed 19.12.23.

Fletcher, Elizabeth, 'Who was Deborah in the Bible?' (2006), https://womeninthe bible.net/women-bible-old-new-testaments/deborah-and-jael/, accessed 19.12.23.

Flood, Michael, 'Men, sex, and homosociality: how bonds between men shape their sexual relations with women', *Men and Masculinities*, Vol. 10, No. 3 (2008), pp. 339–59. https://doi.org/10.1177/1097184X06287761, accessed 19.12.23.

Fonzo, K., 'Procula's civic body and Pilate's masculinity crisis in the York cycle's "Christ before Pilate 1: the Dream of Pilate's Wife"', *Early Theatre* (2013), pp. 11–32.

Forbes, Greg and Scott Harrower, *Raised from Obscurity: A Narratival and Theological Study of the Characterization of Women in Luke–Acts* (Eugene, OR: Wipf and Stock, 2015).

Fricker, Miranda, *Epistemic Injustice: Power and the Ethics of Knowing* (Oxford: Oxford University Press, 2007).

Fry, Alex, 'Clergy, capital, and gender inequality: an assessment of how social and spiritual capital are denied to women priests in the Church of England' (2021) https://doi.org/10.1111/gwao.12685, accessed 19.12.23.

Frymer-Kensky, Tikva, *Reading the Women of the Bible* (New York: Schocken, 2002).

Gafney, Wil, 'When Gomer looks more like God', https://www.wilgafney.com/2018/09/24/when-gomer-looks-more-like-god/, accessed 19.12.23.

Gafney, Wil, *Womanist Midrash: A Reintroduction to the Women of the Torah and the Throne* (Louisville, KY: Westminster John Knox Press, 2017).

Garsiel, Moshe, 'The story of David and Bathsheba: a different approach', *The Catholic Biblical Quarterly*, Vol. 55, No. 2 (April 1993), https://www.jstor.org/stable/43721228#metadata_info_tab_contents, accessed 19.12.23.

Gebara, Ivone, *Out of the Depths: Women's Experience of Evil and Salvation* (Minneapolis, MN: Fortress Press, 2002).

Habermann, R., 'Gospel of John', in L. Schottroff and M.-T. Wacker (eds), *Feminist Biblical Interpretation: A Compendium of Critical Commentary on the Books of the Bible and Related Literature* (Grand Rapids, MI and Cambridge: Eerdmans, 2012), pp. 662–79.

Harries, Martin, *Forgetting Lot's Wife: On Destructive Spectatorship* (New York: Fordham University Press, 2007).

Hertzberg, H. W., *I and II Samuel: A Commentary*, Old Testament Library (London: SCM Press, 1964).

Hobbs, T. R., *2 Kings*, Word Biblical Commentary (Waco, TX: Word Books, 1985).

Hollis, Susan T., 'The woman in ancient examples of the Potiphar's wife motif, K2111', in Peggy L. Day (ed.), *Gender and Difference in Ancient Israel* (Minneapolis, MN: Fortress Press, 1996).

Holt-Lunstad, J., T. B. Smith, J. B. Layton, 'Social relationships and mortality risk: a meta-analytic review', *PLoS Medicine*, Vol. 7, No. 7 (July 2010), https://10.1371/journal.pmed.1000316. PMID: 20668659; PMCID: PMC2910600, accessed 19.12.23.

Hooker, Morna D., *The Gospel According to St Mark* (London: A&C Black, 1991).

Humphreys, Williams L., *Joseph and His Family: A Literary Study* (Columbia, SC: University of South Carolina Press, 1988).

Jacobs, Joseph, Judah David Eisenstein, 'Temple, administration and service of', in the Jewish Encyclopaedia (1906), https://www.jewishencyclopedia.com/articles/14303-temple-administration-and-service-of, accessed 19.12.23.

Jacobson, Lauren, Alexandra Regan, Shirin Heidari and Monica Adhiambo Onyango, 'Transactional sex in the wake of COVID-19: sexual and reproductive health and rights of the forcibly displaced', *Sexual and Reproductive Health Matters*, Vol. 28, No. 1 (2020).

Jamie, Kathleen, 'The Queen of Sheba', https://www.scottishpoetrylibrary.org.uk/poem/queen-sheba/, accessed 19.12.23.

Japinga, Lynn, *Preaching the Women of the Old Testament* (Louisville, KY: Westminster John Knox Press, 2017).

Josephus, Flavius, *The Antiquities of the Jews*, https://www.gutenberg.org/files/2848/2848-h/2848-h.htm#link72HCH0007, accessed 19.12.23.

Kaminker, Mendy, 'The Daughters of Zelophehad', https://www.chabad.org/library/article_cdo/aid/2259008/jewish/The-Daughters-of-Zelophehad.htm, accessed 19.12.23.

Kamionkowski, T., 'Will the real Miriam please stand up?', TheTorah.com (2015), https://www.thetorah.com/article/will-the-real-miriam-please-stand-up, accessed 19.12.23.

Kimball, Alexandra, *The Seed: Infertility is a Feminist Issue* (Ontario: Coach House Books, 2019).

Kinukawa, H., *Women and Jesus in Mark: A Japanese Feminist Perspective* (Eugene, OR: Wipf and Stock, 2003).

Kirsch, J., *The Harlot by the Side of the Road: Forbidden Tales of the Bible* (London: Rider Books, 1997).

Kluttz, Billy, 'Queers in the borderlands: Rahab, queer imagination, and survival', *The Other Journal: An Intersection of Theology and Culture* (September 2015), https://theotherjournal.com/2015/09/21/queers-in-the-borderlands-rahab-queer-imagination-and-survival, accessed 19.12.23.

Krause, D., 'Simon Peter's mother-in-law – disciple or domestic servant? Feminist biblical hermeneutics and the interpretation of Mark 1.29–31', in Amy-Jill Levine (ed.), *A Feminist Companion to Mark* (Sheffield: Sheffield Academic Press, 2001), pp. 37–53.

Kugel, James, *In Potiphar's House: The Interpretive Life of Bible Texts* (Cambridge, MA: Harvard University Press, 1994).

LaHurd, Carol, 'Rediscovering the lost women in Luke 15', *Biblical Theological Bulletin*, Vol. 24, No. 2 (1994), pp. 66–76.

Langer, Heidemarie, 'Letting ourselves be found', *Ecumenical Review*, Vol. 38, No. 1 (1986).

Lassner, Jacob, *Demonizing the Queen of Sheba: Boundaries of Gender and Culture in Postbiblical Judaism and Medieval Islam* (Chicago, IL and London: University of Chicago Press, 1994).

Levenson, Jon Douglas, '1 Samuel 25 as Literature and as History', *The Catholic Biblical Quarterly*, Vol. 40, No. 1 (1978).

Lévi-Straus, Claude, *Elementary Structures of Kinship* (Boston, MA: Beacon Press, 1971).

Levine, Amy-Jill, *Short Stories by Jesus: The Enigmatic Parables of a Controversial Rabbi* (New York: HarperCollins, 2014).

Lorde, Audre, 'The master's tools will never dismantle the master's house', in *Sister Outsider: Essays and Speeches* (Berkeley, CA: Crossing Press, 1984), pp. 110–14.

Lowenthal, Eric I., *The Joseph Narrative in Genesis: An Introduction* (New York: Ktav Publishing House Inc., 1999).

Luger, Steven, 'Flood, salt, and sacrifice: post-traumatic stress disorder in Genesis', *Jewish Bible Quarterly*, Vol. 38 (2010), pp. 124–6.

Ma'at-Ka-Re Monges, Miriam, 'The Queen of Sheba and Solomon: exploring the Shebanization of knowledge', *Journal of Black Studies*, Vol. 33, No. 2 (2002), pp. 235–46.

MacArthur, John, *Twelve Extraordinary Women* (Nashville, TN: Thomas Nelson, 2005).

Maloney, Linda, 'Swept under the rug: feminist homiletical reflections on the parable of the lost coin (Lk. 15:8–10)', in Mary Ann Beavis (ed.), *The Lost Coin: Parables of Women, Work, and Wisdom* (London and New York: Sheffield Academic Press, 2002), pp. 34–8.

McCann, Clinton J., *Judges*, Interpretation Series (Louisville, KY: Westminster John Knox Press, 2002).

McClintock John, James Strong (eds), 'Canticles', *Cyclopaedia of Biblical, Theological and Ecclesiastical Literature*, Vol. 2 (New York: Harper & Brothers, 1891), pp. 92–8.

McDonald, Chine, Marianna Leite, Nadia Saracini and Karol Balfe, *War on Women: The Global Toll of Conflict and Violence* (London: Christian Aid, 2018).

McShane, Albert, *I & II Kings* (Kilmarnock: John Ritchie Ltd., 2015).

Meyers, Carol, 'Rebekah: Bible' (2021), *The Shalvi/Hyman Encyclopedia of Jewish Women*, https://jwa.org/encyclopedia/article/rebekah-bible#pid-13308, accessed 19.12.23.

Mir, Mustansir, 'The Qur'anic story of Joseph', https://www.islamic-awareness.org/quran/q_studies/mirjoseph, accessed 19.12.23.

Mlaba, Khanyi, 'How do women and girls experience the worst of war?', https://www.globalcitizen.org/en/content/women-and-girls-impacts-war-conflict/, accessed 19.12.23.

Mollenkott, Virginia Ramey, *The Divine Feminine: The Biblical Imagery of God as Female* (Eugene, OR: Wipf and Stock, 2014).

Myers, C., *Binding the Strong Man: A Political Reading of Mark's Story of Jesus*, Twentieth Anniversary Edition (Maryknoll, NY: Orbis Books, 2008).

Ndekha, Louis W., 'The daughters of Zelophehad and African women's rights: a Malawian perspective on the book of Numbers 27:1–11', *Journal of Gender and Religion in Africa*, Vol. 19, No. 2 (November 2013).

Nelava, S., 'Smart Syrophoenician woman: a Dalit feminist reading of Mark 7:24–31', *The Expository Times* (2006), pp. 65–6.

Nelson, Richard, *First and Second Kings*, Interpretation Series (Louiseville, KY: Westminster John Knox Press, 1987).

Newsom, C. A., S. H. Ringe, J. E. Lapsley, *The Women's Bible Commentary* (London: SPCK, 2014).

O'Day, G., 'John', in C. A. Newsom, S. H. Ringe, J. E. Lapsley, *The Women's Bible Commentary* (London: SPCK, 2014).

O'Donnell, Karen, *The Dark Womb: Reconceiving Theology through Reproductive Loss* (London: SCM Press, 2002).

O'Nika, Auguste, 'Rape and consent in Genesis 34 and Red Tent', https://popularcultureandtheology.com/2020/06/19/rape-and-consent-in-genesis-34-and-red-tent-part-one, accessed 19.12.23.

Peecook, E., 'Hagar: an African-American lens', *Denison Journal of Religion* (2002).

Rapp, Ursula, 'The vanishing of a wife', in Irmtraud Fischer and Mercedes Navarro Puerto (eds), *Torah* (Atlanta, GA: Society of Biblical Literature, 2011), p. 327.

Reddie, A., 'Reassessing the inculcation of an anti-racist ethic for Christian ministry: from racism awareness to deconstructing whiteness', *Religions* (2020), p. 6.

Reis, P. T., 'The Levite's concubine: new light on a dark story', *Scandinavian Journal of the Old Testament*, Vol. 20, No. 1 (2006), pp. 125–46.

Ringe, Sharon H.,'A Gentile woman's story, revisited: rereading Mark 7.24–31a', in A.-J. Levine (ed.), *A Feminist Companion to Mark* (Sheffield: Sheffield Academic Press, 2001), pp. 91–2.

Roberts, Soraya, 'The classroom origins of toxic masculinity' (2019), https://longreads.com/2019/01/25/origins-of-toxic-masculinity, accessed 07.10.23.

Robinson, B., 'Zipporah to the rescue: a contextual study of Exodus Iv 24–6', *Vetust Testamentum* (1986).

Rozmarin, Miri, 'Living politically: an Irigarayan notion of agency as a way of life', *Hypatia*, Vol. 28, No. 3 (Summer 2013), p. 472.

Rozmarin, Miri, 'Staying alive: matricide and the ethical-political aspect of mother–daughter relations', *Studies in Gender and Sexuality*, Vol. 17, No. 4 (2016), pp. 242–53.

Ruskin, Gila Colman, 'The Shunamite woman: a model of radical empathy', https://www.myjewishlearning.com/article/shunamite-woman/, accessed 19.12.23.

Sakenfeld, Katharine Doob, *Just Wives? Stories of Power and Survival in the Old Testament and Today* (Louisville, KY: Westminster John Knox Press, 2003).

Santos, Boaventura de Sousa, *Epistemologies of the South: Justice Against Epistemicide* (Abingdon: Routledge, 2014).

Sasso, Sandy, 'Bear witness: the story of Lot's wife explored through art, poetry', *News at IU* (2019), https://news.iu.edu/live/news/25906-bear-witness-the-story-of-lots-wife-explored, accessed 19.12.23.

Savage, Anne and Nicholas Watson (trans.), *Anchorite Spirituality: Ancrene Wisse and Associated Works* (New York: Paulist Press, 1991).

Schmidt, Kelly L., 'Strategic leadership as modelled by the daughters of Zelophehad', *Journal of Biblical Perspectives in Leadership*, Vol. 10, No. 1 (Fall 2020), pp. 102–12, https://www.researchgate.net/publication/344829038, accessed 19.12.23.

Schneiders, Sandra M., *The Revelatory Text: Interpreting the New Testament as Sacred Scripture* (Collegeville, MN: Liturgical Press, 1999).

Schüssler Fiorenza, Elizabeth, *But She Said* (Boston, MA: Beacon Press, 1992).

Schwartz, Barry L., *Path of the Prophets: The Ethics-Driven Life* (Philadelphia, PA: The Jewish Publication Society, 2018).

Sculos, Bryant W., 'Who's afraid of "toxic masculinity"?' *Class, Race and Corporate Power*, Vol. 5, Issue 3, Article 6 (2017), https://digitalcommons.fiu.edu/classracecorporatepower/vol5/iss3/6/, accessed 19.12.23.

Setzer, C., 'The Syrophoenician Woman', https://www.bibleodyssey.org/articles/the-syrophoenician-woman/, accessed 19.12.23.

Stinchcomb, Jillian, 'Race, racism, and the Hebrew Bible: the case of the Queen of Sheba'. *Religions*, Vol. 12, No. 10 (2021), p. 795.

Sweeney, Marvin, *I and II Kings: A Commentary* (Louisville, KY: Westminster John Knox Press, 2007).

Taylor, Marion Ann and H. E. Weir, *Let Her Speak for Herself: Nineteenth-century Women Writing on Women of Genesis* (Waco, TX: Baylor University Press, 2006).

Taylor, V., *The Gospel According to Saint Mark* (London: MacMillan, 1953).

Thalabi-Al, *Lives of the Prophets*, trans. W. M. Brinner (Chicago, IL: Kazi Publications, 2019).

Thiede, Barbara, *Male Friendship, Homosociality, and Women in the Hebrew Bible: Malignant Fraternities* (London and New York: Routledge, 2022).

Thomas, R. S., in *R. S. Thomas Selected Poems* (London: Penguin, 2003).

Trible, Phyllis, 'Miriam: Bible', *The Shalvi/Hyman Encyclopedia of Jewish Women* (1999), https://jwa.org/encyclopedia/article/miriam-bible, accessed 19.12.23.

Trible, Phyllis, *Texts of Terror: Literary-feminist Readings of Biblical Narratives* (London: SCM Press, 2002).

Tsymbalyuk, Oleg M. and Valery V. Melnik, 'Rediscovering the ancient hermeneutic of Rebekah's character', *HTS Theological Studies*, Vol. 76, No. 1 (2020), pp. 1–8.

Ulrich, Dean R., 'The framing function of the narratives about Zelophehad's daughters, *JETS*, Vol. 41, No. 4 (December 1998), p. 535, https://www.etsjets.org/files/JETS-PDFs/41/41-4/41-4-pp529-538-JETS.pdf, accessed 19.12.23.

Van der Bergh, R., 'The reception of Matthew 27:19b (Pilate's wife's dream) in the early church', *Journal of Early Christian History*, Vol. 2 (2012), pp. 70–85.

Van Selms, A., 'The origin of the title "The King's Friend"', *Journal of Near Eastern Studies*, Vol. 16, No. 2 (April 1957), pp. 118–23.

Van Tilborgh, Allison J., 'Deborah, Jael, and gender reversal: God favors the trouble makers', https://medium.com/interfaith-now/deborah-jael-and-gender-reversal-dc144e2ac908, accessed 19.12.23.

Wainwright, E. M., 'A voice from the margin: reading Mathew 15:21–28 in an Australian feminist key', in F. F. Segovia and M. A. Tolbert (eds), *Reading from This Place* (Minneapolis, MN: Fortress Press, 1995), pp. 150–3.

Warner, Marina, *From the Beast to the Blonde: On Fairy Tales and their Tellers* (London: Vintage, 1995).

Weinberger, Theodore, 'And Joseph slept with Potiphar's wife', *Literature and Theology* (1997), p. 145.

Wenham, Gordon, *Genesis 16–50*, Word Biblical Commentary (Dallas, TX: Word Books, 1994).

Wilhelm, Dawn Ottoni, *Preaching the Gospel of Mark* (Louisville, KY: Westminster John Knox Press, 2008).

Williams, Delores S., *Sisters in the Wilderness* (New York: Orbis Books, 2013).

Wiseman, Donald J., *1 and 2 Kings*, Tyndale Old Testament Commentaries (Leicester: Intervarsity Press, 1993).

Witherington III, B., *Women in the Ministry of Jesus* (Cambridge: Cambridge University Press, 1987).

Wright, Addison H., 'The widow's mites: praise or lament? A matter of context', *The Catholic Biblical Quarterly*, Vol. 44, No. 2 (April 1982), pp. 256–65. https://www.jstor.org/stable/43709756

Wright, G. R. H., 'Dumuzi at the Court of David', *Numen* (January 1981), pp. 54–63.

Young, Damon, 'Men just don't trust women. And this is a problem', *The Root* (2014), https://www.theroot.com/men-just-dont-trust-women-and-this-is-a-problem-1822523100, accessed 19.12.23.

Index of Bible References

Old Testament

Genesis

1	89	24.30	14	27.42–45	15
1.4	12, 18, 21, 25, 31, 90	24.34–38	14	27.45	20
		24.42–49	14	27.46	15, 20
		24.47	16	29.2	54
2	89	24.50	16, 27	29.12	16
3.15	96	24.55	16	29.15–28	24
12.5	27	24.58	14, 16	29.17	26, 54
12.17	42	24.58–67	14	29.18	32
16.6	2	24.59	16	29.26	26
16.7	2	24.60	16	29.27	26
16.8	1	24.61	16	29.31	31
16.9	2, 3	24.64–65	16	29.32	24
16.11	2	24.65	14	29.33	24, 32
16.12	4	25.20	17	29.34	24
16.13	1, 5	25.21	17	29.35	24
19.1–3	10	25.22	14, 17	30.1	25, 26
19.5–8	10	25.23	17, 21	30.3	25
19.14	10	25.26	17	30.5	25
21.8–21	1, 3	25.28	18	30.8	25
21.10	2	25.29–34	18	30.11	24
21.13	2	26.1–33	18	30.13	24
21.16	1, 2	26.5–16	19	30.14	25
21.17	3	26.6–7	18	30.15	24, 25, 27
21.21	3	26.7	42	30.16	25, 27
24.12–14	15	26.12, 29	19	30.18	25
24.15	54	26.34	19	30.19	25
24.15–21	15	27	42	30.21	32
24.16	17, 54	27.1–4	19	30.23	25
24.18	14, 15	27.6–10	14	30.24	25
24.20	15	27.13	15, 19	31.14b–16	25–6
24.24	16	27.22–24, 27	21	31.30	27
24.24–25	14	27.27	15	31.35	25
24.25	15	27.33	21	32	75
24.27, 35	19	27.39–40	19	32.28	69
24.28	15	27.41	20	33.4	20

34.1	32	2.21–22	55	14.28–35	66
34.2	120	3.1	54, 55, 56	16.1–35	66
34.3	33, 34	4.18	55	16.41–50	66
34.4	31	4.24	55	18.15–16	233
34.7	31	4.25	54, 55	20.1	61, 62
34.10	31	4.26	54, 55	20.4–5	65
34.12	31	12.23	84	20.13	66
34.13	31	13.13	233	21.5	65
34.26	31	14.10–31	60	23.31–33	81
34.27–28	32	14.31	79	25.1–4	66
34.29	32, 35	15.15	79	26.1–2	66
34.30	32	15.20–21	60, 61	26.33	66, 67, 71
34.31	32, 35	15.21	60	26.52–56	66
37.26	40	18.1	56	27.1	67
38.2	40	18.1–2, 5	54	27.2–4	67
38.3	40	18.1–2, 5–6,		27.3	67, 68
38.4	40	9–10, 12,		27.3–4	65
38.6	40	14, 17	55	27.4	68
38.12–23	195	18.2	55	27.5–11	157
38.16	39, 41	18.2, 5–6	55	27.7	69
38.17	39	18.3	91	27.8–11	69
38.18	39	20.10	247	36.2	70
38.23	41	20.13	194	36.5–6	70
38.24	42	22.22–23	227	36.10	67
38.25	39	32	62		
38.26	43	35.2	247	**Deuteronomy**	
39	49, 50			4.39	79
39.1	50	**Leviticus**		6.3	67
39.7	47	12.2–8	233	7.16	84
39.12	47	15.19	121	8.9	67
39.14	48	15.20–21	121	11.11–12	67
39.14–15	47	18.16	207	14.28–29	227
39.17	48	18.17	184	18.11–12	154
39.17–18	47	20.10	120	20.16	84
39.19	49	20.21	207	21.15–17	66, 67
40—42	48			22.23–29	195
41	48	**Numbers**		24.17–21	227
46.15	32	1.1–4	66	33.24–25	234
49.31	20	10.29	54, 55		
		11.1–6	65	**Joshua**	
Genesis Rabbah		12	61	1.2	79
85.4	42	12.1	54, 55, 56	2	81
		12.2	60, 61	2.1–7	195
Exodus		13.31—14.38	66	2.4–5	77
1.15—2.10	80	13.32–33	66	2.8–10	80
2.16	54, 56	14.1–4	81	2.8–13	78
2.18	55	14.2, 4	65	2.9	78, 79
2.21	54	14.4	66	2.10	79

2.11b	79	5.28–30	94	*Ruth*	
2.12–13	83	5.29–30	97	1.1–2	100
2.16	78	14	182	1.1–18	99
2.17–20	82	14.2	181	1.8	100
2.21	78	14.4	182	1.8–9	99
5.24	82	14.6	182	1.9	100
6.23	84	14.8	181	1.11–13	99
6.25	84	14.12	181	1.14, 16–18	100
14.12	70	14.12–14	181	1.15	99
15.16–19	69	14.15	181	1.19–20	100
17	70	14.16	179, 183	1.20–21	100, 101
17.3	67	14.17	181	3.1–4	100
17.4	65, 70, 74	14.18	181	3.1–5	99
		14.19	182	4.13–17	99
Judges		14.20	181		
1.9–15	69	15	182	*1 Samuel*	
1.16	54, 55	15.1	181	1	111
4	91	15.2	181	1.1	113
4.1	91	15.14	182	1.2	113
4.1–7	88, 89	15.18–19	182	1.6	113
4.2	91	16–18	105	1.8	113
4.4	91	16.4	182	1.9	114
4.5	91	16.5	183	1.10, 15	235
4.6	91	16.6	179	1.11	111, 113
4.6–7	88	16.6, 10, 13,		1.15	111
4.6–10	92	16	183	1.18	111
4.7	91	16.9	179	1.20	111
4.8	91	16.9, 12, 14	183	1.22	111, 114
4.9	88, 91	16.10	180	1.26–28	112
4.10	91	16.12	180	1.28	114
4.11	54, 55, 92	16.13	180	2	111
4.13	91	16.14	180	2.1–10	112
4.14	88	16.15	180, 183	2.4–5	114
4.16	92	16.18	180	8.10–22	122
4.17	91, 92	16.20	180	14.49	184, 185
4.18	89, 93	16.20–21	183	14.50	183
4.19–20	93	17.6	181	16.14–15	184
4.21–22	93	19	10	18.10–11	184
4.22	89	19.3	106	18.17–19	185
4.23	95	19.3–9	106	18.20	185
5	88, 91	19.28	106	18.20–25	185
5.2	93	20.5	105	18.27	184
5.4–5	93	21.6	105	18.28–29	185
5.7	93	21.8–23	105	19.9–10	184
5.23	94	21.25	90, 106,	19.9–11	185
5.24	93, 94		181	19.11–17	185
5.24–27	93, 95			19.12	80
5.26	94			19.14	185

20.33	184	11.25	122	14.21	137
25	184	11.26	121, 122	14.25	129
25.43	183	11.26—12.10,		14.28—19.4	136
25.44	185	13–15	117	15.12	119
27.3	184	11.27	123	16.21–22	131
27.5–6	184	11.30	123	20.16	135, 139
28	155	11.31	123	20.17	135
28,12	154	12–20	119	20.18–19	136, 139
28.3	154	12,15–23	122	20.19	139
28.3–35	154	12.1–7	136	20.20	139
28.4–6	154	12.8	183	20.21	136
28.7	154	12.9–10	122	21.1	140
28.9	152	12.10	122	21.1–9	140
28.10	154	12.11–12	122	21.8–9	187
28.11	153	12.14	122	21.8–14	140
28.13	153	12.24	122	21.10	141
28.13–14	154	12b–19	179	21.14	141
28.14	153, 154	13.1	129	23.34, 39	119
28.16–19	155	13.1–17	184	30.16–20	184
28.21–22	153, 155	13.2–5	130		
28.24	155	13.4	136	1 Kings	148, 149
30.1–2	189	13.5–10	130	1.1–4	123
30.1–3	184	13.12–13	129	1.1–40	117
30.16–20	184	13.12–14	130	1.2	187
31.4	186	13.14	33, 120	1.4	187
		13.15–17	35	1.13–14	123
2 Samuel		13.16	129	1.15–40	117
2.2	184	13.19	130	1.17–18,	
3.2	184	13.20–38	131	20–21	123
3.7	140	13.23	136	1.17–21	117, 123
3.12–16	186	13.28	136	1.20	123
6.1–5	179	14.2–3	137	1.25	123
6.16	186	14.4	134	1.28	123
6.20	186	14.5–7	134	1.31	117
6.21–22	186	14.7	137	2.13	118
6.23	186	14.8	137	2.13–18	124
11.1–2	119	14.9	134, 137	2.14	118, 125
11.1–15	117	14.10	138	2.15	124
11.2	120, 121	14.11	135, 138	2.17	187
11.2, 3, 4a	119	14.12	135	2.18	118, 124
11.3	119	14.13	138	2.19–24	124
11.4	123	14.13–17	135	2.20	118
11.4b	120	14.14	138	2.21	118
11.5	117, 120, 121	14.15–17	138	2.22	124, 187
11.6–7	120	14.17, 20	137	2.25	187
11.8–10, 13	119	14.18	135	3.16	147
11.11	120	14.18–20	139	3.16–27	195
		14.19–20	135	3.16–28	147

8.23	79	4.3	166	**2 Chronicles**	148, 149	
10.6–9	146	4.6	165	9.5–8	146	
11—14	152	4.8	167	21.6	159	
11.28	187	4.9–10	165, 167	21.6–13	159	
11.29–40	187	4.13	167	21.18–19	159	
12.4–20	188	4.13b	166	22.1–2	159	
12.28–33	188	4.14	167	22.2	159	
14.1–3	188	4.16	167	22.3–4	159	
14.1–18	188	4.16b	166	22.10—23.21	160	
14.5	188	4.17	167	23.13	153	
14.7–16	188	4.19	168			
14.11	188	4.20	168	**Judith**		
15–21a	152	4.22	166, 168	13.4–10	93	
16.8–20	158	4.23	166, 168	13.17–20	93	
16.30	156	4.24	168			
16.31	156	4.26	166, 168	**Nehemiah**		
17.1, 8–9	156	4.27	168	4.14–23	194	
17.16	156	4.28	166, 168			
17.23	156	4.30	166, 168	**Esther**		
17.24	156	4.36–37	168	1.10—2.4	62	
18.1–39	156	5.1–3	174			
18.4	156	5.3	174	**Psalms**		
18.19	156	5.8	175	45.7	235	
18.28–29	156	7–15c	174			
18.40	157	8.1	169	**Proverbs**		
19.1	157	8.6	169	3.18	196, 197	
19.1–2	207	8.16	159			
19.1–16	152	8.18–19	159	**Song of Songs**		
19.2	153, 156, 157	8.24	159	1.5	147	
		8.26b	159			
19.3–5	157	9.1–13	159	**Isaiah**		
19.3–9	157	9.22	157	8.3	193	
21.1–10	152	9.31	153	61.3	235	
21.4	157	9.33–34	158			
21.5	153	9.35	158	**Ezekiel**		
21.7	153, 157	9.37	158	2.3–4	194	
21.8–14	157	11	159, 161	16	194	
21.9–10	153	11.1	160	16.4–6	194	
21.15	153	11.1–20	160	16.8–13	194	
21.23	157	11.14	153	16.35–42	194	
21.27	157	17.24–41	263	24.16	194	
		22.3–4	159	24.18	194	
2 Kings						
2.2, 4, 6	168	**1 Chronicles**		**Hosea**		
4	169	2.49	69	1.4–8	196	
4.1	165, 166	10.13 AV	154	1.8	196	
4.1–7	166	27.33	119	2.2–12	196	
4.2	165, 166			2.3, 13	197	

14	196	
14.4	196	
14.8	196, 197	
14.8–9	196	
14.9	196	

Joel
2.28	234

Amos
5.10b, 12	231

Malachi
3.5	225

New Testament

Matthew
1.1–16	80, 200
1.5	85
2.1–15	205
2.12	201
2.13	201
2.16	206
2.22	201
4.11	269
5.15	231
6.2	226
6.2–3	231
8.10	85
8.11–12	85
8.14–15	267
9.20–22	264
12.8	248
13.5–7	208
13.13–21	209
13.18–57	208
13.44–45	209
14.5	209
14.7	209
14.8	205, 209
14.9	209
14.13	212
15.10–28	217
15.22	118, 217
15.23	118
15.24	118
15.25	118, 217
15.26	118
15.27	118, 217
15.28	118
23.14, AV	228
26.3–4	201
26.69, 71	201
27.11–14	207
27.11–54	200
27.19	200
27.27–19	202

Mark
1.13	269
1.14–20	224
2.27	248
2.28	248
5.25–34	264
6.7–29	205
6.14–29	205
6.18	207
6.19–20	207
6.20	209
6.21	207, 209
6.22	208
6.22–23	208, 209
6.24–25	205, 209, 211
6.25	208, 212
6.26	208
6.29	208
7.24	118
7.24–37	118, 217
7.25	118
7.26	117, 118
7.27	118
7.28	118, 217
7.29	118
11.27—12.44	225
11.27–33	225
12.1–12, 38–40	225
12.13–17	225
12.18–27	261
12.19–27	225
12.28–34	224
12.29–31	225
12.38–40	225
12.38–44	224
12.40	225, 231
12.43–44	227, 229
13.1	230
13.1–8	224
13.1–37	226
13.2	228
14.40	227
14.45—15.39	213
15.2–5	207
16.6–7	213

Luke
1.13, 60	233
1.25	235
1.42	96, 97
1.48	79
2.22–40	233
2.30–32	233
2.32	236
2.36–37	234
2.37	235
2.38	234, 237
3.1	206
4.13	247
4.14	247
4.15	247
4.18b	247
4.18b, 21	245
4.22, 29	245
4.38–39	267
6.5	248
6.6–11	245
6.7	245
7.11–17	241
8	269, 272
8.1–3	269
8.2	267
8.43–48	264

10	272	23.28–30	267	6.1	227
10.25	226	23.29–30	268	13.22	272
10.38–42	269			24.24	267
12.1	248	*John*		24.25	270
12.2–3	248	1.5	211	25.13—26.32	267
12.15	248	2	262	26.30–31	270
12.16	248	3.2	262	26.31	267
12.17	248	3.10	262		
13	269	3.16	90	*1 Corinthians*	
13.2	246	3.17	262	1.27	79
13.4	246	3.29	262		
13.10–17	245	4.5–42	260	*2 Corinthians*	
13.10, 18	246	4.9	260	4.7	182
13.11	246	4.11–12	260	9.7	230
13.12	246, 250	4.15	260		
13.13	246, 251	4.17	260	*Hebrews*	
13.16	245, 246	4.19	260, 263	11	80
15	256–7	4.25	260	11.1	80
15.1–10	255	4.29	260, 264	11.29—12.2	77
15.7, 10	256	4.29, 39	262	11.31	80
15.9	255	4.39	263		
19.45—21.4	226	20.29	71, 74, 75	*James*	
20.47	227			1.27	227
21.1–4	224	*Acts*		2.25	81
21.5–36	226	2.17–18	234		
21.6	228	2.25–36	272	*Revelation*	
22.62–64	201	5.1–11	267	2.20–21	158
23.27	269	5.8	267		

Index of Names and Subjects

Aaron
  Miriam and 61, 62
  against Moses's marriage 56, 57, 58
Abel-Maacah, Wise Woman of
  speaks to Joab 139
  words of 135–6
Abiathar the priest 117, 124
Abigail, wife of David 183, 184, 189
Abimelech 42
Abishag 124, 126
  caught in power politics 187
  story of 180
Abner the general 140, 186
Abraham/Abram
  disguises wife 19
  Hagar and 1–3, 6
  Rebekah and 15–16, 262
  tricks Pharaoh 42
Abraham, 'daughter of' 269
  healing of 245–54
  homiletic points and collect 254
  mustard seed parable and 249, 253
Absalom
  return of 137–9
  revenge rapes 131, 132
  Tamar and Amnon 129–31, 132, 136
  Wise Woman of Tekoa and 136–9
Achish, King of Gath 184
Ackerman, Susan 56
Adonijah
  asks for Abishag 187
  coup attempt 123, 124, 126
  succession bid 117, 118
adultery, Egyptian law and 49–50
Afghanistan, gender-based violence 94,
  97
Age Concern UK 238

Agrippa I, Herod 270
Agrippa II, Herod 270
Ahab, son of Omri 156, 157, 159
Ahaziah, son of Athaliah 159
Ahijah the prophet 187–8
Ahimaaz, Ahinoam and 183–4
Ahinoam, daughter of Ahimaaz 180,
  183–4
Ahinoam of Jezreel
  fallout from marriage 189
  story of 180, 183, 184
  Tamar and 130
Ahithophel 119
Akhmatova, Anna 10
Amalekites, David attacks 184
Ambrose, on Claudia Procula 200
Amnon 184
  Absalom murders 132, 136, 138
  rapes Tamar 33, 129–30, 132
Amos, justice and 108
Ananias 270
Ancrene Wisse 118
Anna, daughter of Phanuel
  background to her story 233–5
  'Eleanor Rigby' and 238–9, 240
  great age of 235, 239
  homiletic points and collect 239–40
  insight of 236–7
  life of 235–6
  as a prophet 234–5
  the Temple and 233, 236–7
Arab Spring 258
Aretus, King of Arabia 206
Argentina 258
Aristobulus, son of Herod the Great
  206
Asher, tribe of 234, 239

Asherah, Jezebel and 156
Athaliah
 character of 160–1
 story of 159
 words of 153
Augustine of Hippo xiv
Austen, Jane 113
Azizus, Gaius Julius 270

Bailey, Randall C., on Bathsheba 118,
 122
Barak *versus* Sisera 91–2
bathing, ritual 120–1
Bathsheba 276
 David sees 118–20
 homiletic points and collect 127
 loses a child 122, 125
 power rape of 118–21, 124
 ritual bath 120–1
 Solomon and 122–4, 126
 Uriah and 119, 120, 121–2
 words of 117–18, 124–7
The Beatles
 'Eleanor Rigby' 238–9, 240
Beckford, Robert, on incarnation 271
Benjamin, tribe of 105, 108, 139
Bernice, daughter of Agrippa 268,
 270, 272
Bethuel 14
Biden, Joe 142
Bilhah, bears sons to Jacob 26
bleeding woman 269
Bliss, Shepherd xii
Boaz, Naomi and 99–100
Boer, Roland 147
Bonhoeffer, Dietrich 206
Bosnia, Mehmedović and 142–3
Brueggemann, Walter 140
Bryars, Gavin 242
Budde, Rt Revd Mariann Edgar xiv
Burkhill, Alec 220

Caleb 66, 70
Calvin, John 32–3
Cambridge University 63
Canaan
 'evil report' on 66
 God's promise 80–1

uncomfortable narrative 89–90
Carden, Michael 106
Chalmers, John xi–xii, xiv
Cherepakha, Kateryna 104
Christ, Carol 130
Christian Aid
 War on Women report 43
Church of England
 Past Cases Review 2022 50
churches
 keeping victims quiet 12
 sexism in 61
 as unjust places xiii
circumcision
 Jacob bargains with Hivites 31–2
 Zipporah's son 54–5, 56, 57–8
Clarke, Adam 175
Claudia Procula, wife of Pilate 201, 275
 Duffy's poem 202
 homiletic points and collect 203–4
 story of 200–1
 words of 200
'Clearing' (Postlewaite) 198
community
 loneliness and 257–8
 woman with lost coin and 257
compassion 242–4

David
 Ahinoam and 183–4
 Amnon and Tamar 129–30, 132
 ancestry of 160, 161–2
 the ark of the Lord and 186
 attack on Gibeonites 140
 Bathsheba praises 117
 blaming Bathsheba 118
 danger to wives 189
 despotism 122
 a man after God's heart 272
 Michal and 80, 185–7
 moved by Rizpah 141
 murders Uriah 121–2
 old age 123, 126
 rapes Bathsheba 124
 reigns in Judah 184
 Rizpah's resistance and 143
 Saul and 184
 sees Bathsheba 118–20

Solomon and Bathsheba 121, 123–4, 126
Wise Woman of Tekoa and 136–9
women and conflict 180, 183–7
Deborah
  the Prophetess 193
  Song of 91, 93–4, 95
  story of 91–2
  troubling character of 89
  words of 88
Delilah
  Samson and 182–3
  words of 179–80
dignity in knowledge 174
Dinah 276
  family relations 31–2, 32
  homiletic points and collect 37–8
  interpreting her story 33–4
  powerlessness 34–5
  rape of 31–7, 32–3, 120
dogs, Syrophoenican woman and 218, 219–20
Dolansky, Shawna 33–4
drinking, Hannah and 111
Drusilla, daughter of Agrippa 268, 270, 272
Duffy, Carol Ann 200
  'Pilate's Wife' 202
Dufton, Francis 219

Eastern Orthodox Churches
  Anna the Prophetess 238
  Photini and 263, 265
Eaton, Jessica 33
Egypt, Hagar and 2
Elah, King 158
'Eleanor Rigby' (Lennon–McCartney song) 238–9, 240
Eleazar the priest 67, 70
Eli the priest 113, 114, 115
Elijah the prophet 156, 157, 160
Elisha
  Elijah and 168, 169
  Naaman's wife's maid 175
  the Shunammite Woman and 167–9
  the Widow and 166–7, 169–70
Elizabeth
  on conception 235

Zechariah and 233
Elkanah, son of Jeroham 113–15, 114, 115
Endor, the Medium of
  ambiguous character of 154–5
  summons Samuel to Saul 154–5
  words of 152–3
Epiphanes, Gaius Julius Antiochus 270
Er, son of Judah 40–1, 42, 44
Esau
  born to Rebekah 17
  family relations 18–22
  Jacob flees from 26
  murder plans 15
Esquivel, Julia 92
Ethbaal, King of Sidonians 156
Ethiopia, Queen of Sheba and 147, 148
exile, God's harshness and 194
Ezekiel the prophet, wife of 194

Felix, Antonius 270
feminism, Queen of Sheba and 148
fertility and infertility 111–15
  Jesus on 268
  mandrakes 26–7, 28
  Rachel and Leah's competition 26–7
Fricker, Miranda 174
Frymer-Kensky, Tikva 121

Gabriel names John 233
Gafney, Wilda
  on Gomer 195–6, 197
  preaching Hagar 5
Gath, Ziklag and 189, 191
Gebara, Ivone 27
Gehazi, Elisha's servant 167, 168
generational problems 11
Gibeah, men of 105–6
Gibeonites, Rizpah and 140–1, 143
God
  chosen people 90
  the concubine and 107
  covenant and land 66
  destruction of Sodom 10
  femininity of 256
  Hagar and 2–3
  healing and 251

Jeroboam and 188
Jezebel and 156–7
love of Israel 146
Moses and 54–5, 56
punishments 90, 194
Queen of Sheba ideal 149–50
Rebekah and 21
sees the unseen 6
the Widow's oil and 166–7
'with breasts' 101
works with us 169–71
Zipporah and 57–8, 58
Gomer, wife of Hosea
children of 196
promiscuity 195–6
Gross Domestic Product (GDP) 51

Hagar xiii, 275
first to name God 2
homiletic points 7
'One Who Sees and Lives' 1–7
racism and sexism 3–5
as a slave 2, 5–6
story of 1–3, 5
as unseen 5–7
women's interpretations of 3–5
Haggith 126
Hamor, bargains for Dinah 31–2
Hannah
desire for a child 111, 113–15
'favour' 235
homiletic points and collect 116
redeeming 114–15
words of 111–12
Harries, Martin 9–10
Hayworth, Rita
Salome 208
Heber the Kenite 92, 95
Hebrew language
'ah' name endings 67
hesed/kindness 83–4
laqach/take 120
mitqaddešet/purifying 121
miṭṭum'ātāh/period 121
pilegesh/concubine 104
rōḥeṣet/bathing 121
Shaddai/God with breasts 101
Herod Antipas 206

John the Baptist and 206–13
marries Herodias 206
Herod Philip I 206
Herod the Great 205–6
Herodians, hostile towards Jesus 225
Herodias, daughter of Aristobulus
John the Baptist and 207, 209,
209–13, 211–13
marries Herod Antipas 206
words of 205
Hertzberg, H. W. 118
Hilary of Poitiers 200
Hindley, Myra 160
Hirah 39–40, 41, 44
Hittite women 15
Hivites, Dinah and 31–2
Hoglah, daughter of Zelophehad
65–75
Holofernes 93
hope and resistance 141–3
Hosea, Gomer and 195, 197
Huldah the Prophetess 193

Idit, Lot's wife xiii, 275
homelitic points 13
looks back 9–10
story of 9–11
trauma of 11–13
idolatry
Baal worship 90, 156, 157
Jeroboam's punishment 188
incarnation, taking seriously 271–2
injustice and inequality xi, 174–6
in our own parish 108
Isaac
family relations 18–22
marriage and children 17–18
plays with Ishmael 2
Rebekah and 15–16, 20–2
supplanted by Jacob 17–18
trickery 42
Isaiah, justice and 108
Ishbosheth, son of Saul 140, 186
Ishmael 2, 5
Islam, Joseph and Potiphar's wife 48
Israelites
God's love for 146
land rights for women 65–75

Rahab and 83
through the Red Sea 80-1
uncomfortable narrative 89-90
war with tribe of Benjamin 105

Jabin, King 91, 92, 94-5
Jacob
born to Rebekah 17
deceives Isaac 20-2
Dinah and 31-2, 32, 35, 36
family relations 18-22
Leah and Rachel 26-30
meets Rachel 262
Jael
homiletic points and collect 96-7
interpretation of 94-6
murders Sisera 92-3, 94-6
troubling character of 89
words of 89
Japinga, Lynn 33, 155
Jay (Alexis) Report 36
Jehoiada, priest 162
Jehoram, King of Israel 159
Jehoram, King of Judah 159
Jehosheba 275
character and story of 161-3
homiletic points and collect 163
secures line of David 160
Jehosophat, King 159
Jehu, King 157-8, 159
Jericho
Rahab and 77-86
Yahweh's conquest of 80
Jeroboam, King of Israel 180, 187-8
Jeroboam's wife
carries message 187-8
story of 180
Jerusalem, women of 268
Jesus Christ
Anna and 233, 236-7
black women and suffering of 3-4
Christian behaviour 4
compassion of 242-4
crushes serpent's head 96, 97
'daughter of Abraham' and 245-54
depictions of 271
healing 218-19, 242, 245-9
incarnation 271-2

inclusion in heaven 85
John the Baptist and 208-13, 215
miracles of 209
parable of the mustard seed 249, 253
political troubles 225-6, 245-6
prophets without honour 208
Sabbath-breaking 247
Samaritan woman at the well 261-5
the Syrophoenician Woman and
218-22
in the Temple 225-8
widow of Nain 241-4
women in his story 36, 200
women of Jerusalem 269
Jethro/Reuel 55, 56
Jezebel
Baal and 156, 157
character and story of 155-60
daughter Athaliah 159
Jehu and 157-8
as scapegoat 158-9
words of 153
Jezreel, son of Gomer 196
Joab 124
with Adonijah 123
Wise Woman Abel-Maacah and 139
Wise Woman of Tekoa and 135,
136-7, 139
Joash, son of Jehosheba 160, 161-2
John the Baptist 235
homiletic points and collect 214-15
Mark on 208-9, 211, 213, 214
sermon perspective 209-14
stories of death 205, 206-13
Jonadab, Absalom's friend 136
Jonathan, son of Saul 141, 185
Joram, son of Jezebel 157-8
Joseph of Nazareth 233
Anna and 236
Claudia's dream 201
Joseph, son of Judah 40
Joseph the slave 47-51
Josephus, Flavius 118
Joshua 66, 70
Judah, son of Jacob
friendship with Hirah 39-40, 44
sons of 40-1
Tamar and twins 41-2

Tamar tricks 44–5
use of women 43–4
Judaism
  bravery against Holocaust 162–3
  Jesus and the Samaritan 263
  Joseph and Potiphar's wife 48
Judith (in Apocrapha) beheads
  Holofernes 92–3

Kamionkowski, Tamar 61–2
Kennedy, Robert F. 108
Kimball, Alexandra 113–14
Kinukawa, Hisako 219
Kluttz, Billy 78
knowledge, dignity and 174
Korah 66
Kugel, James 48
Kuznets, Simon 51

Laban
  daughters and 26–7, 28
  Rebekah and 15–16, 20
  teraphim 27, 29
Laban's sister 15
Langer, Heidemarie 256
Lappidoth 91
Leah
  daughter Dinah 31, 32
  Rachel and 26–30
  words of 24–5, 25–6
leprosy, Naaman and his wife's maid
  174–6
Leroy, Catherine 189
Leszcynska, Stanislawa 162–3
Letby, Lucy 160, 163
Levenson, Jon Douglas 183
Levi, son of Jacob 32, 35, 36
Levine, Amy-Jill 256
Levite's Concubine 276
  homiletic points and collect 109
  raped and dismembered 104–6
Lo-Ammi, son of Gomer 196
Lo-Ruhamah, daughter of Gomer 196
Lorde, Audre 50
Lost Coin, Woman with the
  her words 255
  homiletic points and collect 258–9
  story of 255–8

Lot 10
Lot's daughters
  incest with Lot 10
  Lot tries to trade 10
  story of 9–11
  trickery and 42
Lot's wife see Idit, Lot's Wife
Luwum, Janani 206

Maacha, daughter of Talmai 129, 130
McCann, J. Clinton 181
Magi, Claudia Procula and 201
Mahlah, daughter of
  Zelophehad 65–75
Malawi land rights 66
male friendship, sex and 41
Maloney, Linda 255–6
Manasseh tribe 65–70
Mariamne I, wife of Herod 206
marriage
  infidelity 195–6, 197
  levirate 69
  loss of land and 70
  as a transaction 197
  unlawful Herod 207
  woman at the well 261
Martha of Bethany 269
Mary Magdalene 275
Mary of Nazareth 275
  Anna and 236
  purification after childbirth 233
Masemola, Manche 207
Medium of Endor see Endor, the
  Medium of
Mehmedović, Hatidža 142–4
Menelik I, Emperor of Ethiopia 147
menstruation
  Bathsheba and 121
  Laban thwarted by 27, 29
  period poverty 29
  as pollution 27
Merab, daughter of Saul 276
  David and 185
  traumatic losses of 140
Messiah, expectation of
  Samaritan Woman 253, 260
Methodist Covenant Prayer 237–8
#MeToo xii

Micah 108
Michal, daughter of Ahinoam 184
  saves David 80
  spurned by David 185–7
Midianites, Zipporah's story and 55,
  56–7
Midrash, Miriam and 61
Milcah, daughter of
  Zelophehad 65–75
Miriam
  homiletic points and collect 63–4
  leading the women out 62–3
  leprosy 58, 61
  against Moses's marriage 56, 57, 58
  as Prophetess 193
  story of 60–2
  words of 60
Mladić, General Ratko 142
Mollenkott, Virginia Ramey 101
Monges, Miriam Ma'at-Ka-Re 148
Moses
  inheritance for women 65
  inter-racial marriage 56
  Korah leads rebellion against 66
  on leaders of Moab 79
  leads to men out 62–3
  mother defies Pharaoh 80
  promises of land 70
  saved by Pharaoh's daughter 57
  saved by sister Miriam 60–1
  sister Miriam and 62–3
  symbolic circumcision? 56, 57–8
  on tribe of Asher 234
  Zelophehad's daughters and 67
  Zipporah and 54–5, 57–8, 262
Mothers of Srebrenica 142
Mount Carmel, Elijah and 156
mustard seed, parable of 249, 253
Myers, C. 219

Naaman the Syrian 174–6, 245
Naaman's Wife's Maid 275
  homiletic points and collect 177–8
  story of 174–6
  words of 174
Nabal 184, 189
Naboth the Jezreelite 153, 157
Nain, widow of

  homiletic points and collect 243–4
  story of 241–2
Naomi 275
  homiletic points and collect 102–3
  interpretation of 101–2
  Mother God 101
  Ruth and 100–2
  story of 100
  words of 99–100
Nathan the prophet 122, 123, 126,
  136
nazirites, Hannah's deal and 113
Ndekha, Louis W. 66
Nelavala, Surekh 230–1
Nero, Photini and 263
Nicaragua 258
Nicodemus 262–3
Noadiah the Prophetess 193
Noah, daughter of Zelophehad 65–75

Obama, Michelle xii
obedience, Idit, Lot's wife and 9,
  11–12
O'Donnell, Karen
  on Hannah 113
  on trauma 132
Og 77
Old Woman Reading (Rembrandt) 236
Onan, son of Judah 40–1, 42, 44

Palti, son of Laish 185, 186
patriarchy
  Hagar's story and 3–5
  Laban sells daughters 26–7
  land rights and 65–75
  the Levite's concubine and 105–6
  men protest for 69–70
  Naomi and 100–2
  widow of Nain 241
  see also power relations; women
Paul on giving 229–30
Peninnah, Hannah's co-wife 113, 114,
  115
personhood and being unseen 5–7
Peter
  on Ananias 270
  servants recognize 201
Peter, mother-in-law of 272

story in Gospels 268–9
Peterson, Jordan 197
Pharaoh, Abraham tricks 42
Pharisees, Jesus and 225, 245, 248
Philistines
  Samson and 180–2, 183
  Woman of Timnah 180–2
Phoenicia, the Syrophoenician Woman
  217–19
Photini 263, 265
Pilate, Pontius 201–3
Pilate's Wife see Claudia Procula, wife
  of Pilate
'Pilate's Wife' (Duffy) 202
Piper, John 261
Plaskow, Judith 130
Postlewaite, Martha
  'Clearing' 198
Potiphar 47–51
Potiphar's wife
  homiletic points and collect 52
  Joseph the slave and 47–51
  unpaid domestic work 51
  words of 47
poverty
  widows 225–30, 242–3
  woman with the lost coin 255–6
power relations
  Abishag's body 187
  being powerless 107–8
  David spurns Michal 185–6
  land and 69–70
  more power and 106
  power rape 34–5, 120
prayer, Thomas on 102, 103
Prophetess, unnamed 193
Punch board meeting cartoon 176,
  177

Qur'an on Queen of Sheba 147

Rachel
  chosen 54
  Jacob and 32, 262
  Leah and 26–30
  words of 25–6
racism
  being unseen 6

Hagar's story and 3–5
  White exceptionalism 269
Rahab
  Company of the Faithful 80–1
  faith and action 78–9, 81–6
  homiletic points and collect 86–7
  intertextuality 80
  otherness of 78, 81–6
  story of 77–80
  words of 77–8, 79
rape and sexual abuse xi
  being seen 35–7
  Dinah and 31–7
  distance and admission 108
  gang rape as punishment 194
  the Levite's concubine 104–8
  Lot's family and 11–12
  power and 34–5, 107–8, 120
  revenge rape 131
  shame 130–1
  statistics of 107
  victim blaming 32–3, 118–19
  in war 104
Rape Crisis
  incidence of sexual abuse 34
  rape unprosecuted 45
Rapp, Ursula 56
Rashi, Rabbi 48
Rebekah
  Abraham and 42, 262
  betrothal of 15–16
  chosen 54
  family relations 18–22
  God's prophecy to 21
  homiletic points 22–3
  marriage and children 17–23
  son Jacob 16
  tricks Isaac 19–22
  words of 14–15
Red Tent mini-series 33
Reddie, Anthony 269
Rembrandt van Rijn
  Old Woman Reading 236
Reuel see Jethro
Rizpah 140–1, 143–4, 276
Romero, Oscar 206
The Root magazine 49
Rotherham sex abuse 36–7

Rozmarin, Miri 10, 27
Ruether, Rosemary Radford 271
Ruskin, Rabbi Gila Colman 167–8
Ruth, Naomi and 100–2

sacrifice, the Medium of Endor and
155
Sadducees 225
Salome
family network 206
John the Baptist and 207–13
story of 205–6
words of 205
Salome (film) 208
Samaritan Woman at the Well
discussion with Jesus 261–5
homiletic points and collect 265–6
marital status of 261, 264
Photini 263, 265
witness of 263–5
words of 260
Samson
Delilah and 180, 182–3
flawed character of 181–3
Woman of Timnah 180–2
Samuel, born to Hannah 114
Santos, Boaventura de Sousa 175
Sapphira 272
story of 270
words of 268
Sarah/Sarai
Hagar and 1–3, 6
Isaac and Rebekah 16
Sasso, Rabbi Sandy Eisenberg 9, 10
Saul 80
David and 184
death of 141, 154–5, 186
expels mediums and wizards 152, 154
Michal and David 185
Rizpah and 140
wife Ahinoam 183–4
women and conflict 180, 183–6
Schneiders, Sandra 262
scripture and injustice to women xi
Sendler, Irene 162–3
sex
Mrs Potiphar and 48
promiscuity 195–6

as survival tactic 43–5
sexual abuse see rape and sexual abuse
shame
gender difference in 195
Tamar 130, 131–2
Sheba, Queen of 275
legacy of 148
story of 147–8
substance and wisdom 148–50
words of 146
Sheba, son of Bichri, Joab and 139
Shechem, son of Hamor, Dinah and
31–2, 33–4, 35, 36
Shelah, son of Judah 40, 42
shepherd and lost sheep 256, 257
Shercliff, Liz, 'One Who Sees and
Lives: Hagar' 1–7
Shua's daughter, Judah and 40, 43
Shunammite Woman
character and story of 167–9
Elisha and 169–71
God works with us 169–71
homiletic points and collect 172
words of 165–6
Sihon 77
Simeon of Jerusalem 233–4, 236
Simeon, son of Jacob 32, 35, 36
Sisera the general 88, 91–2, 93, 97
slavery
Hagar and 2, 3–5
Laban sells daughters 26–7
women as 'booty' 36
Sodom, destruction of 10
Solomon
Adonijah and 187
Bathsheba and 117, 123–4, 126
on God's uniqueness 79
Jeroboam and 187–8
Queen of Sheba and 147–9
two women claim baby 147
Storkey, Elaine, introduces War on
Women report 43
La Strade Ukraine 104
Syrophoenician Woman
homiletic points and collect 222–3
social outcast 220–1
story of 217–19
words of 217

Talmai, King of Geshur 129
Talmud
  on levirate marriage 69
  Sheba as kingdom 147
Tamar 276
  Amnon rapes 33, 130–2, 184
  context of Genesis 42–3
  homiletic points and collect 45–6,
    132–3
  Judah and 41–2, 43, 44–5
  marries Er then Onan 40–1, 42
  shame and 130, 131–2
  story of 39–42, 129–31
  words of 39, 129
Tate, Andrew xi, 197
Taylor, Marion 4
Taylor, Vincent 220
Tekoa, Wise Woman of
  story of 136–9
  words of 134–5
teraphim, Laban and 27, 29
terrorism; 9/11 attack 9–10
Thomas, R. S.
  'Folk Tale' 102, 103
Till, Emmet, death of 142
Till–Mobley, Mamiee 142, 143, 144
Timnah, Woman of
  story of 180–2
  words of 179
Tirzah, daughter of Zelophehad
  65–75
tithing 229–30
trauma
  Lot's wife 11–13
  Merab and 140
  mothers in resistance 141–3
  protecting the tribe 12
  shame and 131–2
  see also rape and sexual abuse
Trible, Phyllis
  on Miriam's voice 61
  on Naomi 100
trickery in Genesis 42
Trump, Donald xiv

Ugandan women 257
Ukraine, war rapes in 104
uncleanness 121

United Nations High Commissioner for
  Refugees 94, 97
United Nations Security Council 269
United States, slavery and 3
Uriah
  Bathsheba and 119, 120
  David murders 120, 121–2, 125

Vashti, Miriam and 62
Vietnam, woman fleeing in 188–9

War on Women: The Toll of Conflict
  and Violence (Christian Aid report)
  43
Weir, Heather 4
Well, Woman at the see Samaritan
  Woman at the Well
Wenham, Gordon
  on Shechem's feelings 35
  victim blaming 33
  women as 'booty' 36
West, Rose 160
Widow of a Prophet
  character and story of 166–7
  God works with us 169–71
  homiletic points and collect 172
  words of 165
Widow with Two Coins
  in Common Worship 224
  homiletic and collect 231–2
  story of 225–6
Williams, Dolores 3–4
Wise Woman see Abel-Maacah, Wise
  Woman of; Tekoa, Wise Woman of
Wise Woman of Tekoa 137–8
Witherington, Ben 219
women
  anger on behalf of xi–xiv
  asking questions 63
  bent double 269
  conflict and war 94, 97, 179–92, 269
  Court of Women in Temple 226
  Dinah unseen 34–7
  domestic world 256
  fertility of 111–15
  God speaking through 61
  of Jerusalem 268
  land rights and 65–75

leadership 60–2
Leah and Rachel together 24–9
as pawns 42–3
Punch board meeting 176, 177
scapegoating 158–9
shocking evil 159–60
silenced 63
in Solomon's realm 147
unnamed 193–4
unpaid domestic work 51
War on Women report 43
widows 225–30, 238, 261
wisdom of 196, 198
see also patriarchy; rape and sexual
  abuse
The Women's Bible Commentary 140
Women's Voices Conference, 2022 78,
  84
Wood, Sammy 36–7

Yankunytjatjara xiv
Yee, Gale 195
Young, Damon 49

Zarephath, widow of 245
Zechariah 233
Zelophehad's daughters
  challenge for land rights 65–75
  homiletic points and collect 75–6
  sermon suggestions 71–5
  words of 65
Ziklag 189, 192
Zilpah 26
Zimri 153, 158
Zipporah 275
  circumcises son 54–5, 56
  homiletic points and collect 58–9
  ignored by Moses? 55
  inter-racial marriage 56
  meets Moses 262
  as a priest 56, 57–8
  story of 54–5, 57
  words of 54